Marking Time

Marking Time charts a genealogy of alternative practices of theatre-making since the 1960s in one particular city – Cardiff. In a series of five itineraries, it visits fifty sites where significant events occurred, setting performances within local topographical and social contexts, and in relation to a specific architecture and polity. These sites – from disused factories to scenes of crime, from auditoria to film sets – it regards as landmarks in the conception of a history of performance. And it uses performance and its places as a means to reflect on the character of the city itself – its history, its fabric and make-up, its cultural ecology and its changing nature. Weaving together personal recollections, dramatic scripts, archival records and documentary photographs, it suggests a new model for studying and for making performance . . . for other artistic practices . . . for other cities.

Marking Time is an urban companion to the rural themes and fieldwork approaches considered in *'In Comes I': Performance, Memory and Landscape* (University of Exeter Press, 2006).

Mike Pearson is Leverhulme Research Fellow and Professor of Performance Studies at Aberystwyth University. He is co-author with Michal Shanks of *Theatre/Archaeology* (2001) and author of *'In Comes I': Performance, Memory and Landscape* (2006); *Site-Specific Performance* (2010); and *Mickery Theater: An Imperfect Archaeology* (2011). He has made theatre professionally for over forty years, notably with Brith Gof (1981–97) and Pearson/Brookes (1997–present). With Mike Brookes, he co-conceived and co-directed *The Persians* (2010) and *Coriolan/us* for National Theatre Wales, the latter in collaboration with the Royal Shakespeare Company as a contribution to the World Shakespeare Festival/ London 2012.

Exeter Performance Studies

Series editors: **Peter Thomson**, Professor of Drama at the University of Exeter;
Graham Ley, Professor of Drama and Theory at the University of Exeter;
Steve Nicholson, Professor of Twentieth-Century and Contemporary Theatre at the University of Sheffield.

From Mimesis to Interculturalism: Readings of Theatrical Theory Before and After 'Modernism'
Graham Ley (1999)

British Theatre and the Red Peril: The Portrayal of Communism 1917–1945
Steve Nicholson (1999)

On Actors and Acting
Peter Thomson (2000)

Grand-Guignol: The French Theatre of Horror
Richard J. Hand and Michael Wilson (2002)

The Censorship of British Drama 1900–1968: Volume One 1900–1932
Steve Nicholson (2003)

The Censorship of British Drama 1900–1968: Volume Two 1933–1952
Steve Nicholson (2005)

Freedom's Pioneer: John McGrath's Work in Theatre, Film and Television
edited by David Bradby and Susanna Capon (2005)

John McGrath: Plays for England
selected and introduced by Nadine Holdsworth (2005)

Theatre Workshop: Joan Littlewood and the Making of Modern British Theatre
Robert Leach (2006)

Making Theatre in Northern Ireland: Through and Beyond the Troubles
Tom Maguire (2006)

"In Comes I": Performance, Memory and Landscape
Mike Pearson (2006)

London's Grand Guignol and the Theatre of Horror
Richard J. Hand and Michael Wilson (2007)

Theatres of the Troubles: Theatre, Resistance and Liberation in Ireland, 1980-2000
Bill McDonnell (2008)

The Censorship of British Drama 1900–1968: Volume Three, The Fifties
Steve Nicholson (2011)

British South Asian Theatres: A Documented History
edited by Graham Ley and Sarah Dadswell (2011)

Critical Essays on British South Asian Theatre
edited by Graham Ley and Sarah Dadswell (2012)

Victory over the Sun: The World's First Futurist Opera
edited by Rosamund Bartlett and Sarah Dadswell (2012)

Marking Time

Performance, archaeology and the city

Mike Pearson

UNIVERSITY
of
EXETER
PRESS

First published in 2013 by
University of Exeter Press
Reed Hall, Streatham Drive
Exeter EX4 4QR
UK
www.exeterpress.co.uk

British Library Cataloguing in Publication Data
A catalogue record for this book is available
from the British Library.

Hardback   ISBN 978 0 85989 875 1
Paperback   ISBN 978 0 85989 876 8

Designed by Steve Allison, The Design Stage
Typeset in Adobe Systems Warnock Pro
and Ahmet Altun's Halis Rounded.

Printed in Great Britain by Short Run Press Ltd, Exeter.

CONTENTS

LIST OF ILLUSTRATIONS

Cover: Cardiff Laboratory Theatre, *Hunt the Wren*, December 1978 (Steve Allison)

ACKNOWLEDGEMENTS

My enduring thanks are due to many former professional colleagues: Jane Woddis – Theatre in Transit, 1970–72; George Auchterlonie – Transitions, 1971–72, particularly for locating and making available the Transitions archive; Professor Georgiana Gore (Blaise Pascal University, Clermont-Ferrand) – Keele Performance Group, 1972–73; Mick Brennan – RAT Theatre, 1972–73; David Baird, Richard Gough and John Hardy (Royal Welsh College of Music & Drama) – Cardiff Laboratory Theatre, 1973–80; Lis Hughes Jones, Richard Morgan and John Rowley – Brith Gof, 1981–97. And as ever to my close collaborator in Pearson/Brookes (1997 to present) Mike Brookes, whose conceptual acuity and artistic vision is fundamental to our work together, particularly in Cardiff.

I owe my gratitude for insightful conversations to Janek Alexander, former director of Chapter; Geoff Moore, director of Moving Being; Professor André Stitt (Cardiff School of Art and Design); and David Wheeler (IOU).

To Ed Thomas and Keith Wood for permission to include extracts from their dramatic works.

To Mick Pearson and Nia Wynn Dafydd (National Library of Wales); to Dr Louise Ritchie (Aberystwyth University); and to Professor Steve Daniels (University of Nottingham) for introducing me to the field of cultural geography.

To my editors Anna Henderson and Simon Baker.

For permission to include illustrations: Steve Allison; Phil Babot; Cardiff City Hall; Cynulliad Cenedlaethol Cymru/National Assembly for Wales; Andy Freeman; Paul Jeff; Keith Morris; National Theatre Wales/Mark Douet; Michael Shanks; Pete Telfer; Theater Instituut Nederland; Trace Archive; David Wheeler.

For permission to include the itinerary maps, the Ordnance Survey: all maps contain Ordnance Survey data © Crown copyright and database right 2013.

Marking Time takes up themes first mooted in *Theatre/Archaeology* (2001), and I am indebted to Professor Michael Shanks (Stanford University) for the considerable stimulus provided by our renewed conversation.

Two individuals provide constant inspiration: poet/walker/cyclist/psycho-geographer Peter Finch whose journeys in Cardiff, particularly in his *Real Cardiff* volumes – now much emulated – map the territory, geographically and historically; and Professor Heike Roms (Aberystwyth University) whose 'What's Welsh for Performance?/It was Forty Years Ago Today' projects address cognate subject matter through a range of innovative research practices including mapping exercises, restagings and public conversations in which I have from time to time participated. Her aim is to provide a sense of the ecology and context for performance, and to track the coming of styles and the founding of institutions. The debt to both may be insufficiently cited herein.

My final appreciation is of Steve Allison, a friend whom I first met in 1970 and whose fine sensibilities infuse his photographs of my earliest attempts at theatre making and the design of this volume forty years on.

Marking Time: Performance, archaeology and the city is achieved with the support of a Leverhulme Research Fellowship, as the keystone in a two-year project (2012–14) that includes public talks, walks, demonstrations and the restaging of workshops and performances from the early 1970s. I owe the Leverhulme Trust an enormous debt of gratitude for its support.

INTRODUCTION

CITY

Cardiff author Lloyd Robson has the first word:

> so this is my home. This morose dump this castle ground this moggy swamp
> this swab of land this marsh growth this tamponing town of urban blood &
> brown this festering hole this rising damp. (2003: 95)

In 1800, Cardiff was a small port of less than 2,000 souls, huddled close to the castle; by 1901, its population was 164,333. Its boom resulted primarily from the entrepreneurial activities of the 2nd Marquess of Bute (1793–1848), who in 1839 built the West Dock with the twin objectives of exploiting the mineral wealth of the extensive inland properties he inherited through his mother and of controlling its transport for maximum profit via family-owned land in Cardiff. It grew as a company town with one principal landlord, founded on the export of a single commodity – coal. At the peak in 1913, 13.7 million tons left its wharfage.

The 2nd Marquess would become one of the richest men in Britain: he was 'a product of his age, a mixture of evangelical earnestness, aristocratic arrogance and the confident ruthlessness of an early nineteenth century industrialist' (Davies 1981: 13); 'He was irresistible. He owned everything' (Finch 2004: 160). But he never owned ships. The system developed by Cory Brothers and other shipping companies was to dump steam coal at stations around the globe – from Aden to Buenos Aires – and return their vessels with skeleton crews under ballast, which from 1845 included Irish immigrants. It was a simple, efficient concept but as a result the city never acquired industries based on returning imports – apart from the East Moors works of the Dowlais Iron Company opened in 1891 – although there were major repairing facilities for the empty vessels. By the end of the nineteenth century, Cardiff was the largest steamship-owning centre in the world; the boardrooms, banks and exchange that sustained the enterprises of the trade still stand around Mount Stuart Square.

Tramping shipping drew crews from many locations, leading to the growth – as sailors awaited a berth – of a multi-cultural community, mainly in the area of Butetown, though in truth we who live in Cardiff all inhabit 'Bute's Town'; in 1911, there were in Tiger Bay, as it was commonly known, 181 boarding houses – '10 Arab, 4 Chinese, 26 Greek, 13 black, and 24 south European' (Daunton 1988: 217), leading to the not always substantiated claim – *pace* the riots of 1919 – of local racial tolerance.

John Patrick Crichton-Stuart, the 3rd Marquess, was only six months old when his father died. He grew up to be intensely religious and studious: he was the inspiration for the central character in Benjamin Disraeli's novel *Lothair* (1870) – 'Lothair's over-intense religiosity, his fondness for religious paraphernalia and his desire to escape the burdens of wealth were all characteristics of the third Marquess of

Bute' (Davies: 21). In 1868, he converted to Catholicism. In 1869, he commissioned William Burges to begin the extravagant refashioning of the castle: Burges's stylistic preference for French Gothic would have a marked effect on the subsequent look of Cardiff. In 1872, Bute married Gwendolen Fitzalan-Howard; their four children included Ninian (b. 1883) and Colum (b. 1885).

Further Bute docks opened – East Dock (1859), Roath Basin (1874), Queen Alexandra Dock (1907) – but from the 1850s, tensions grew between 'castle' as the sole provider of facilities and 'wharfmen' who regarded the Butes's intransigence to wholesale expansion, and the family's monopoly of ownership, as a brake on progress. Between 1852 and 1895, the Liberals held the parliamentary seat with 'wharf' backing.

Yet despite the frictions, the city prospered:

> It now possesses all the characteristics of a comfortable, improving town, being well drained, watered and lighted: having good hotels, respectably conducted shops, banks, museum and literary institutions, schools and various charitable establishments, the latter of which are supported with great liberality ... Masses of buildings are springing up like mushrooms. (Charles Martin 1878: *Historical and Descriptive Guide to Cardiff and its Environs*, in Evans 2003: 109)

The huge influx of foreigners was not however always regarded positively, incomers viewed as being marked by 'ignorance, infidelity, intemperance, immorality, pauperism and crime' (Evans 1984: 366).

In 1875, town boundaries were extended to include rapidly expanding inner suburbs – Canton, Roath and Splott. In 1905, following a period of relentless 'boosting' of its attributes, Cardiff was designated a city

> ... an impression of modernity and progressiveness, of spacious streets and buildings, of docks and ships, and of great commercial activity which well merit the epithet 'the Chicago of Wales'. It is both ancient and modern; Celtic and Cosmopolitan; progressive; wealthy; enterprising, and a centre of learning. There is a Metropolitan ring about its large ideas and "go" which makes all other Welsh towns seem parochial in comparison. (*Cardiff Times* 1 April 1905)

In the early twentieth century, a civic enclave inspired by examples in Philadelphia and Washington – city hall, law courts, national museum, university – was erected in Portland stone in Cathays Park; an increasing sense of destiny led, for example, to substantial support for Scott's *Terra Nova* Expedition (1910–12) to Antarctica. Scott named Cardiff his vessel's homeport.

But the city's fortunes, based on the transshipment of one commodity with few ancillary activities, would always be precarious: 'The Bute docks were the very raison d'être of Cardiff, but also its principal weakness' (Daunton 1977: 36). When exports declined dramatically after the First World War with low prices and lack of commerce, only its sheer size saved it. Major shippers departed; grain and timber imports continued, though at nowhere close to the volume of coal. The last coal left the port in 1964. But it long retained its carboniferous *noir-ish* cast: 'Cardiff, city of darkness, drizzle and smoke' (Finch 2005: 7).

In 1987, the Cardiff Bay Development Corporation was established to oversee redevelopment of the largely abandoned docks, including a waterfront regeneration programme with Baltimore as its putative model. Its key component is a barrage across the entrance to Cardiff Bay. A lagoon now fronts a city with one of the largest tidal ranges in the world.

Cardiff became capital of Wales in 1955, and post-devolution in 2000, the seat of the Welsh Assembly Government. Its economy is currently based on service industries, education, retail and leisure. Since the launching of Welsh-language broadcaster S4C in 1982 and the opening of the BBC Drama Centre in 2011 at Roath Dock, it has been a hub of media production.

In its layout and toponymy, Cardiff is indelibly marked – haunted even – by the Butes. Its streets are named for Bute estates and mansions in Scotland; Bute ancestors, family members and their titles; and Bute agents, managers and engineers. Its central area is dumbbell shaped – the commercial dockland linked to the castle by the isthmus of Butetown; or perhaps, rather, Y-shaped, with the castle symbolically in the cleft and the large Bute-owned parks preserved from residential development as its arms. And although the Bute Estate constructed few houses, by vetting the plans, materials and site layouts of leasehold developers, it ensured a quality of construction that avoided mid-twentieth century mass clearance; many of Cardiff's residents still live in late-Victorian and Edwardian terraces.

Cardiff stands on the alluvial plain of three rivers – Ely, Rhymney and Taff: its bedrock is far down. It has limited subterranean space, and until the advent of recent construction developments offered few panoptic views – of Michel de Certeau's 'gigantic mass ... transformed into a texturology' (1984: 91). It is, in general, low and walkable terrain.

It is a young city – of surface rather than stratigraphy, of locales rather than depths – never quite sure how it came to be so quickly and what sustains it: 'Cardiff is forever looking for itself. For the places of its origin. For the spots where history launched. For the locus of just what made it' (Finch 2009: 136).

Why Cardiff? Since the late 1960s, Cardiff has accommodated and nurtured innovative practices of theatre making, initially through the activities of companies such as Cardiff Laboratory Theatre, Diamond Age, the Keith Wood Group, Moving Being, Pauper's Carnival, Red Light Theatre; only in 2010 was National Theatre Wales launched. It is at and in the many spaces of Bute's Town – street corners, adventure playgrounds, public halls, youth centres, private houses, empty shops, former schools, abandoned docks, disused factories and *terrains vagues* – that artists have devised, rehearsed and presented performances. For forty years, I have periodically made theatre in Cardiff.

PERFORMANCE

The late 1960s and early 1970s witnessed a burgeoning of alternative theatre in Britain, with the appearance of new modes and practices – physical theatre, devised performance, site-specific work, community-engaged events – albeit in nascent forms and rarely identified as such at the time; and novel approaches to making and presentation involving physical training, participatory workshops, individual improvisation and group collaboration. Developed in and through local residencies, regional and foreign touring, and international co-production (see Ansorge 1975; Craig 1980). Such aesthetic and political initiatives – in both institutional and independent contexts – were inspired by European and US innovators and exemplars: from the intense, corporeal productions of Polish director Jerzy Grotowski whos Teatr Laboratorium toured Britain in 1967 to the sprawling, confrontational shows of the Living Theater, who, with other American companies including La Mama and Bread and Puppet Theatre, appeared in newly established venues such as The Roundhouse in London in 1968–69. These practices were elaborated and espoused by British companies whose existence was facilitated by the appearance of a circuit of venues – arts labs and centres, the 'black box' studios of new-build theatres, festival programmes – and by a period of Arts Council policy supporting innovation. Their attitudes and methods were emulated in a radicalized student world: the National Union of Students (NUS) Drama Festival became an important forum for showcasing pioneering groups and incoming work from Europe.

As an undergraduate archaeology student in Cardiff in 1969, I performed in a masked version of Dylan Thomas's *Under Milk Wood* (1954), in a university lecture theatre – a play that I knew only from pianist Stan Tracey's eponymous jazz suite (1965) and tenor saxophonist Bobby Wellins's peerless playing on the sublime 'Starless and Bible Black'.

In 1970, inspired by – though with little understanding of – Jerzy Grotowski's *Towards a Poor Theatre* (1969), we presented a wordless version of Homer's *Odyssey* in a faculty coffee bar.

In 1972, with community arts group Transitions, we helped local children make a horror film, set in 'Dracula's Castle' constructed on a disused railway embankment.

In 1973, RAT Theatre performed *Blindfold* in a studio fashioned in an empty engineering lecture room that was opened to encourage audiences prior to the launching of the university Sherman Theatre. With the Casson Studio Theatre and artist-run Chapter Arts Centre, it joined the emerging number of venues staging key visiting companies of the period: the Pip Simmons Theatre Group, The People Show, the Ken Campbell Roadshow.

In 1974, Cardiff Laboratory for Theatrical Research staged *The Lesson Of Anatomy*, after texts by Antonin Artaud, with the recently dedicated hexagonal Sherman Arena Theatre doubling as a dissection theatre.

In 1977, Cardiff Laboratory Theatre devised *special events* – fleeting occupations of locations, quickly conspired, barely rehearsed – that in their themes and forms celebrated places, dates, people and past events: in a youth centre, a parish hall, a deconsecrated church.

In the 1980s and 1990s, Brith Gof conceived performances for reconstructed buildings at the Welsh Folk Museum – cock-fighting pit, barn – and later large-scale architectonic works in disused industrial spaces. *Gododdin* (1988), based on a sixth-century Welsh battle elegy, was mounted in the former Rover car factory, with a scenography involving hundreds of tons of sand, dozens of trees and wrecked cars, and thousands of gallons of water that gradually flooded the setting during the performance.

Between 2001 and 2004, artist and designer Mike Brookes and I, as Pearson/ Brookes, mounted a series of multi-site, peripatetic performances that existed at dispersed locations across Cardiff, appreciating and reflecting the city as 'an amalgam of often disjointed processes and social heterogeneity, a place of near and far connections, a concatenation of rhythm; always edging in new directions' (Amin and Thrift 2002: 8). And concurring that: 'We no longer know where to look to find the glorious ensembles and performances that we once called "the city"' (Kwinter 2010: 92).

In *Carrying Lyn* (2001), as they crossed the city on a single evening, performers repeatedly dispatched video footage and still images of themselves by cycle courier to Chapter Theatre. There it was projected in parallel with recordings of the same actions and routes undertaken earlier, at midday: the juxtaposition illustrating changes in the city's diurnal constituencies and ambiences.

In *Polis* (2001) (Roms 2004; Pearson 2007), groups of audience went out by taxi to locate and then video isolated performers in the city: working in a coffee bar, standing in a telephone kiosk, singing in a club. Only when the recordings were returned to Chapter Theatre and played in combination was it apparent that these were figures in a single story. This process was then repeated, the performers having in the meantime moved to different locations. A performance potentially as large as the city but refusing to make itself available for total scrutiny, there being no one place from which to view it *in toto*, demonstrating 'An increasing awareness of and challenge to the theatrical representational apparatus' (Roms: 179). *Polis* was archaeological in form: to understand its scale, let alone its narrative, the individual spectator pieced together video sequences, photographs, maps, texts, overheard conversations and interrogations in acts of interpretation: in a reconstitution of the immediate past from its surviving, though recently generated, fragments.

The organization of these works was facilitated through the annexation and employment of urban transport and information intermediaries and systems. They drew attention to a city composed of a multitude of circulatory dynamics, mobilities and rhythms, of barely discernible temporalities and manifold narratives. They proposed the use of time as a structuring device in performance – their dramaturgies were composed as schedules to be met as much as places to be – as indeed it is in the city itself: 'The city is a device for measuring time' (DeLillo 1992: 27). They tested the feasibility of works occurring within the urban everyday; and the use of low-grade technology in the almost instantaneous re-presentation of ephemeral occurrences – that which happened 'just now, but elsewhere' – in mediated forms that problematized presence and visibility as defining notions of the theatrical contract. They were of course of their time. What was then a matter of analogue tapes and discs could all now be achieved on mobile telephony.

Raindogs (2002) (Pearson 2011) included ten suited performers who were videoed – for timed durations – in the city: 'It rained and they lost the scent, all trace of the way home' (production publicity). In one sequence, five men were recorded travelling by train, bus, car, boat and at the airport; in a second, the other five were required to remain motionless at certain locations in Cardiff whilst being recorded for three minutes by police CCTV cameras. These latter figures were both embedded within and aesthetically distinct from the urban flux: quietly resisting the circulations of consumption around them, their loitering a potential provocation to public order in the management of 'what should happen, and who should be, in the spaces and times of cities' (Graham 2000: 247). Their very stillness drew all that surrounded them into a frame of representation. With the performers present yet palpably restrained, attention was deflected towards the crowd and its make-up, to the kinetics and choreographies of passers-by, to the details of architectural style, composition and fabric: the eye turned forensic.

In *Raindogs*, there was a shift from visitation to site by audiences to a form in which often inaccessible places were instead brought to an audience in Chapter Theatre, and familiar places presented from unusual viewpoints. As a consequence, 'ecologies of ignorance' were disclosed: 'gaps, blind spots, mistakes, unreliable paradoxes, ambiguities, anomalies, invisibilities which can only ever be partially taken in, since they are, to an extent, one of the means by which knowledge itself is created and justified' (Amin and Thrift 2002: 92). The city was drawn into the studio, a locale once defined by its exclusivity – cutting itself off from 'an implicitly corrupt and false social world outside', effectively obliterating 'all social signals from its interior' (Wiles 2003: 257) – now become porous. 'Oh, look where they are now,' the audience repeatedly uttered. The effect was to open a new kind of perceptual space in performance that can encompass varying degrees of spectatorial interest and competence in its rapidly shifting citations, asides and allusions rather than ensuring the singularity of attention to the motives and actions of the context-less characters conventionally encountered in the black box theatre.

Performance here made no attempt to re-enact the multitude of events that may have happened at a particular point in the city; but through its fleeting presence, it served to highlight and increase awareness of the material and human environment, the urban present, dwelling as is. In concatenations of word and image, of factual and fictive, of dramatic and mundane, of aesthetic and ordinary, of hidden and overt, performance might actively encounter and divulge that which escapes the attention and concerns of instrumental discourses of urbanism: the daily lives of citizens in all their disconcerting complexity.

To map and document such multi-site and mediated performances is not easy, as they move across platforms and across the urban terrain. Any subsequent account risks collapsing time and space into an impression that these were discrete and coherent instances of exposition, counter to their very intentions and their sprawling manifestations. It demands a disciplinary shift from regarding site as an analogue of the auditorium to attending to the very particularities and details of its engagement *in* and *with* a location, to the nature and conditions of its specificity, to all that might impact upon theatrical composition and its reception, be that physical or virtual.

All the performances above are sufficiently past for them to become hazy in memory, and for their sites to have altered in the interim: the university refectory has been consumed by internal revamping; the railway embankment levelled; the Sherman Arena Theatre modified by refurbishment; the car factory demolished; the places in *Carrying Lyn* redeveloped.

Many of these practices were never systematically recorded: there is imperfect visual evidence, and only scant written description. With the accent upon 'seizing the time' and live-ness, there was neither the purpose nor will nor indeed the apparatus available to capture transient and ephemeral events. Ironic, given recent disciplinary preoccupation with documentation and archiving. They survive as increasingly distant memories, on the point of disappearance as their practitioners retire or pass away. We risk losing authentic accounts of the nascence and early years of forms, techniques and terminologies that are now an undifferentiated though vital facet of British theatre and drama education.

■ What then remains of performance and its places, and what can we make of its remains?

Whatever the original purpose of performance documentation, it is also a fragment of social history, a snapshot of the city, albeit with equipment that may itself now be obsolete.

PREMISE

Marking Time aims to recover, account for, reassess and evoke a range of performances, their related generative practices and their genealogies; and to chart their manifestations within particular topographical, environmental, social and cultural circumstances in one city: 'Art and the equipment to grasp it are made in the same shop' (Geertz 1976: 1497).

■ To locate and describe instances and procedures of production and presentation as they were enacted at a variety of scales within one specific urban geography, architecture, vernacular setting, ambience and populace.

■ To regard and categorize such performances not purely as examples of genre, or idiolect, or ascribed order, or modish nomenclature (post-dramatic; immersive; alternative even), nor as aesthetic singularities, but to consider them with other artistic and quotidian activities as aspects of a wider cultural ecology, as functions and reflections of cityscape, as distinct – if minor – moments within civic history, with a biographical inflection. 'Moment' here is a 'function of a history, the history of the individual', possessing form, content and memory: as constituted *'by a choice which singles it out and separates it from a muddle or a confusion, i.e., from an initial ambiguity'* (Lefebvre 2008: 343–45).

■ Further, to attend not only to aesthetic endeavours but also to the performance of everyday life: that dramaturgy of gestures and narratives, 'characterized as chains of *operations* done on and with the lexicon of things' (Certeau et al 1998: 141).

■ As a complement: to occasion reflection on the city itself and its performative nature. And on the passage of time in a place as memories mesh with cultural meanings, as particular emotional geographies of drives, compulsions and confounded obsessions overlay experiences of habitual dwelling – 'An everyday urbanism has to get into the intermesh between flesh and stone, humans and non-humans, fixtures and flows, emotions and practices' (Amin and Thrift 2000: 9).

As it identifies and visits sites, *Marking Time* regards performance through the city and the city through performance, employing them as mutually reflexive aides-memoire or mnemonics, with archaeology as the intervening critical optic, or way of focusing attention – in either direction.

It juxtaposes the materiality of the city (architectures, layouts, fabrics) and the materiality of performance (sites, scenographies, objects); it assembles, fuses and agglomerates fragments of the city (events, histories, narratives, beliefs and manners) and fragments of performance (documents, accounts, residual practices, bodies) – material remains and faint recollections, existing on the ground, in the archive and in memory – to explicate artistic impulses and procedures within the tenor of their times: 'Worldbuilding. Modeling worlds on the basis of fragments' (Shanks 2012: 148).

It is an attempt at a lesser theatre historiography within a single urban milieu – performance as an adjunct to city rather than an affiliate of a classificatory order – that evinces the grain of a place that is being constantly transformed through use. And this through reading onto (in creative writing) as much as reading from (through academic analysis): 'even adding other layers derived from elsewhere – from other cities, other parks (a palimpsest)' (Tschumi 1994a: 191–92).

It contemplates the fit between performance and its contexts of exposition:

☐ as performance inhabits 'set aside' spaces (in ways often utopian): as places of escape and brief respite, of exceptionality, of defamiliarization, of conviviality, where daily conventions don't hold, including sites primarily intended for certain practices that are 'able to be bent to others' (Amin and Thrift: 119);

☐ or as it exists in public within the urban flux (in ways often heterotopian), as a challenge to, or subversion of, or reiteration of quotidian flow and convention.

Performance as temporary densities or concentrations of people, objects, institutions and architectural forms: as 'the gathering of assemblages of people and things in dynamic fields' (Read 2006a: 78); as local eruptions or thickenings, where site and event collapse together to generate friction and innovation. Aesthetic performance as transitory exception – characterized by a set of circumscriptions and levels of engagement and artifice: as a distinct 'place-marker' (Sante 1992: 87).

Marking Time describes performances about the city – that in their historical and cultural themes may be transformative of attitudes to dwelling and to interpretation of urban realities. And performances of the city – that in their concepts and structural conceits may lay bare conventions and anxieties of inhabitation. City not simply as scenic backdrop, but as sets of material and social conditions that may inform and prefigure the nature of performance. Or indeed that may be effectively ignored in order to confront and challenge urban prescriptions.

It figures city as ruin, in the survival of architectures of various periods and in the relic customs of its inhabitants: 'attesting to the tastes and attitudes of generations, to public events and private tragedies, to new and old facts' (Rossi 1982: 22).

> Through the material fact of preservation, time challenges time, time clashes with time; habits and values carry over beyond the living group, streaking with different strata of time the character of any single generation. Layer upon layer, past times preserve themselves in the city until life itself is threatened with suffocation. (Mumford 1938: 4)

And it casts past devised performance too as ruin, shakily constructed from 'this' and 'that': existing momentarily, surviving as documentary vestiges and recollections that may – incidentally, *en passant* – give glimpses of the city itself.

Performance as sedimented into the city's history and fabric: as archaeological 'context' whose meanings can be recovered only through 'a symbolic archaeology; the act or art of memory' (Donald 2000b: 150).

In its appeal to archaeology, *Marking Time* does not advocate excavations such as those undertaken at the Rose Theatre (see Bowsher 2007), where wear and tear on the floor might indicate the presence of the standing audience close to the stage. Neither does it employ drama as metaphor: the city as 'a theatre of new, unforeseen constellations' (Benjamin 1985: 169); as 'a fascinating theatre' (Certeau et al: 141); as akin to David Harvey's series of stages upon which individuals could work their own distinctive magic while performing a multiplicity of roles (see Edensor 2005: 81); as 'the fixed stage for human events' (Rossi: 22). Nor does it regard citizens as 'on the stage with the other participants' (Lynch 1960: 2), 'following incomprehensible scripts, full of shifting scenes, juxtapositions and random movements coming from a range of angles' (Edensor: 81). Nor is the city envisaged as a ground awaiting 'some sort of [Situationist] performance, one that would treat all space as performance space and all people as performers' (Sadler 2001: 105).

It does however conceive of the city as 'a field of events' – of presence and encounter – within which: 'Each urban moment can spark performative improvisations which are unforeseen and unforeseeable'; 'Each urban encounter is a theatre of promise in a play of power' (Amin and Thrift: 4); 'the social is constructed, formed and transformed *through* the multiple performances that define it' (Read 2006a: 78).

It concurs that:

> Gestures are the true archives of the city …
>
> As gestural "idiolects," the practice of inhabitants creates, on the same urban space, a multitude of possible combinations between ancient places (the secrets of which childhoods or which deaths?) and new situations. They turn the city into an immense memory where many poetics proliferate. (Certeau et al: 141)

The city as a realm of wordless histories, communal traditions, timeless events, of non-cognitive imperatives and 'things that escape attention' (Amin and Thrift: 93), that 'make people believe and do things' (Certeau et al: 142), and that might ultimately require conservation and renovation as much as buildings.

It identifies places of past performance that may now be substantially modified. These it employs as a spur to rumination not only upon events and their constitutive feelings, but also upon changes in the city. It recalls places, incidents and people from a personal history of performance making in Cardiff that coincidentally reflect the city's cultural makeup and varying fortunes over time. It traces the origins of an individual practice: the development of site-related performance and ultimately the elaboration of dramaturgical structures based on network and schedule. And it recalls related practitioners and performances that are frequently 'documented but unaccounted for' (Roms 2013).

■ *Marking Time* develops and recommends a transferable methodology that might be pursued with other practices and other histories, elsewhere.

THE MAP OF THE BOOK

Marking Time is a personal quest for performance, and a quest for personal performance, in one city – Cardiff. In structure and content, it has a biographical aspect. It traces practices of alternative theatre making, commencing in the late 1960s, the principal manifestations of which are listed before the Bibliography; it suggests approaches to the apprehension of performance other than through those of authorship, period and genre. Its enquiry triangulates location, encounter and record: it conjoins sites, documents and memories.

The introduction delineates the critical field in which performance, archaeology and the city conjoin and describes the optics through which its subjects are regarded. The text then maps five itineraries and possible perambulations in Cardiff – North, East, South, West, Central – each of which passes through ten resonant locations: places of past events, places of cultural and civic importance, places of individual significance – 'I cannot place the event that occurred there precisely to a date, even a year ... but the geo-reference is clearly recalled; the spatial coordinates are accurately given on my mental map' (Schofield 2009: 5); 'Two things about memory and the city are clear: the narrative quality of memory, and the essential temporality of the city. There is a city formed from strata of recollected events and ascribed stories' (Donald 2000b: 150). The book concludes with extended ruminations on the city and on archaeology – after walking.

Each location on the itineraries prompts reflection upon aesthetic performance within the context of municipal history and the built environment; upon the performance of the city in its everyday guises; and upon the city itself. A combination of anecdotes, analects or parables of practice, enigmas, critical observations and recollections: risky accounts 'to register the queerest idiosyncrasies of the humblest actors' (Latour 2005: 121); 'Space is less the already existing setting for such stories, than the production of space through that *taking place*, through the act of narration' (Donald 1999: 183).

It is drawn to personal and public landmarks – 'one element from a host of possibilities' (Lynch 1960: 48) – to orientate the 'recalling of incidents, feelings and experiences that were constitutive of that individual's understanding of the life world'; 'the knowledge produced is importantly different: atmospheres, emotions, reflections, and beliefs can be accessed, as well as intellects, rationales, and ideologies' (Anderson 2004: 258;.260). It plots a 'knitted order of places', 'determined by preference' (Kittlausz 2006: 184).

Its scope is broad: it visits disused factories and scenes of crime, auditoria and film sets; it pauses on street corners and in *terrains vagues*; it describes displays of architectural confidence and conjures literary and media imaginaries; it recollects past incidents and their constitutive feelings, and it contemplates changes in the character and configuration of the city. So the National Pageant of Wales (1909), the race riots of 1919, J. Lee Thompson's film *Tiger Bay* (1959), RAT Theatre's *Blindfold* (1973) and BBC Television's *Doctor Who* inhabit the same landscape: the city accommodating and prescribing modes of performance within its built structures, the rhythms and schedules of its temporal cycles, and the ambiences and occlusions of its spatial and social networks.

In the invitation to participate, its walks may be undertaken physically in the field or imaginatively at a distance: to orientate the reader, each itinerary has an accompanying map; each location has a pertinent image, though there are few panoramic views; each halt has a consideration of performance and its documentation, of materiality, and of political and social history.

There is an alternation of sauntering and loitering: pausing at notable sites and undistinguished places – pointing to, or pointing out, this or that, before moving on in both space and time: 'geography and history are cosubstantial. Placeless events are inconceivable, in that everything that happens must happen somewhere, and so history issues from geography' (Macfarlane 2012: 147).

The walks embrace places that survive unaltered or that through processes of demolition, redevelopment and renewal may now be changed beyond recognition. They focus variously upon events, fabrics and surfaces, temporalities, appellations, demographics, planning and regeneration from several disciplinary perspectives: performance studies, archaeology, cultural geography and urban theory. They reference a range of related practices enacted there, and their practitioners, equally now changed or disappeared. Sites of commemoration (of blue plaques, statues, monuments); of daring solo deeds (balloon flights and murders) and collective demonstration; of baroque interiors and surviving facades; of erasures, losses, and hauntings; of decay and absence; of stirred reminiscence. A meditation on the passage of time in a place and in biography.

These are not the *dérives* of Situationist psychogeography – with their concomitant appeal to chance – though they do contain elements of reverie, and they are drawn back to old neighbourhoods, recording them for posterity (see Andreotti and Costa 1996). The object is to think topographically and pragmatically, the ambition 'to read landscapes back into being, and to hold multiple eras of history in plain sight simultaneously' (Macfarlane: 147).

Marking Time is a chorographic account that acknowledges 'the constitutive co-ingredience' (Casey 2001: 684) of people and places. Strictly local in aspect, it concerns specificities, particularities and peculiarities. In so doing, it disregards other places that fall outside its sphere of interest. It demonstrates partiality; its outcomes are prejudiced. Its accounts draw together diverse phenomena into a heterogeneous collection that evokes the tenor of place and time. Performance finds itself adjacent to, drawn into juxtaposition with, other *things* – mutually illuminating things, awkwardly dissimilar things – across the terrain and embedded through time within a particular region. Avoiding comparison with its supposed generic type elsewhere, in that taxonomic ordering by genre that pervades performance scholarship, it becomes a local feature of, and an active contribution to, the distinctiveness of a city; it may indeed be the most interesting thing that has ever happened at this site. Ed Casey's *things* (1998: 34) – his constituents of a choric region – may include all manner of celebratory, ludic and performative activities, as well as topographical features: contemporary devised theatre; international rugby matches; and monumental statuary are potentially co-present.

It is a work of micro-history, combining, overlapping and layering moments, things, places and people, in the conjunction of archive and personal experience. Its substance is defined by emotions, affects, anxieties, compulsions and obsessions as much as verisimilitude; it remembers forces and effects now invisible either on the ground or in the document; it is aware of the largely unnoticed, the in-between, the banal. The knowledges employed – often without citation – may include common, local understandings and hearsay that spring from being hefted to a place (see Lorimer 2006). 'A body is shaped by the places it has come to know and that have come to know it – come to take up residence in it, by a special kind of placial incorporation'; 'The reverse is also true: places are themselves altered by our having been in them' (Casey 2001: 502). We are held 'by various sensory and kinaesthetic means and in memory' (p.687) in 'robust places' that engage our concernful absorption, subjection and tenacity. Topography and somatography are merged.

The signature style is theory-inflected storytelling, including discursive, descriptive, creative and analytical voicings and various levels of rhetorical engagement. It is a concatenation of memoir – 'a dramatization of the past with yourself as both actor and spectator' (Donald 2000b: 149); scenographic depictions; passages of dramatic script; analysis of dramaturgical procedures and theoretical deliberations on urbanism. It works through forms of inscription that foreground its performative nature: 'In order to imagine the unrepresentable space, life, and languages of the city, to make them liveable, we translate them into narratives' (Donald 1999: 127). It involves interpenetrations of the historical and the contemporary, the political and the poetic, the factual and the fictional, the colloquial and the theoretical, mindful that in memory 'impressions of fictional stories and images, one's own imaginings, wishes and anxieties are assimilated as well and stain the individual ways of experiencing the world around' (Kittlausz 2006: 198).

Marking Time addresses Eyal Weizman's call for 'a complex methodology aimed at unlocking histories from the things that they saturate' in which 'the built environment must rather become a protagonist in the unfolding of incidents': 'the murky ground of a "fuzzy" forensics of probabilities, possibilities, and interpretations' (2010: 61).

It pursues routes akin to those charted in Jo Robinson's 'Mapping the moment:

Performance culture in Nottingham 1857–1867' project (Robinson 2013) and Nick Kaye's 'SiteWorks: 288 events/sites, San Francisco 1969–84'.

It takes inspiration from the work of Nicholas Whybrow, in his considerations of art and the city (2005; 2011); of anthropologist Kathleen Stewart, in her direct appeals to the reader to 'picture' this and 'imagine' that (Stewart 1996: 9–10); of architectural critic Jane Rendell in her *site-writing* and consideration of a site's 'material, emotional, political and conceptual' constituents (Rendell 2010: 1); and, in its selectivity, of chorographer Tim Robinson – 'I concentrate on just three factors whose influences permeate the structures of everyday life here: the sound of the past, the language we breathe, and our frontage onto the natural world' (2008: 3).

It is a guide to shrouded histories and indistinct occupations. In touching upon revenant histories – in conversations between past and present – it is often melancholic or elegiac in tone, with shades of nostalgia for entropy itself. Its small narratives help delineate particular origins; they may also subvert canonical trajectories of theatre historiography.

> And the theatre demands a writing appropriate to it, a writing of gesture, posture, and breath. (Nancy 2005: 65)

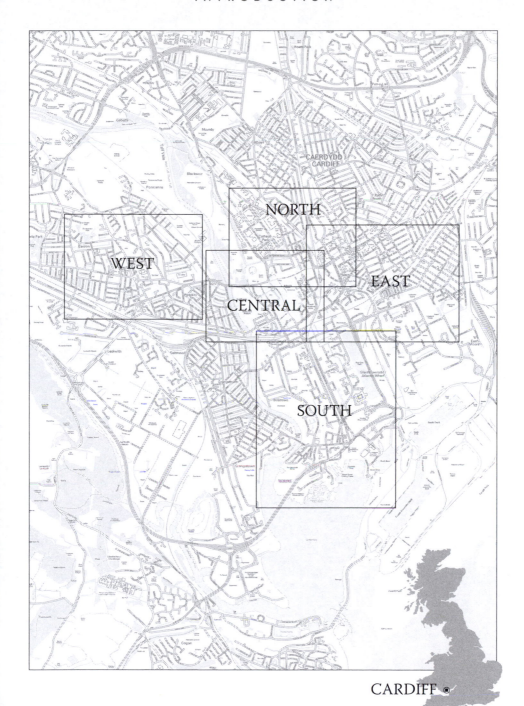

NORTH

WEST

CENTRAL

EAST

SOUTH

CARDIFF

ITINERARIES

1 University Arts Building

2 University Main Building

3 University Assembly Hall

4 47 Park Place

5 Sherman Theatre

6 Sherman Arena Theatre

7 Cathays Park

8 National Museum Wales

9 Park House, 20 Park Place

10 University Engineering Building

NORTH

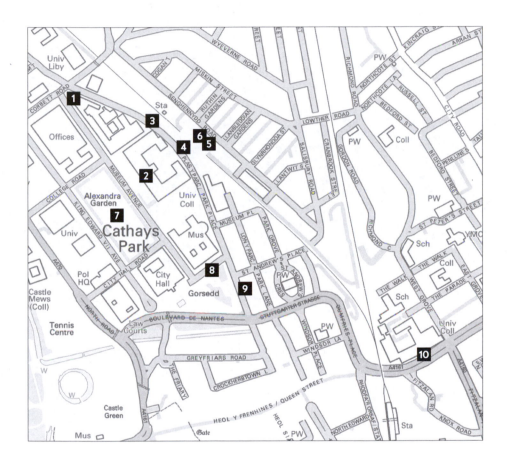

Theatre in Transit, *The Odyssey*, February 1970

1. University Arts Building

It fits the northern apex of the university site: a V-shaped, snub-nosed building by Cardiff architect Percy Thomas faced with vertical, fluted Portland stone, opened as the Faculty of Arts in 1962. The main lecture theatre appears unchanged: a small semi-circular dais with two risers faces tiered rows of fixed desks, though the entrances to toilets at front left and right that expedited entrances and exits in student drama productions are gone.

Here English lecturer Terry Hawkes rehearsed ideas towards his scholarly monographs *Metaphor* (1972) and *Shakespeare's Talking Animals* (1973): that human communication involves complex sets of inter-related non-verbal signalling 'systems' including gesture, paralanguage, noise, spatial and temporal relationships; that 'nobody just *talks*' (p.15). Inadvertently, he provided intellectual licence for a theatre based on physical expression, interaction and imagery, within which metonym and synechdoche might be key functions, and for which, after Claude Levi-Strauss, ritual and *bricolage* might inform both dramaturgical structures and approaches to improvisation and scenography.

Here in 1969, I played Captain Cat and Eli Jenkins in Dylan Thomas's *Under Milk Wood* (1954): one group in masks silently miming the action on the dais, the others reading the play behind the audience as in the original radio play. Visual and aural frames coming apart.

And here in on 24 October 1970, we presented the Pip Simmons Theatre Group in *Superman* – 'a comic strip play', a combination of fast-moving cartoon-style acting, live rock band and papier-mâché carnival heads. 'Simmons is speaking to a generation in England which has grown up on a diet of American films, TV, pop music, writers, comic books and coke. Americana' (Ansorge 1975: 31). Standing on the dais today is to appreciate the conditions facing the new touring companies and the need for flexibility in their stagings. And as Jimmy Olsen received messages from Superman through his electric guitar, the hired amplification repeatedly relayed the voices of passing Cardiff taxi drivers.

The script for *Superman* is published (Simmons 1972), though Simmons's disclaimers evince its devised origins: 'It is probably more useful to consider it as a scenario – written after the play was performed' (p.89). It includes extensive sections in parenthesis that describe non-verbal scenes, characterizations and musical atmospheres, in order to manifest emergent facets of theatre production: 'It was not our intention to provide a working script but to suggest possibilities to a group with five months spare time' (ibid.).

We had the time, but not the patience. Returning from the 15th National Union of Students Drama Festival held in Manchester over New Year 1970, Theatre in Transit created *The Odyssey* in two months. Making no claims to originality, we aspired to emulate the productions we had seen in Manchester – Keele University Drama Group's version of Megan Terry's *Viet Rock* (1966) with live band and spinning human helicopters, and Andrew Wistreich and York University Actors' Workshop's version of *The Ancient Mariner*, with the white bird in female form carried aloft; companies we had not seen, such as Nancy Meckler's Freehold – 'It is the body which has to bear the main burden of the theatrical expression involved: the text is often viewed as a disguised tool of repression' (Ansorge: 26); and companies we were unlikely ever to see, glimpsed in copies of *The Drama Review* held in the university periodicals library – the Living Theatre, the Open Theatre, the Performance Group, La Mama. And to employ exercises learned on a visit from Jane Howell of the Northcott Theatre, Exeter and those culled – though barely understood – from Grotowski's recently published *Towards a Poor Theatre* (1969). The beginnings of an archaeology of practice.

Following Peter Brook's prescription of 1968, our 'empty space' was the adjoining student coffee bar.

In the twelve surviving postcard-sized prints, more shades of grey than black and white, the padded leatherette benches are pushed back to form a rectangular performance area; a black sheet covers the noticeboard on the rear wall; the blinds are drawn. A transient occupation of a familiar place. Performers, barefoot either to aid purchase or after the fashion of the day, wear dark t-shirts and jeans, chosen from their own wardrobes; nothing else crosses the threshold of a theatrical scene barely set aside and marked only by degrees of rhetorical, physical activity. Without lighting, make-up, properties, scenery, costume, this is Grotowski's 'poor theatre' enacted programmatically: theatre as 'what takes place between spectator and actor' (Grotowski: 32).

Bodies pose and arms wave. We form a human boat, hands on shoulders – with Odysseus as the prow, outstretched palms together – passing between a grasping six-armed Scylla and a spinning two-woman Charybdis, knees flexing as the vessel plunges; we feel the walls of Cyclops's cave in front of the audience whilst the monster lies on his back, hands forming a circular eye before his face; Odysseus's ears are stopped as the Sirens call. Other photographs show enigmatic, blurred actions and momentary pauses as performers attend to events happening off camera. Naïve certainly but with some sense of physical and spatial composition. We turn our backs on spectators seated around; we appear three-dimensionally, but absorbed as much in the task at hand as in acknowledging their presence. We call it a 'theatrical experiment'; in the final photograph, cigarette in hand, I sit under audience interrogation.

It lasts twenty-nine minutes: the clock on the wall shows Cyclops's cave at 7.45, the boat caught in a rough sea at 8.00; and Scylla and Charybdis at 8.03. There are no negatives to indicate either the order of photographs or of the narrative trajectory, but the programme – from *Odyssey II* presented at the Edinburgh Festival in August 1970 – gives an inkling of the original structure: I. The Trojan War; Cyclops; The Lotus Eaters; Circe; The Court of Alcinous; II. The Book of the Dead; III. The Sirens, The Island of Calypso, Homecoming.

> The first and last parts are largely simplifications of the tale told in mime drama. They demand, and deserve and reward a certain degree of concentration for the sensitive details of the mime have as much to offer as the telling of the tale. (*Infringe* 4, Friday 28 August 1970)

Four pages of hand-written notes record sequences of events: groping for terminology in personal shorthand and obscure notations, now largely indecipherable:

> 3. <u>Circe</u>: boat stops. Jane goes upstage as Circe, Od [...] at side, crew explore island arriving at Circe's door. Suddenly opened – TABLEAU enticed in by [...], et, degenerate into pigs, freeze as pigs.
>
> <u>Enter Odysseus</u>, meets Circe; wants to go with her but can't move without the crew – this having been established by Od, is released by Circe who frees the crew, who discover themselves, go to help Od who rejects them; freeze
>
> Od. goes off with Circe. All neutralize. Form a boat. Sail.

The Odyssey included indexical tableaux and sequences: figurations, embodiments, impersonations and illustrations of people and phenomena from Homer – including held pauses that we referred to as *images* – with more elusive metaphors, allusions and physical citations. A 'mime drama' lacking spoken text: the programme perhaps as essential guidebook.

Ten minutes later, the configuration of the coffee bar was restored. It has long since vanished, colonized by offices and corridors installed in the present Law Department. The photographs of *The Odyssey* may constitute one of its few records.

University Main Building, 2013

2. University Main Building

In the foyer of the main university building sits the first principal John Viriamu Jones – 'relaxed but contemplative' – in white marble by W. Goscombe John. From this 'delightful space', 'long, vaulted corridors tunnel away' (Newman 2004: 234): their original wood panelling and floors remain intact, virtually unchanged.

Here, one weekend early in 1971, we played hide-and-seek with Bruce Birchall: 'a student drop-out from whom the term "filthy hippy" must have originated' (Walton 2013). More challenging was his stipulation that we walk to the building by a different route each morning, as we lived on Colum Road barely two hundred metres away. Strategies intended to challenge social convention and disrupt normative routines.

At university, Birchall had produced Peter Weiss's *Marat/Sade* (1963): 'Apparently, they'd gone round Cambridge after performances singing the songs in the streets and then went on to more practical attacks – window smashing and graffiti' (Walton 2013); at the NUS Drama Festival in Manchester at New Year 1970, he was instrumental in the student takeover; on 8 November 1970, he was in the group that forced the live David Frost Show featuring American activist Jerry Rubin off air. With PSST! (Please Stop Screaming Theatre) he made agit-prop and political street theatre: 'For Birchall, revolutionary theatre, which uses theatre as a weapon, is autonomous of society' (Craig 1980: 36); by 1977, he was arguing that cooperating with the state through accepting Arts Council grants was undermining revolutionary ambitions (see Kershaw 1992: 145).

Birchall's ideas – a combination of Situationist, libertarian, anarchist, socialist and Yippie attitudes and polemics – are enshrined in a samizdat publication entitled *Radical Arts* that circulated amongst a network of university and independent groups: 'What's this you're holding in your hands? It's about a problem: bringing together Art and Politics. Which means it's about bringing together "art people" and "political people".'

It includes interviews, accounts, exercises, scripts and articles such as 'Abbie Hoffman Rapping', and Jean-Jaques Lebel's 'Notes on political street theatre, Paris 1968, 1969'. Birchall's own contributions are two-fold:

'A Living Theatre'
Some Aims for a Living Theatre: (Find More)
– to use places imaginatively – to release their full potential …
– to slow down the pace of city living so experience may be deeper and more intense …
– to remove the tyranny of one specific use of objects and places, of one repeated activity being associated with all that a person is capable of.

And with Chris Rawlings and James Allen:

'Street Theatre – How to do it'

How to start: First get your group …

Suggestions: Props should be big. Collect them – you can use them over and over again. Exaggerated top hats for capitalists, big hands and fists on sticks, £ sign and dollar sign, banners spelling out key slogans. Step ladders are a very good image – easy to take with you, gives several different acting levels – for capitalists to look down on workers, teachers on students etc.– and for the authority-figures to be deposed from during the action …

In a play lasting 10–15 minutes you've inevitably got to simplify so your initial concept has to be very clear to avoid distortion …

Try to find central image (e.g. the educational race, the exploitation machine, the building and destroying of Cabora Bossa Dam) central ideas or central characters. Then you can improvise around these. Or choose known dramatic or entertaining images e.g. circus, auction, horse race, beauty contest, fashion show, tug of war, wrestling match … and transfer your political situation and characters to that framework. This is easiest accomplished if <u>verbally</u> the recognisable political clichés of the scene you're illuminating are put over simultaneously with the <u>visual</u> movements of the image you're transferring it to.

We too appear, in an act of confrontation:

Cardiff University group did a play in the very alienated atmosphere of students union at lunchtime: satirising the 'conversations' about work and sex which fly around in that atmosphere: one device being of two people who apparently did not know each other jumping into the automatic-kind of conversation straight away: worked best by not obviously being actors, just speaking slightly too loud, so they'd be overheard.

Inspired by contact with Birchall, Theatre in Transit created its third production as agit-prop theatre: *Welcome to the degree factory* was performed on 29 November 1971 in the Engineering Building Studio, and later at the 17th NUS Drama Festival in Bradford.

A schematic scenario – copied on a Gestetner duplicator with small hand-etched cartoons – was circulated to the network for comment: 'We hope this will be the first in a series of theatrical notes exchanged between universities and other groups'. It contains contemporary allusions and points of reference, not always easy to fathom: untutored 'hopes for great happenings' (Hunt 1976).

OUR SCRIPT

The action is based upon conveyor belts i.e. the mass production aspect; the boxes (sentry boxes, coffins etc.) – the selection and alienation aspects. Maybe the action could follow the journey of one individual through the mill. The whole thing is cartoon-like and taken at a fast rate. In the acting space – big

shiny brightly coloured boxes. Each box represents a college building – Arts and Social Sciences, Engineering etc. and one represents the union building. Note: Faculties should not mix; movement will be by conveyor belt regulated by academic clowns. Perhaps also chessboard pattern could be used, students as pawns.

The action begins at the general station where the students are met, given a slip of paper, a mock degree and advice to take the next train home.

1. Auction by Mr F.U.C.C.A., a northern comedian (introduced by Country Joe "Fish" chant). Auction six-formers – take account of A-levels, nice legs etc. Dim view of clearing; look down on less well-known universities …

11. Finals. Man with watch times students – metronomic, machinelike – as if for an egg ('How do you like them sir, soft, hard boiled' etc.) At end, let them out onto production line – given cursory handshake.

12. Stage divided as a pinball machine, as in Oxford's Tommy. Shunt candidates into the degree boxes – buffers have titles, such as department, faculty etc. Test candidates for [length of] hair etc.

Once in boxes cowboys come along and brand them – BA, BSc etc.

It elicited a response – from Harrow Youth Movement Street Theatre Group: 'A suggestion. Possibly some symbolic figure representing the forces of society (economic and economo-social) slowly putting chains or blindfolds or blinkers etc. onto students to make education etc. more to society [sic].'

The production programme asserts:

It takes a look at university life from the inside and presents it in cartoon form. … as a skeletonal [sic] structure, it may be performed in different ways to different effects. For example, to accompany a demonstration against the Thatcher proposals for the destruction of student unions. … after the show, we would welcome any concrete ideas or chat about the group and the show.

The extent to which its objectives were achieved is unattested: neither photographs nor final scenario exist.

Radical Arts stalled with us: we should have passed it on, kept it circulating. The yellow card cover is now shredding down the spine, the three staples rusty: quietly falling apart – transient in ideology and substance

John Viriamu Jones meanwhile remains institutionally secure: resilient, unchanging and unmoved.

RAT Theatre, *Hunchback*, Mickery Theater, Amsterdam, December 1973

3. University Assembly Hall

It was the largest room available for booking: a place to stage concerts – Roy Harper, Kevin Ayres and the Whole World – and mass examinations. Here too on 29 January 1972, the Keele Performance Group presented *Hunchback*.

The letter from director Pete Sykes:

> This construct began as a fairly free-form interpretation of the dominant moods and images of Victor Hugo's novel. But as a result of the social and political climate at Keele at the time of its conception, it took on – and has retained – a far greater significance. It is an examination of the relations and inter-relations of a society and an object regarded as outside that society … the conflict that is caused by the emergence of a sub-culture and its attempts at interaction with the culture; and most important, how the establishment seeks to resolve this conflict.

> Length: this construct is approx. 75 minutes in length.

> Lighting: no extraordinary lighting effects are needed. In fact, it can if necessary be done with only a very few lanterns and fit within set positions.

> Staging: there are no sets for this construct. However a rostrum (3 ft long 2 ft wide and 2 ft high) is necessary. It is best if this construct can be performed with audience on three sides and on a floor area of 50 × 50, into which is fitted the performing area (25 × 25 approx.) and the audience seating.

Simple to install, we arranged it against the long east wall in the large open space; the old cabinet provided as a rostrum quickly collapsed under the weight of several bodies.

In various guises, the Keele group presented increasingly provocative performances at the NUS Drama Festival: *Viet Rock* (Manchester, 1969); *Paradise Lost* (Southampton 1970); *Fallacy* (Bradford 1971). *Hunchback* was created post-Southampton, using a combination of yoga, theatre games, military training and exercises gathered from the Living Theatre, Grotowski and Freehold.

The publicity reads:

> Hunchback developed through improvisations and workshop situations, and it continues to expand as a result of continued exploration in performance, as well as in workshop.

> Hunchback explores in terms of a sequence of physical images the relationship between the structured group and an individual alien to that group; it explores the conflict that this attempted integration by the alien precipitates; and finally it explores the attempts made by the group to resolve the problem.

> Interspersed with these structured passages are open sections which allow

us to maximize the energy, and the dynamic force that is injected into the situation by the presence of a live audience. This allows us to make a step into the realms of the unknown; that area of theatre which it is impossible to experience in the confines of the workshop, and that is why performance is important to us; it opens up a situation where some form of positive communication is possible … but that does not mean to say it is always achieved. And that is why our work continues.

A sequence of tableaux, choreographed sections and open passages in what they termed a 'construct': fermented in the over-heated environment of a campus university and presented in the barest of conditions.

Simple to disassemble, not easy to forget. But what is the nature of remembering performance? Does duration inevitably collapse into a few images and impressions?

In the chapter 'Crippling Inadequacies' in his *Staging Real Things* (1994), Geoff Pywell recalls in shocking, often poetic detail a performance of *Hunchback* by RAT Theatre, which he takes to stand for 'Real and True Theatre' (p.13).

At the opening: three silent, statuesque women …

> [and] a prone figure, wearing only a loincloth, the body twisted horribly. His cheek was pressed to the floor, his neck obliquely angled, his face turned away, and the curve of the spine seemed impossible, alien. He was completely, inhumanly, still. (p.14)

Time passes. Then in response to a giggle in the audience, the figure responds with a slight movement of the head. And then again:

> This time a slow and exquisite swan-curving of the neck toward the sound, a yearning of the ear to catch the slightest repetition should it come. The figure in its absurd contortion was suddenly pitiful, achingly vulnerable. This is important because without this dimension, without the awful pity, the terror that followed would be even more inexplicable (p.16).

First physical response, then vocal mimicry as he begins to copy coughs and noises from an increasingly proactive audience. Suddenly it changes: 'Any noise now was greeted with a swift turn of the head and a piercing, totally intimidating, glare'; 'Both the atmosphere and our perceptions, already heightened by the sensory engagement, were re-arranged in an instant' (p.20). The hunchback grabs a female performer by the hair:

> … and in a single, rapid motion brought her face down on to his raised knee. I could hear the sharp crack of a bone. Her nose opened up. He lifted her head, still held by the hair and showed us the blood covering her face as her knees went from under her so that she seemed to be swinging like a grotesquely abused doll from his grasp. He held her there for a few seconds and then let her drop unceremoniously to the floor. Without removing his eyes from us, he ground his heel into the face beneath him. She didn't move and I believe at that point she was unconscious. (p.21)

Spectators begin to leave and shout obscenities as he attacks other performers, whilst continuously regarding the audience: 'I think he hit her three times before she collapsed' (p.22). Mayhem ensues as two men leap on stage and grab him:

> He fought back and I saw one of his first assailants felled by a vicious butt to the head. The actor lashed out in a Dionysiac frenzy, kicking and clawing and screaming. The actor, honestly spent and probably hurt, began to laugh as they struck him. (p.22)

Hunchback was profoundly disconcerting for Pywell, in the realization that it never entirely stopped being theatre. Is this then what we saw in Cardiff? I remember the violence and the nudity certainly. But Pywell's experience resembles a psychic dislocation in which memory and imaginings coalesce, in which for him anything might have happened, might have been true: 'Once again I felt that I didn't know where I was' (p.21). One female allegedly receives a hairline fracture; 'Pete' later commits suicide …

From hearsay, he then describes a subsequent performance called *Cripple* in which the male actor locks an audience in a gymnasium, lurching around on crutches, cursing, before attacking them in the semi-darkness.

> There was a general panic and confusion and when the lights were turned back on, he was once again restrained by the audience. His final act was to try and swallow the key to the building. (p.155)

An illusory conflation of Keele's *Paradise Lost* and RAT Theatre's *Blindfold*? Myth-making of which Pete Sykes would surely have approved. And now we cannot enquire: Pywell died shortly after publication, and Sykes passed away in 2006.

On 9 December 1972, we performed *Hunchback* at the Institute of Contemporary Arts (ICA) in London, three men and Sykes in the first professional constitution of RAT Theatre. For us, it was never so bloody, though always surprising: at the Chieri Festival in Italy in June 1973, Sykes climbed Quasimodo-like to the top of the altarpiece in the church in which we performed.

Biomechanic training, October 1972

4. 47 Park Place

The offices and consultation suite of the student health centre now occupy the lower floor. Of the original room, only the patterned windows remain, and the composite floor, its impacts still residing in hips, knees and elbows: 'Give blood – or we'll come and take some' resembles an admonition from the past.

Former features – door, skirting board, radiator – appear occasionally in twenty-nine colour transparencies: as three hirsute men in black t-shirts and knee-length tights are captured, sometimes airborne, though frequently bending, breathless, head down; or squatting in rest positions.

After the Cardiff performance of *Hunchback*, I travelled to Keele to be inducted into the training technique the group acquired during the summer of 1971 from Swiss company Les Treteaux Libres – seemingly a distortion of the exercises of Grotowski and Eugenio Barba, and already attaining a mystique. Pursued daily, they termed the practice *biomechanics*, though it bore little resemblance to Meyerhold's system of that name.

It consisted of four phases: preparation; floor exercises; wall exercises; and *plastiques*.

Preparation featured impulsive movements: 'picking apples' rapidly around the body and 'firing ball-bearings' from the fingers; 'electric yoga' – the rapid alternating of *asanas*; rising from kneeling by lifting the pelvis.

The floor exercises comprised a vocabulary of forward and backward rolls, handstands and dives; jumps in various attitudes; sitting and squatting positions; lifts, catches and carries; equilibriums and shoulder-stands.

The wall exercises were five standing positions, hands against a wall at different angles – two forward, two in reverse, one handstand – in which vigorous motions of the pelvis were transferred to spine and shoulders. In addition, the 'cat' was performed on the floor in a contracted 'push-up' position, requiring similar thrusts and feline emulations.

Most difficult were the *plastiques*: a series of flicks, kicks and jerks of isolated body parts, combined into a standing, writhing motion.

A training session would include repeated transitions from one phase to another – through personal preference or by instruction – creating energetic excitation in the room. Objectives included building stamina and endurance, and occasioning contact: men and women, body to body, from all angles. Gradually, the lexical moves of the floor exercises were strung into long-form, individual improvisations; then, with growing cognizance of others, tuned to foster encounters, making oneself available to lift, to be lifted, revealing physical interactions that might ultimately inform moments of performance.

It was arduous, grinding, achieved without either mats or compromise; and it was crude, undertaken by un-athletic bodies, oblivious of present concerns with fitness. It was achieved without either mirrors or the video recording that might have given some external impression of how it looked; and in the absence of viable, portable playback systems, without musical inducements. This was physical theatre before contact improvisation, and before the application of the term to dance-inflected approaches.

And it was psychologically taxing. In Keele, the group constantly urged each other on through imputation and abuse. In the scrutiny of interpersonal relationships and confrontations with self and others, and putative ecstatic release through pelvic and spinal articulation, R. D. Laing and Wilhelm Reich were required reading, as was Mircea Eliade's *Shamanism* (1964), in an attempt to distinguish these activities from actorly practices.

Biomechanics necessitated uninhibited commitment to action in a scene of exposure. It was exhausting: one quickly reached thresholds of decision on whether to go on in the development of dynamic and energetic flow. 'The techniques that are used are designed to push both the mind and body to the very edge of their endurance ... and ultimately over that edge', publicity reads.

A letter from Pete Sykes:

> University of Keele Student's Union, 22 Feb 1972.
> ... at least physically your body and senses are still ticking over after the ordeal of your initiation ...

> Since you left we have had ups and downs group-wise ... the bio-mechanics have taken their toll on us ... mentally and physically ... and on me personally the whole of my stomach armouring is it seems disintegrating. Head consequently is suffering a kind of information chaos ... but I go on. And in the end 'ON' is the only way to go ...

In October 1972, behind closed doors at 47 Park Place, Mike Baker, Mick Brennan and I begin to train and to develop a performance inspired by two sources: Pieter Breughel's painting of a file of blind men falling, and the story of Siamese twins Chang and Eng. A notebook records our further interest in Artaud and psychology. We work in blindfolds and we tie ourselves together: to create purposeful disabilities, conditions to be explored through extemporization. Provisionally, we call it *Les Aveugles.*

In July 1972, I had received an unexpected letter from Pete Sykes: 'What it comes down to is this ... R.A.T.T. is me ... there is no group at present.' In October, he comes to train with us; within a fortnight we are RAT Theatre though whether Real and Actual, Ritual and Actual or Ritual and Tribal is never made clear.

In January 1973 we premiere *Blindfold* at the 18th NUS Drama Festival in Durham. Later, *contra* accusations of being 'barbaric, sadistic, pointless, or even reducing theatre to the animalism of the wrestling ring', Mike Baker would write:

'We do not see violence in performance as being in essence more than an extension of the physical language that we use to explore the situations that we stage to reflect our experience of life.'

The publicity flyer is both idealistic and belligerent; backs against a wall, we look like a rock band:

> All these doubts, all these fears have to be confronted and overcome before we can expose ourselves to a performance situation. But this does not necessarily ensure that new ones cannot and do not emerge in the immediacy of the performance. Without exception every performance creates new and unforeseeable difficulties for us.

> And this is why we go on.

> These difficulties are not solely our property; they affect the audience, they affect the world. A call is thus made to the 'humanity' of the audience.

> Or perhaps it is this 'humanity' that is being called into question …

> We do not pretend to be the Living Theatre … We do not identify with Grotowski's Laboratory Theatre … we do not choose to follow their well worn and crowded paths.

> We are R.A.T. Theatre and the direction we have chosen is the one which is particular to ourselves. We have made a conscious choice to express ourselves in this way, in this medium, in this day and age.

> Tomorrow, who knows …

On 17 November 2007, a symposium on RAT Theatre was held in Aberystwyth University (Hulton 2007b): to recover the company's work, to examine the cultural, political and artistic contexts within which it existed, and to celebrate the life of the late Pete Sykes. It drew together the reminiscences of former company members and surviving documentation in an evocation of times past, in presentations, interviews and discussions.

And a group of Aberystwyth students under Louise Ritchie demonstrated biomechanics: despite advice to the contrary, men of mature years attempted to reveal some of the finer points. How training might lead directly to forms of sophisticated, free-flowing group improvisation is apparent in the video documentation (Hulton 2007a). But when demonstrated live – without academic parenthesis – at the British Grotowski Conference at the University of Kent in June 2009, it caused uproar: a mix of concern for participants' safety, and affront. As if, briefly and sensationally, RAT Theatre and 1973 and the temper of the times were revenant.

Brith Gof, *Patagonia*, 1992

5. Sherman Theatre

It was a gift of Harry and Abe Sherman of the Cardiff-based football pools company: a sequestered space 'of dark brown brick, virtually windowless, giving nothing away' (Newman 2004: 236).

The proscenium of Alex Gordon's main stage is wide, its aspect open. It survived the recent refurbishment (2010–12) which clad the exterior in scale-like metal plates, though the original seating has been replaced and the hydraulic orchestra pit removed.

Stage and auditorium are two interior spaces built around the principle of separating the 'see' from the 'being seen': the one, often a place of darkness that tends to be sociofugal, positioning spectators and fixing sight-lines; the other, of illumination, of focused scrutiny, where anything might be adjudged significant. Theatre as a relatively static object whose structure is regarded as unchanging, where perception is limited and representation fixed; where architectural configuration and scenographic principles influence the type, nature and quality of techniques of exposition employed, and their reception. Theatre as a locale of concrete and conventional and increasingly fixed social practices. Imagining aesthetic and political change has frequently involved imagining a new role for the spectator: by taking them elsewhere, by re-orientating them spatially; or by transgressing the boundaries of the auditorium, the divide of them and us, 'in here, out there'.

Here in 1973, audiences crossed the proscenium in Joint Stock's production of Heathcote Williams's *The Speakers* (1982) which features a quartet of Hyde Park orators, including the fearsome Jacobus Van Dyn, whose face is tattooed with bows and roses, hearts, flowers, twigs and butterflies. The speakers stood around us on milk crates; in the middle of the stage, the 'Town and Country' refreshment stall served tea. An ebb and flow of language and opinion, of acute social observation, of prejudice, of rambling invective; and of spectators too as we shifted from speaker to speaker. Aware as we peered into the darkened 'wings', where access was prohibited, that we were adrift on stage.

Brith Gof's *Patagonia* (1992) attempted to unite the spaces by creating another, all-embracing architecture of sound (see Pearson 1996). With radio microphones on stage and audio speakers around the auditorium, voices could be distributed, moved and overlaid, removing from performers the need to project, allowing them to employ modes of address and intimate tones unusual in this context; enabling live voices to be mixed with pre-recorded samples and soundtracks, the visual and aural sliding out of synchronicity to suggest the disorientations of this truly foreign land.

Patagonia took the story of the assassination of Llwyd ap Iwan in 1910, allegedly by Butch Cassidy and the Sundance Kid, as its spine; this was elaborated and illuminated by descriptive, discursive, tangential texts creating a kaleidoscopic picture of Welsh emigration to Patagonia.

Four performers – two men and two women to add further tensions to the story – in the costume of the late-nineteenth century, worked in varying combinations of solo, duet, trio, quartet, allowing a simultaneity of different activities on different areas of the stage. The text included monologues; hymns; field recordings; extracts from imaginary guide books; lists; descriptions of artifacts, photographs and women; and a radio play. Springing from the company's experience of having visited that landscape in South America in 1984, of having met the descendants of those emigrants. Significantly, the various fragments of material were not ascribed to particular individuals before rehearsals began.

Imagine this. Cliff McLucas's scenic design utilized the full width of Gordon's stage in emulation of Cinemascope: a strip of sand and a skeletal scaffolding frame represented the trading post in the desert where ap Iwan was gunned down. The focus of activity gradually moved from left to right, crossing the thresholds from desert to steps, verandah, store, office, and strongbox. This formal setting resembled a diagram or architectural drawing: the picture was flat, filmic, lacking perspective, without any impression of depth.

Synechdochic in nature – sand=desert, frame=house – it drew together the fabricated and the found – contemporary scaffolding and antique artifacts – in composing a separate theatrical reality, complete, if schematic, in its parts.

Patagonia had nine sections. Sections 1–7 each consisted of an *event* of one-minute duration, followed by a *state* of six to ten minutes. Section 8 comprised a radio play and the resolution of the physical activity presented in the preceding sequence of events, with a replay of the death of ap Iwan. Section 9 was an epilogue of 'lies told about Patagonia'.

The sequence of events leading to the assassination used the conventions of the earliest silent movie acting: non-stop movement, acting in different styles within a single frame. Each event began and ended with a freeze or tableau as the camera 'turns over' or 'runs out': before each event the stage was 'wiped clean' by the passage of two large, suspended light-boxes, the freeze appearing in silhouette. The soundtrack that accompanied the events of Sections 1–7 resembled a film score, composed as a single basic theme that gradually accumulated more layers of orchestral voices. These were fully expounded and remixed in Section 8. This climactic orientation in the events provided the dynamic impetus of the performance; it provided the only sense of a narrative through-line.

The states included material of different orders: personal reflections, tall tales and fictions, dialogues and Biblical quotations. English and Welsh texts travelled in sequence and in parallel, with little direct translation. The performers were free to use a variety of performance modes – from hymn singing to story-telling, from manual rhetoric at static microphones to choreographed enactment – in the exposition of this material.

The fractured nature of the scenario allowed the employment of formal and informal performing modes and various acting styles, with the possibility of repeatedly stepping in and out of both character and narrative; of addressing the audience directly and retreating into mimetic reconstructions; of confounding practices and conventions that the stage/auditorium boundary might presuppose.

As commentator/narrator/director, I sat facing the stage in the semi-lowered orchestra pit throughout; finally, I climbed onto the stage to take the role of ap Iwan.

In Eddie Ladd's *Cof y Corff/Muscle Memory* (2007), the auditorium was recast as 'digital environment'. Audience members wore headphones to hear the bilingual text spoken by Ladd. They sat in groups clustered around small screens on which they could watch her captured live, on cameras that tracked and followed her choreography on stage – sometimes out of plain sight – with the images processed and manipulated on set: 'A true post-modern experience that enabled the audience to become an agent of the performance by choosing to watch what was on stage or on the screen or to focus on the sound, both outside and inside the headphones' (Kasner 2013).

'The real crux of the project was altering the existing spaces' reveals architect Jonathan Adams of the refurbishment. 'As we peeled away the layers of plaster and fake ceilings we uncovered quite a lot of structure that we didn't know was there' (*Wales Online*, 2 February 2012). Downstairs, the white rehearsal room where Cardiff Laboratory for Theatrical Research presented its first production *Abelard and Heloise* in February 1974 – two men and two women in black – has gone: 'The spectators sat in two rows facing each other, forming an aisle. At either end were the set images; the central area was open for free activity. It was as if the spectators were a jury' (Pearson 1980: 22).

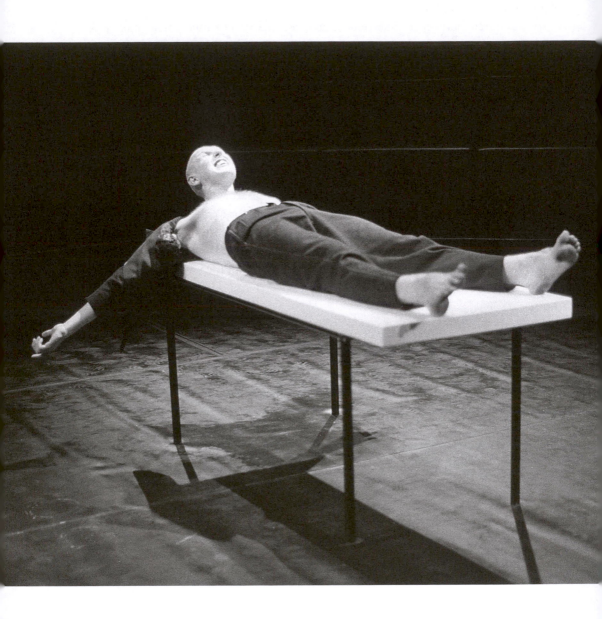

Cardiff Laboratory for Theatrical Research, *The Lesson of Anatomy*, July 1974

6. Sherman Arena Theatre

The hexagonal arena studio was opened in 1973 by Welfare State International: a morning lion hunt for children in the surrounding wasteland located a moth-eaten stuffed creature that was subsequently burned; the evening event included a cake in the shape of a swimming pool ('We made a mistake'); Sir Lancelot Quail constructing a brick wall ('Haven't built bugger yet'); and the illuminated, Perspex model of the Sherman being gradually and poignantly buried in sand and surrounded by monoliths of ice.

The arena was not a black box. And the planned retractable bleachers under the surrounding walkway were never installed. Instead, fixed seating rakes surrounding seventy percent of the performing area created a configuration – of audience proximity to performers, of spectators observing spectators – and an intimacy that favoured direct address: in Peter Weiss's *Marat/Sade* (1975); in Joint Stock's *Fanshen* (1975). Here, on 5–6 July 1974, Cardiff Laboratory for Theatrical Research presented *The Lesson of Anatomy: the life, obsessions and fantasies of Antonin Artaud.*

The concept of French directors Jean Gremion and Patrick Guinand, whom I had met when RAT Theatre performed *Blindfold* at the World Theatre Festival in Nancy, France in May 1973, was to employ the inflammatory, accusatory and disturbing texts Artaud produced mainly towards the end of his life – 'Van Gogh, The Man Suicided by Society'; 'To Have Done With the Judgment of God'; 'Artaud Le Momo'; 'Les Tarahumaras' – in a performance of four sections, corresponding to his various views of the body: 'Flesh' on the body physical; 'Bardo' on the dream body of the Tibetan Book of the Dead; 'The Other Body' on his desire for a different physicality; and 'Asylum ' on the body social. Eventually, I performed 'Flesh' and 'Asylum' alone.

They imagined the arena as an anatomy or autopsy theatre, a marble slab at its centre; they arrived with the medical section of Denis Diderot's Encyclopaedia, and ambitions for me to appear wearing a mouthful of dental clamps.

In 'Flesh', the proposal was for a man alone, obsessed with his own body. Initial compositional work included abstract sculptural poses, isometric contortions, physical dynamism and the parodying of liturgical postures – but just too athletic for Artaud. Change came with an appreciation of his dark humour and ability to distance himself from his own most horrific statements; and with the acquisition of an old dinner suit. Gradually, a figure emerged, fascinated by the functions and mechanics of his body: erratic, comic, desperate, disturbing.

In the one hundred and eighty-two black and white photographs, I appear shirtless and shoeless, dressed in the shabby garb. By pulling the jacket over the head, or rolling the trousers, fractured images could be presented, starkly black and white; parts of the body could be isolated, as if for dissection. The suit as both straightjacket and comfort blanket. The continuous search for imperfections and preoccupation with orifices and facial appearance became behavioural traits; smoking was both nervous habit and delineation of inhalation and exhalation; playing with matches potentially dangerous. Ears, eyes, mouth; touch, smell and taste became the focus of actions: fingers crept into holes and into trousers; saliva covered the face and shaven head; cigarettes were stuck in ears; outbursts of swearing were recurrent. A thin line between artifice and reality:

> He bites himself, scratches, preens his head. He casually finds words on the back of a matchbox or on the label inside his jacket. Sometimes he dances; sometimes part of his body crashes to the table. He tries to get his nipple into his mouth; his fingers attach to his tongue, deforming speech.
> (Pearson 1980: 12)

Under close scrutiny in the immediate setting of the arena – in ironic reference to theatre convention and practice, and allusion to analogous contexts elsewhere – the figure could by turn resemble medical patient, deranged variety act, after-dinner speaker, confessional tramp, naughty child, vampire and self-regarding dandy given to embarrassing silences and ecstatic outbursts.

A mortuary slab was always impracticable: what infections might lurk in the veins of marble? Instead, a white table became demonstration worktop, soapbox, park bench and life raft; instrument of torture and haven; territorial marker and choreographic reference point – 'The floor as crap, the ceiling as God. Man pinned between the two' (ibid.). And the figure was able to engage the audience directly and to reference the distinction between me 'out here, on view', and you 'over there', watching me – as entertainer, lecturer and exhibit.

In 'Asylum', based on texts produced during years of confinement and experiences of electro-shock treatment, the figure wandered in dressed in white shirt and trousers, hand lightly on the face for comfort, the limbs shaking. Yet the movement to the table was swift and definite:

> There was an alternate tensing and relaxing of the body, having a marked effect on the curvature of the spine, extended during a direct attack on Western culture, collapsed during personal reflection. There were almost imperceptible movements of the hands. And above all there was the action of the eyes, piercing, powerful and focused during tirade, dilated during withdrawal, sometimes like mirrors, at other times like magnifying lenses for the spectators.
>
> ... accusatory outbursts, on the breath, to the world outside the theatre, almost on behalf of the spectators. There was the lecturer and monologue on the technical matters of psychiatry; also a dialogue concerning experiences under electric shock ... there were personal reflections, single words, whispers, revealing a world of innovations, hallucinations and distractions, and speech addressed to self, stimulated by private jokes and invisible connections. It was

as if the performer could see a series of radiating circles, each of which could
be spoken to, and accompanied by relevant focusing of the eyes. (ibid.)

A conflation of patient and performer: whether before a group of consultants or
a demanding audience, similar questions – 'How can I make them understand my
experience?' 'Can you accept me as real in this artificial situation?' (ibid.).

The form of the Sherman Arena survived refurbishment, though the seats are
removed and entry is now at ground level. Here on 5–6 July 2014, on the fortieth
anniversary of their initial staging, I intend to perform 'Flesh' and 'Asylum'– or at
least to attempt to perform them – revealing the effects of ageing whilst summoning
modes of confrontational performance long extinct. As reference, there are personal
notebooks, though no video. Of the photographs, I make a number of suppositions:
that they were shot during one non-stop rehearsal; that the films were numbered
in the order that they were exposed; and that if the photographs were shot in the
order of the performance, then the numbered series of the negatives should indicate
the sequence of that performance. The arrangement of the images in order will
then provide a relative chronology – how time passed – but without any sense of
duration. Time between one exposure and the next remains uncertain, or indeed
whether the photographs record moments of stillness, or of actions stilled. I have
only vague intimations of how long sections lasted.

And yet all is not quite as it seems. In one frame, the jacket is on the right arm,
slightly later it is on the left. Perhaps there are retakes here, or images printed in
reverse: conundrums of documentation incidentally registered, and lacking regard
for forty years hence.

Albert Hodge, 'Mining' (1908–12), February 2013

7. Cathays Park

Once site of a short-lived mansion (1812–25) built by the 1st Marquess of Bute, the corporation first tried to acquire Cathays Park in 1858; instead, Sophia Gardens – named for the widow of the 2nd Marquess – was transferred to the town as open public space. The 3rd Marquess of Bute relented in 1896 and sold the fifty-nine acres of the rectangular park for £159,000, strictly for the construction of public architectures.

The competition for a new town hall was announced in 1897. Won by the 'swaggering Baroque' of the young firm of Lancaster, Stewart and Rickards, Cardiff was pronounced a city – and this its City Hall, 'Villa Cardiff' – at its opening in 1905. It was gradually joined by an ensemble of monumental classical buildings in the creation of 'the finest civic centre in the British Isles' (Newman 2004: 220): law courts, university, museum, county hall. And it set precedents: the taste for classical design, the use of Portland stone as facing material and the establishment of a cornice line respected by subsequent buildings, leading to a sense of coherence, uniformity, harmony and proportion. Two types of Portland stone are even employed in Alex Gordon's bunker-like Welsh Office, designed after the bombing at the Temple of Peace in 1968 by Mudiad Amddiffyn Cymru.

Fired by 'boosterism' – asserting growing civic confidence and international aspirations – individual plots were laid out along broad boulevards: 'It's what I imagine imperialist capitals in Africa or Australia look like' (Hatherley 2010: 268). This civic enclave and landscape, where building ceased in 1972, continues to orientate the circulation of the city.

It is a place of war memorials. And of dedicatory statues: the 1st Viscount Tredegar (1909), survivor of the Charge of the Light Brigade in the Crimean War, in uniform on horseback; John Cory (1906) – 'Coal Owner Philanthropist by his friends and fellow citizens as a token of their appreciation of his world wide sympathies' – in Astrakhan coat, top hat in his left hand on hip, open papers clutched in the right; Lord Ninian Edward Crichton-Stuart (1919), Member of Parliament for Cardiff, Cowbridge and Llantrisant who fell on 2 October 1915 at the Battle of Loos – in British Expeditionary Force uniform of jodhpurs, laced boots, field glasses in right hand, swagger stick in left.

Crichton-Stuart was the guarantor of the lease on the city's football ground, as, in 1908, Riverside Albion became Cardiff City AFC; Ninian Park was named for him. The 'Cardiff Bluebirds' themselves are allegedly nicknamed after Maurice Maeterlinck's children's play *The Blue Bird* presented at the New Theatre in 1911.

Whether distinguished by class or trade, these are forthright men, meeting the world on the front foot, performing confidently in perpetuity: all caught in bronze by Cardiff sculptor W. Goscombe John.

Inside City Hall, in the Marble Hall are the ghostly and ghastly figures in white Serraveza marble presented to the City in 1916 by Viscount Rhondda of Llanwern: St David (by Goscombe John, inevitably), Giraldus Cambrensis, William Morgan translating the Bible, Henry VII after the battle of Bosworth, Owain Glyndŵr. Their unveiling by David Lloyd George is recorded in a massive painting by Margaret Lindsay-Williams.

> The imposing statues … will ever bear tribute to the part which Wales has borne in the civilising and elevating influences of the Empire. (*Illustrated Catalogue of the Welsh Historical Sculpture*, Cardiff, 1916, in Evans 2003: 124)

Outside, Welsh dragons are everywhere, notably on the dome. There are also elaborate sculptural groups and friezes that conjoin figures, symbols and objects from mythology, commerce and industry: a three-dimensional world that enacts, displays, projects and exudes civic self-assurance as much as enshrining allegorical connotations. Vivid, vertiginous and performative groupings of people and things cluster on the cornice: in dramatic, often pyramidal compositions around a central figure, in which left and right match without mirroring.

On City Hall: 'Poetry and Music', and 'Welsh Unity and Patriotism' with a dozing lion; and panels representing cardinal compass points – 'North' with walrus, pole star and icy curtain, 'West' with bananas, bison and tomahawk. Most striking are 'The Sea Receiving the Severn', an erotic fishy charge of entwined tails and scaly torsos, as Neptune receives a fluid, nubile Severn. And looking down are 'The Taff, the Rhymney and the Ely', the water-swept models of Cardiff's three rivers.

On the Law Courts: 'Science and Education' in which a seated figure engrossed in study reads a scroll, whilst another holds an open book towards us. In 'Commerce and Industry' there are bare-chested miners with chains and cogwheel, and merchant and mariner with ropes, nets, and anchors.

Flanking the entrance to Glamorgan County Hall are two colossal groups of excessively muscular and veined figures by Albert Hodge (1908–12): in 'Mining', helmeted Minerva and grimacing, gaping, semi-naked toiling miners, bent in the effort, pulling and pushing; in 'Navigation', a manic Neptune and half-submerged, rearing, straining horses, literally bursting out of the plinth but arrested by isometric tension. Frozen ensembles that read like a performance or film as one circles them, discovering fresh juxtapositions of bodies, creatures and objects from different aspects. But faces are beginning to erode, fingers and toes to go missing, lichen and moss to encroach, stains to appear.

The 3rd Marquess, heavily robed and magisterial, is in Cathays Park; the 2nd Marquess moves around the city, though he always looks towards the castle not his docks. He is currently on the desolate roundabout that is Callaghan Square – in ermine and gartered tights, and bright green verdigris. He stood first outside the Town Hall in the middle of St Mary Street; in 1879, he relocated to the bottom of

St Mary Street, close to the canal. He now faces nondescript office blocks.

John Batchelor (1886) – 'The Friend of Freedom' – Liberal mayor and opponent of castle influence sometimes shifts slightly too on The Hayes, to accommodate the latest traffic layout (see Morgan 2006). He and Aneurin Bevan (1987) frequently wear traffic cones on their heads, in mockery of their oratorical poses.

Rugby player Gareth Edwards (1982) is all action; but boxer 'Peerless' Jim Driscoll – 'The greatest exponent of the straight left' – allegedly nicknamed by Bat Masterson, sheriff of Dodge City, is four square.

For Aldo Rossi, monuments are primary elements in the city: persistent and characteristic artifacts, with symbolic function in relation to time that can both retard and accelerate processes of urbanization:

> Certain works which participate as original events in the formation of the city endure and become characteristics over time, transforming or denying their original function, and finally constituting a fragment of the city …
>
> Other works signify the constitution of something new and are a sign of a new epoch in urban history; these are mostly bound up with revolutionary periods, with decisive events in the historical course of the city. (Rossi 1982: 115)

Monuments may be 'the tangible trace of collective memory, or perhaps as the mnemonic device that can reactivate accumulated memories' (Kerr 2001: 72); they may 'give every individual the justified feeling that, for the most part, they pre-existed him and will survive him. Strangely, it is a set of breaks and discontinuities in space that expresses continuity in time' (Augé 1995: 60).

If, that is, we ever notice them: silent actors suspended in preternaturally long durational performances, marked only by processes of erosion and decay, and ghostly shifts.

Detail, Paul Brewer, 'A Section of My Studio Floor', 1981

8. National Museum Wales

Although George V and Queen Mary laid the foundation stone in June 1912, the National Museum did not open until 1927. In Portland stone, it completes the frontage of the civic suite, though in a monumental American Beaux-Arts style rather than the adjacent Baroque. The courses of its basement are at the same level as those on City Hall, and the cornice line of the side elevation is at a matching height (Newman 2004: 228), enhancing visual continuity and creating a datum. The sculptural groups show archaeological 'ages': the 'Modern' has man with telephone, aviator in flying helmet, and female graduate in mortarboard.

At the opening ceremony in 1927, Lord Pontypridd called it 'a shrine of Welsh antiquities' and 'a monument to the Welsh people' (Redknapp 2011: 1). And here are the iconic objects – a combination of the purposefully preserved, the intentionally deposited, the accidentally lost, the incidentally recovered – through which a national history is constituted: the twin-headed Iron Age fire dog, evocative of tribal feasting; the Llyn Cerrig Bach gang chain, with its neck rings for five slaves or prisoners; the rood figure of the crucified Christ from Kemeys Inferior Church, one of only four such pre-Reformation figures in Britain – gaunt, bare-chested, worm-holed, eyes downcast.

Sir Cyril Fox, museum director from 1926 to 1948, included the rooms of a Welsh farmhouse, and a replica coalmine in the basement; in the archaeological gallery, he introduced models – of the Neolithic long barrow at Tinkinswood, a Roman hypocaust. But the conventions of display were strictly typological and periodic: stone axes in serried ranks, all Bronze Age rapiers together.

Post-devolution, the gallery has shifted from storehouse to a narrative of inclusivity: the exhibit 'In search of early Wales?' is subtitled 'Who are we?' The narrative is of origins, emergence and continuity: materials are displayed in a timeline from front to back, in tall vitrines that allow objects to be glimpsed through objects. The icons remain, but amended by the outcomes of advanced archaeological investigation – Neanderthal teeth from Pontnewydd Cave, Mesolithic children's footprints from the Severn shore. No mention of the shadowy Celts or of the racial characteristics that once marked a distinct and separate Welshness.

It also includes works by contemporary artists. Mary Lloyd Jones's hanging banners feature quotations from early Welsh poetry and a vocabulary of marks from the Neolithic tombs on Anglesey – circles, spirals, wavy lines, dots and dashes. Blaenau Ffestiniog sculptor David Nash's 'Charred Panel: 3 Cuts Down, 3 Cuts Across' is a four-metre obelisk, black and scored: 'Three elements build from the ground: first a blank; then subdivided left and right by a vertical; then the vertical repeats with a horizontal added. This could then be read as a cross'; 'Charred wood is a mineral, and no longer vegetable; a dark surface reflects but does not absorb.' These works extend claims – that museums are inspirational, that we Welsh continue to be creative – whilst inadvertently problematizing archaeological attributions based solely upon functionality and value. What would be made of Nash's sculpture were it to come from a Bronze Age context? What were 'we' doing when we weren't merely surviving? And perhaps throwing interpretive imaginings onto less immediate objects: the supposed Neolithic bone flute, the Iron Age trumpet mouthpieces.

The Museum houses the major collection of Gwendoline and Margaret Davies, granddaughters of industrialist David Davies Llandinam: paintings by Corot, Corbet, Manet, Monet, Pissarro. But four artists are vernacular in their attention, and archaeological in their resonances.

In 1774, Thomas Jones (1742–1803) painted 'The Bard', the eponymous figure with long white beard, hooded robe and harp about to leap off a cliff to escape the persecution of Edward I, a stone circle based on Stonehenge in the background. It is an over-familiar image, imitated and parodied by Welsh performance artist Bedwyr Williams (Williams 2013): his re-enactment is entitled 'Bad Attitude'. But two small *plein air* oil sketches record scenes from Jones's visit to Italy: 'Houses in Naples' (1782) and 'Buildings in Naples with the North-east Side of the Castle Nuovo' (1782). These are detailed, close-up views from the open windows of his lodgings near the harbour: of the backside of the city; of crumbling, pock-marked plaster, exposed stonework, shuttered windows and doors, dark interiors, peeling paint, lines of washing, wisps of smoke. In 'A Wall in Naples' (around 1782) in the National Gallery, London, the wall is pitted with scaffolding holes and stained by dirty water tipped from the balcony. They are strikingly modern: flat geometric shapes, slanting shadows, subdued tones and cropped images. And they record the quiet decay of the everyday: an early document of contemporary archaeology.

In February 1966, Mark Boyle and his wife Joan Hill organized 'The Annual Dig of the Institute of Contemporary Archaeology' on a roped-off section of a site in Shepherd's Bush that had been an ornamental garden statue factory. As demolition was already under way and permission not forthcoming, Boyle produced a bogus letter from the Institute authorizing him to undertake clearance: 'Thirty or so diggers in three hours excavated hundreds of broken statues, molds, tools and a magnificent stretch of early 20th Century concrete paving' (Boyle 2013). An early coinage of contemporary archaeology: part actual act of recovery, part performative artwork.

In September 1968, the Boyles commenced their project 'Journey to the Surface of the Earth', subsequently pursued with their children as 'The Boyle Family'. They selected one thousand sites in the world at random, by throwing darts at a map; they then visited each site and identified a square of six feet, depending on the terrain, the bottom edge delineated by throwing a carpenter's right-angle. Amongst their strategies was then to preserve and exactly recreate the surface and texture of the square using a process of casting and sampling. In the 'Manual for the Journey' (ibid.), they outline their approach. For solids they advise – 'Take the actual surface coating of earth, dust, sand, mud, stone, pebbles, snow, moss, grass or whatever; hold it in the shape it was in on the site. Fix it. Make it permanent.'

Part archaeological document, part artwork, the resulting 'multi-sensual presentations' exist somewhere between the real and the replicated: fragments of the material world, records of the mundane and ordinary. The National Museum's 'London Study' (1965–66) is one of a hundred earlier studies in 'The London Series'. It includes a paper bag and a piece of newspaper on an anonymous pavement.

Paul Brewer's 'A Section of My Studio Floor' (1981) is exactly that – an embellished latex mold of the parquet floor in the artist's former studio in Chapter Arts Centre: dirty cream in hue, encrusted, scratched, with scraps of newsprint attached, Hung vertically, it was shown in the Museum's National Museum of Art inaugural exhibition in 2011.

At the international Artes Mundi 2012 exhibition, winning Mexican artist Teresa Margolles, who has a background in forensics, showed a section of the tiled studio floor, bearing a small smear of red paint, upon which artist Luis Miguel Suro was found murdered: 'The empty surface, which has borne witness to the horrific crime, marks the absence of the person, showing loss as a result of the act rather than evidence of the act itself' (Margolles 2013). An attestation of acts unimaginable, a testimony to a crime that remains unsolved.

Park House, 20 Park Place, February 2013

9. Park House, 20 Park Place

20 Park Place, currently the Park House club and restaurant, was designed by William Burges for James McConnochie, dock engineer to the Bute Trustees. In a simplified early French Gothic style, its asymmetrical front elevation has a pillared lateral entranceway and steeply angled, gabled roof. Built between 1871–74 by Bute workmen from the docks – the new Roath Basin opened in 1874 – this was Burges's first building in Cardiff. It was to be a paradigm for the city's architecture: it provided a template, giving status to a style and establishing both look and fabric. Grey, snecked, rock-faced Pennant sandstone with dressings of beige Bath stone and Gothic arches, embellishments and coloured glass ran through the castle, churches, chapels, libraries, schools, arcades, mansions and residential terraces, as late Victorian architects and speculative builders aped Burges's proclivities.

As the city burgeoned, the Bute Estate – together with the Tredegar and Windsor Estates – declined either to sell its land, or to build mass housing. Instead, it granted ninety-nine year leases whilst retaining rights to the final approval of designs, elevations, construction materials and standard of workmanship: 'The builders must be seen as the *agents* of the city building process, but with very little responsibility for the *character* of that process' (Daunton 1977: 89). They built in bulk, resulting in 'a housing stock of uniform size and appearance' (Finch 2004: 93); in the inner suburbs, inhabitants live in houses of only two or three basic internal plans.

The close attention of the estates led to a housing stock that was generally of high quality but often beyond the means of working families; properties quickly became multi-occupancy – in 1911, 36.2% of families were sharing houses (Daunton: 98). And leases were strict, with requirements to repaint the exterior every three years and outside every seven, and to insure the house.

If districts are defined by 'thematic continuities which may consist of an endless variety of components: texture, space, form, detail, symbol, building type, use, activity, inhabitants, degree of maintenance, topography' (Lynch 1960: 48–9), distinctions may be difficult to discern in a period of rapid, homogeneous development.

'The alignment of most of the streets of the Cathays, Adamsdown, Riverside and South wards of modern Cardiff, and the layout of substantial areas of the suburbs, are the work of Bute officials' (Davies 1981: 201). Bute houses frequently have bay windows and small front gardens; in Adamsdown and Splott, the building line of the humbler terraces of the Tredegar estate is directly on the street. Bute planning often included squares and parks; and the refusal to lease Cathays Park and Bute Park preserved large open tracts in the city centre.

As a visitor, districts are known through imprinting of nodes, routes and landmarks; as an inhabitant, their associations are 'soaked in memories and meanings' (Lynch: 1). For both in Cardiff, there may be subtler aspects that mark an area: the play of light; the acoustics; the feel of its surface under foot; the circulation and choreography of its everyday.

Cardiff is Bute in character, weighty and well built: large areas of the late Victorian/ Edwardian low-rise city survive intact. But this was not foregone. By the mid-1960s properties were deteriorating rapidly and leases beginning to fall in. At the end of a lease, the property reverted to the ground landlord – by this time Western Ground Rents – which it could have chosen to demolish, develop and rebuild.

> With so much of Cardiff having been built between 1870 and 1914 and buildings usually lasting about a hundred years before they fall down, the old Marquess of Bute's cunning 99-year leases would have had a devastating effect on the shape of the city and its social character. (Morgan 1994: 53)

Without the Leasehold Reform Act (1967), Cardiff might have looked completely different. Drafted by Pontypool MP and homosexual rights campaigner Leo Abse, brother of poet Dannie Abse, it enabled the tenants of houses held on long leases at low rents to acquire the freehold, or an extended lease on fair terms. With the introduction of Improvement Grants in 1969, tenants were able to buy freeholds and start renovation. Large areas were prevented from further decay and avoided clearance: 'Cardiff was reclaimed for its citizens' (p.54). And amongst the latter were artists, for whom Cardiff proved a relatively inexpensive place to live.

The Gothic architectural style endures externally and internally as a familiar, as context and ambience for performance, in a city well suited for it: 'a wet climate – with thunderstorms, humidity and damp – seems to play a major, arguably indispensable, role in the Gothic imagination' (Manaugh 2009: 92). Whether its ambience leads to feelings of 'dread, constriction, obscurity, transgression' (p.91) is debatable, though much performance considered in this volume does lack Baroque extravagance.

Edwin Seward's Royal Infirmary (1882–1908) is strictly Gothic, though his Central Free Library (1882) of Bath stone with Portland columns and finials is more 'Elizabethan': it marks the first appearance of a new material. The use of Portland Stone in the civic buildings – to mark distinction, to demonstrate confidence – was unprecedented.

A single company, E. Turner and Sons Ltd., whose catalogue of 1929 (see Anon.) is modestly called *Superb Buildings*, constructed most of Cardiff's early major buildings: City Hall, Law Courts, National Museum, University College of South Wales and Monmouthshire, Glamorgan County Hall, Fire Station, Post Office, Coal and Shipping Exchange, School of Medicine, Duke Street Arcade. Also, the now demolished: the Capitol Cinema with seating for three thousand persons and standing accommodation for fifteen hundred, and a second-floor dance-hall with Austrian oak floor; the three-tiered Empire Theatre – 'The proscenium is surrounded with Greek Gipolino Marble and the Act drop is a view of the Acropolis (Athens)' (p.40). And the much altered: David Morgan's former department store

(1891–1904) in Bath, Portland and Forest of Dean stone, though the Morgan Arcade still functions as intended. Turner's also built the offices of John Cory on the corner of Mount Stuart Square and the enormous National Westminster Bank that spans the block between Bute Street and West Bute Street.

The company's masonry works was on Ninian Park Road: here gantry cranes could lift twelve-ton blocks. 'Every stone is shewn for fixing purposes on a key plan which is delivered to the site of the building, and shewing clearly its position thereon, with comparative ease' (p.11).

The catalogue also contains advertisements for suppliers and contractors: B. Ward and Co. for wood block and parquet floors; Bristow Wadley and Co. Ltd. for stained glass and leaded lights; The Marble Mosaic Co. for 'wall lining and tiling and all kinds of marble work.' The pediments, architraves, tiles and chimney pots eventually stacked in the reclamation yard on Ferry Road: the city in pieces. All that had fallen off, fallen out, become rendered surplus to requirements; that didn't survive home improvements and the ravages of do-it-yourself in the 1970s; that couldn't resist the installation of central heating. Still present at the Pumping Station on Penarth Road: fireplaces to doorknobs on sale. Traces of resolute advancement and idle vandalism: sought out in the recreation of domestic interiors similar, but not too similar to Victorian antecedents.

After Rossi, the city as archaeological artifact: the perpetuities of Bute's actions configuring and conditioning daily life, sustaining values and functions in ways barely perceptible: in dwelling together.

RAT Theatre, *Blindfold*, January 1973

10. University Engineering Building

Another room impossible to locate: a lecture hall in the University School of Engineering and Physics – constructed as the Medical College by Turner's in 1918 – converted into a studio by Sherman Theatre director Geoffrey Axworthy in 1972, prior to the opening his theatre, to encourage student audiences. In-filled by later spatial reorganization: gone without a trace.

Here the Pip Simmons Theatre Group performed *Do It!* – 'Half-way between fantastic recreation and crisis documentary' (Craig 1980: 26) – after US Yippie Jerry Rubin's polemic text (1970). The first half climaxed with the storming of Chicago Democratic Convention in 1968, the theatre filling with noxious smoke; the second half, featuring giant marionettes, focused on the trial of Rubin and the so-called Chicago 7. But Simmons's attitude was ambiguous and even cynical: 'It caught the image of a society during a potential moment of breakdown and, above all, the hysteria of its youth reflected in the rhythms, power and even obscenities of the language and music' (Ansorge 1975: 33).

For The People Show, chairs were arranged on stage: 'The most important part of the show became where we were doing it, the space in which we were doing it and the people who were there. We worked out situations that were flexible and could react totally to the people, to the space. There was no commitment to return to a prop, not even a commitment to a character' (Long 1971: 54). 'It has decided and recognized its materials – space, light, sound, people and all that entails – colour worn or animated, objects worn or animated. The fact that these materials are more used by "The Theatre" than any other art form is neither here nor there. It is the conflict of these materials, these images played out in an audience environment that becomes the Show' (Theatresurvey 1971: 63). In Cardiff, Mexican performance artist Jose Nava smeared a box of Shredded Wheat cereal with butter and then attempted to eat it, box and all.

Here on 12–13 January 1973, RAT Theatre presented *Blindfold*.

> In "Blindfold" everything revolves around a cripple, sole survivor of an ecological catastrophe who brings up three children, whom he has torn from their mothers' wombs, with a blindfold over their eyes so that they do not become aware of his infirmity.
> All their education is conducted to the sound of blows, let loose at random with long sticks of wood and with a heavy crutch. In the course of the show the sticks break on backs shining with sweat, on legs marked by bruises and abrasions or even on the faces of the actors. (*Panorama*, Chieri, Italy, 12 July 1973)

The makeshift adaptation of the hall is evident in the sixty-one black-and-white photographic prints of *Blindfold*, unobscured in the production's lack of emplaced scenography: a carpeted tier replaces the rows of desks at the front; heavy curtains hide flanking walls; at the rear of the area that now functions as a stage, the panelled entrance doors are covered and painted black.

The audience sits close to the action in two rows to either side and on the rake in front: a ground-plan repeated elsewhere and recorded in a small blue sketch-book – back wall, bare performing area, audience on three sides. Spectators draw back, legs extended protectively; or push forward, hands clasped, apprehensively. One individual covers her face, another is agape.

Before them: three figures in tattered loincloths and blindfolds, long hair gathered in topknots; the sighted fourth in a shirt. Only several broom handles, a wooden crutch, and a bowl for burning human hair enter the scene. This is Breughel's *The Blind Leading the Blind* (1568) in action: muscular men feel, lift and embrace each other; they focus, listen, anticipate and beseech; they climb, cling, cower and link; they are dragged by the hair; they receive navel, oral and sexual gratification; they explore and seek out with the sticks; they participate in rituals of rebirth. For them, the blindfolds set a condition, an ergonomic impediment. Their only sense of orientation – of approaching threat, succour and comfort – is provided by sound that might issue from many sources, in a room fraught with peril:

> Every sound means danger. Every cough or shuffle from the audience means, for the players, fear and possible pain. They react heavily to every sound, which creates an enormous tension between the audience and the actors. You see those three people suffering and that is a terrible thing to see. You hold your breath and try not to move. (Jac Heijer, *Haarlems Dagblad* 6 December, 1973)

They are blindfolded; and in their relationships and interactions they are a blind fold.

After the dramaturgical signature of RAT Theatre, I was social outcast, though become Messianic figure, teacher, leader, guide. If the portrayal of disability is difficult to condone today, its metaphorical resonances and complexities are apparent in critical reviews, the relationship variously taken to represent state/individual, tyrant/oppressed, God/mankind, father/son, guard/prisoners, handler/beasts. In retrospect, *Blindfold* mirrored Simmons's disillusion and frustration with a youth culture grown complacent and rendered ineffective by growing economic realities and industrial dispute. It was aggressive, confrontational, disturbing, insolent and preposterous but only ever about itself: a provocation in the moment – form and content locked in one semi-coherent outburst of energy; proto-punk in attitude.

I toy with the audience in a hideous circus: the threat of violence is always greater than violence itself. In the end, as I grasp the legs of the audience, crutch broken, Pete Sykes removes his blindfold, looks around as if in accusation, and then replaces it.

The dramaturgy included fixed images, choreographed sequences and longer improvised sections that 'allow us the possibility of exploration in the presence of an audience' (publicity flyer, 1973). There is sufficient documentary material to provide some sense of a trajectory that always began with Pete Sykes diving in over the audience's heads.

> Blind rise, slowly, jerking, impulses off the sounds in the room. Audience realise sound is their world. Make noises – they control the blind. Blind panic if noise builds. Find each other – impulse together – climbing. Searching – if touch audience, retract immediately (from a schematic scenario).

But only a fragment of film shot at the World Theatre Festival in Nancy and discovered in the archive of the Institut National de l'Audiovisuel (INA) in Paris demonstrates the kinetic awareness and empathy of the blind as they jump, lift and fall regardless of risk. Most striking is the film's colour when the photographs render the performance's themes and atmospheres, its world, black and white. And the sound of ricocheting broom handles is a perfect sonic mnemonic. 'This was brutally realistic – with the marks to prove it and riveting to watch' (*The Guardian*, 7 February 1973).

Returning to the photographs:

> Certainly, it was bloody, accidentally if not systematically. If you look closely you can still see the stitch marks above my right eye where the crutch flew from my hand, opening it like a boxer's cut. I spent the rest of the performance streaming blood, which is of course what the audience had paid to see. Ironically, my fellow performers didn't realise it had happened, as they were all wearing blindfolds.

Performance engraved on and in the body, as scar and worn joints; and ingrained too as barely acknowledged dispositions – physical, artistic, political.

1 Bridgend Street
2 Topaz Street
3 Ruby Street
4 Metal Street
5 Sanquhar Street
6 Moira Place
7 Adamsdown Cemetery
8 Howard Gardens
9 'The Vulcan'
10 'The Big Sleep'

EAST

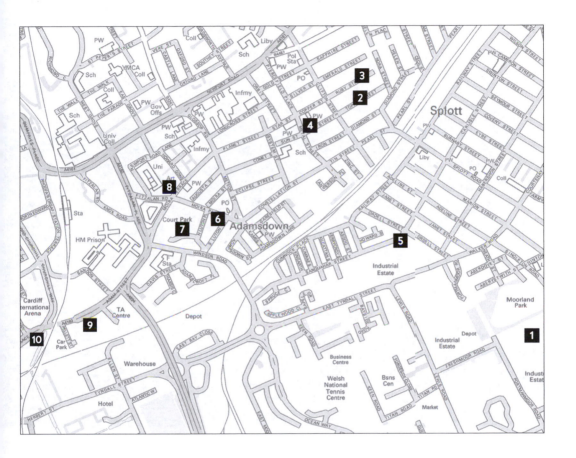

Transitions, *Captain Confusius*, 1971

1. Bridgend Street

Picture this: three spacemen in silver vinyl suits on Bridgend Street – Captain Confusius, Spacewoman Wotsit and Astronaut Arbuckle.

And you will need to envisage both figures and ground. Of the Welsh towns only Aberdovey and Aberystwyth survive intact; Neath and Swansea are now cut short by the grassy patch that is Moorland Park, muddy goalmouths betraying recent exploits; Bridgend, Caerphilly, Llanelly, Pontypridd, Tenby and Milford are gone. So too Menelaus, Layard, Enid, Elaine and Cornelia, relatives and associates of ironmaster Ivor Bertie Guest. All are amongst the fifteen streets demolished between 1972–78. The only mark of East Moors Iron and Steel Works is in names on the Portmanmoor Industrial Estate that squats its site – Guest Road, Keen Road, Nettleford Road and Dowlais Road.

Until 1850, Splott ('God's plot') was a moory waste with three farms (see Childs 1995; Childs 2012). In 1887, the Bute estate leased one hundred acres to the Dowlais Iron Company – with wharfage on Roath Dock – as it relocated from Merthyr Tydfil, seeking a coastal site giving readier access to materials now economically unviable inland. Two blast furnaces were blown in 1891; steel production commenced in 1895. In 1902, the company became Guest, Keen and Nettlefolds (GKN), one of several subsequent guises; in 1978, the British Steel Corporation closed the works, making eight thousand people redundant. Parallel to the works, east of now-attenuated Portmanmoor Road, the company built terraced housing for its workers: 'a bewildering maze of houses, shops, taverns, and Board Schools' (*St Peter's Chair* June 1891, in Childs 1995: 151).

It was in the Welsh towns – already scheduled for demolition, already partly abandoned – that community arts project Transitions worked in the early 1970s. In its *game-plays*, costumed figures appeared at a play-site or scheme and in a short dramatic introduction – including songs and improvised passages, and involving imaginative play and suspensions of (dis)belief – outlined a theme and posed a problem to be solved in a day of participatory craft activities, construction, processions and performances.

In *Jack Russell's' Circus* (1972), a ringmaster and two clowns arrive alone. The rest of the circus has been sent to China: unfortunate, as Lady Fiona Ffinch Ffish, 'the most important lady in the world', is to visit that afternoon. Children take up the challenge: creating costumes and devising acts for a show of talents for Lady Fiona. Each staging culminates in a rough-and-ready cavalcade of clowns, strong-men and part-human lions, elephants and camels through the neighbourhood.

> I'm Captain Confusius the best spacemen yet,
> I'll go to the moon it's an even bet,

And when I get there everyone will say,
Confusius the best in the land.
Chorus: Heigh-ho what shall we do
Go to the Moon, you can come too,
Heigh-ho, we'll all lend a hand,
To Confusius the best in the land.

The fantastic, though robust, conceit of *Captain Confusius* (1971) is that Confusius believes he has landed on the moon: his ambition, to found a school. He is ready to start building when it is pointed out that he is not on the moon but at a certain play-site, and that the children are not the 'moon creatures' he has assumed them to be, as he attempts to communicate in the 'moon language' in which he is the professed expert. Wotsit reveals them to be humans: 'Hello, what's your name?'.

'Can't you see what this means? All my hopes destroyed! I'll be a laughing stock! I'll look a complete fool! What can I do?' Confusius laments.

Disappointed, he is urged to make a bargain: that if they help him to get to his destination, he will take them too. He is not easily persuaded and raises a series of objections that must elicit creative responses if the notion is to proceed; his indecision is constantly countered by sung ripostes, and through problem solving. For example, as the children won't know how to walk on the moon, Confusius, 'the greatest teacher in the universe', instructs them in a mimetic movement sequence. Later, all are invited to speak 'moon language' – a combination of gobbledygook and hand gestures – to each other and to Confusius himself; to fight moon-men in slow motion; and to decide what they will teach on the moon. Arbuckle chooses maths and spelling, instigating a game in which children physically form numbers and letters by lying on the floor and which culminates in a boisterous competition on a lunar theme between two teams.

Confusius's final objection is to the lack of suitable equipment, but he promises that if they're ready at 3pm, he will relent. The cast then withdraw and change out of costume; for several hours, with other helpers, they guide the making of spacesuits, helmets, breathing apparatus, passports and capsule – from paper potato sacks, cardboard boxes, discarded scrap and waste material, suitably painted and adorned.

The acceptance and implementation of the challenge varies by group, individual and age range: at Llanover Hall Youth Arts Centre, the constructed capsule has roll-down hatch cover and approach steps, wall maps, portholes with star paintings behind them, moon-men identification charts, a huge nameplate and egg-box driving apparatus.

As the day proceeds, participants are repeatedly recalled to the 'astro-teaching circle': to review progress, introduce further instructions and renew impetus towards task completion. The songs – similar to children's rhymes – taught during the initial performance and frequently repeated, help reiterate the plot and sustain the conceit. Several have interrogative or call-and-response structures that can incorporate individual contributions: 'Who saw what on the moon?'; 'Susan saw stars'.

The return of Confusius is accompanied by checks and double checks: 'lunar explorer' photographs are taken; participants learn the 'Take-Off Chant', and how to brace themselves in flight. On landing, Wotsit undertakes a series of interviews and the assembled crew completes a space walk. A new 'moon-man attracting' song – 'Come to school, come to school, come to school on the moon, You'd better come quick, so you'll get here soon' – succeeds and in a comic scene the monster (two volunteers as a four-armed, four-legged creature) learns English in order to examine the passports. It is then questioned about life on the moon. In response, in the 'Lunar Clapping Game', it asks them their favourite foods. The evanescent fantasy climaxes as the moon-man sends everyone back to Earth – by putting their helmets on the wrong way round and spinning on the spot; a parade sometimes follows. The characters finally remove their costumes and reveal their identities: I am Confusius.

In the Welsh towns: 'the day's activity had been frenetic; almost the whole of the area's young population, around seventy, had been working on space suits and then gone out onto the streets' (Pearson, 1973: 161).

Two photographs: in the *South Wales Echo* (10 August 1972), Transitions's George Auchterlonie, 'The Pied Piper of the 1970s', leads a gaggle of children on Portmanmoor Road, guitar in hand – 'The Splott children helped to make costumes and built a town [sic] of cardboard boxes'; sometime in 1975, a woman sweeps the pavement in front of her house on Portmanmoor Road (Briggs 2002: 144) – a daily task given the dust and grit generated by the steelworks, and necessary when the front door lets directly onto the street. An enduring practice, though this community surely knows its fate: a display of domestic fastidiousness all but vanished.

Transitions, announcing *Dracula's Castle*, August 1972

2. Topaz Street

Picture this: a video camera, reel-to-reel recorder and monitor on Topaz Street, during Adamsdown Community Week, 5–10 August 1973. The poster reads: 'Our own community tele – keep an eye out for the cameras which will be recording events and doing interviews.' Enabling startled residents to see themselves 'here, just now' without recourse to processing, often for the first time; or 'these events, later'. A Transitions initiative presaging Cardiff Street Television and Chapter Video Workshop. An envisioning that might have been additionally difficult.

To the west of Clifton Street are the metals: Zinc, Tin, Iron, Lead, Copper, Silver, Gold. To the east the precious stones: Agate, Pearl, Diamond, Topaz, Ruby, Emerald, Sapphire. Tight terraces lacking front gardens: streets laid out on Tredegar Estate land between the late 1860s and 1890, 'a homogeneous area of artisan housing' (Newman 2004: 311). In the 1960s, they were almost cleared.

Cardiff: Development and Transportation Study (1966) by Colin Buchanan and Partners regarded the city centre as 'worn out, inconvenient, drab and downright dangerous.' Buchanan's 'transport-driven land-use planning, based on high-growth projections' imagined Cardiff 'studded with high-rise office complexes and criss-crossed by urban motorways to allow people to drive into the city and park on the edge of the ring road, encircling a largely pedestrianized shopping area' (Punter 2006: 123). Thirty-six miles of new urban motorway would require the demolition of three thousand, three hundred homes: the Central Primary – the Hook Road – would drive through the precious stones, meeting the Southern Primary at the Splott Interchange, towards the southern end of Clifton Street at the Tredegar Hotel. Buchanan himself acknowledged the extreme difficulty of inserting new structural features into a standing fabric and the likelihood of disturbance to property and livelihoods.

The proposal for a citadel city on razed foundations included inducements: a national theatre, an opera house, and extensions of the University and National Museum. But opposition was fierce from local residents' groups, and in Parliament from Ted Rowlands, Labour MP for Cardiff North: 'People worried about the effect of roads on their homes and lives and on their neighbourhoods are not Luddites' (Rowlands 1968: 573); 'I believe the City Corporation has not even begun to count the social cost involved' (p.575). Buchanan's plan was never realized but its ambitions were taken up in 'Centreplan 70', a collaboration with private developers Ravenseft that would have levelled much of the existing core: 'a modernist vision of office towers (up to twenty-one storeys) and covered shopping centres linked with first-floor pedestrian decks to multi-storey car parks across the city centre' (Punter: 125). This too included library, facilities for adult education, youth activities, the arts, entertainment, design, exhibitions and conferences – all financed from projected commercial revenue. At 56 St Mary Street, a large wooden model was displayed for public inspection. The scheme foundered in the property slump and fuel and industrial crises of the early 1970s, leaving the integrity and distinctiveness of residential areas relatively intact but the corporation in possession of the many properties it had compulsorily purchased. This would result in more piecemeal commercial development, though the ensuing St Davids 1 and St Davids 2 shopping malls fulfil Centreplan by default, occupying much of its proposed site.

In 1972, Transitions was able to secure a house on Topaz Street, rent-free from the vacated housing stock, as a base for its activities in Adamsdown and Splott,

Founded in September 1971 by George Auchterlonie, Jill Taylor and myself (see Pearson 1973), Transitions was one of a number of companies – notably Interplay in Armley, Leeds – inspired by the philosophy and practices of Interaction: 'Ed Berman's master-plan for revitalizing the community through the use of drama' (Theatresurvey 1971: 62). Launched in 1968 by former Rhodes scholar Berman in Camden, London, Interaction engaged in a wide variety of dramatic and art activities, through the Ambiance Lunch Hour Theatre Club, the Dogg's Troupe street theatre group, the Fun Art Bus and the experimental TOC. It was the enhancement of community cohesion and advancement through the application of specialist artistic skills in the field of social work, particularly through the involvement of children, that progressively became its aim, against a perceived lack of opportunity and space for creative interaction and expression in urban milieux: 'I am suspicious of statements on politics which are not borne out by actions' (Berman quoted in Itzin 1980: 51).

A key component of Interaction's approach was the participatory workshop and its attendant repertoire of theatre games and exercises: 'It's based on children's games and not on verbal or intellectual ability' (p.52). These group sessions offered frameworks for participation through play, aiding the development of individual and social capabilities. Guided by trained 'enablers', they offered a flexible and transferable, though controlled, environment; essentially, they required participants explicitly to 'contract in', underscoring the need for self-discipline and helping shape relationships.

These formats were transferred into Dogg's Troupe *game plays*: *Moonmen* commenced with the arrival of Dr Watt and six padded creatures on a playground; a series of participatory games then ensued to reveal the Moonmen as fakes. *Make a Circus* began with a parade:

> Beating drums, wheeling cartfuls of old clothes, paper and assorted junk, and armed with megaphones, they invited any children in the vicinity to join in.
> A startling pied-piper effect soon turned a trickle of curious passers-by into a parade which was led into a park or playspace where the children would gather round a makeshift ring to watch a circus performance by the group. Afterwards the children were encouraged to perform their own circus – this

> could involve such improvised props and menagerie as a distinctly human-looking lion jumping through a hoop comprising two twelve-year-olds. (Asquith 1980: 92)

Interaction's achievement – in a period of provisional and short-lived self-help and pressure groups – was to institutionalize itself as a charitable trust with a viable business structure and to build relations with statutory authorities: its enablers were accredited by the Inner London Education Authority and worked in contexts such as the Henderson mental hospital: 'a redistribution of resources and engagement as a means of building critical ability, voice and argument' (Amin and Thrift 2002: 147).

In Cardiff, the aim of Transitions was to make the creative arts 'more relevant to, more readily available to and more responsive to various communities and their particular environment', 'to the aspirations and needs of the participants' (Pearson 1973: 59).

> Our aim is to offer involvement and active participation in artistic activities. We further believe that involvement and active participation in such creative activity performs a vital educative function on both a personal and social level, since it offers the individual an opportunity to explore both himself and his relationship and behaviour with others. (Company statement, March 1972)

Activities were focused in areas of Adamsdown and Splott both reprieved and scheduled for demolition, in corporation property with both long-term and shifting populations, and in analogous communities elsewhere.

Transitions presented game plays and organized workshops and dramascapes, emulating the methodologies of Interaction, and of Interplay whose object was 'to make the arts more relevant to education, to environment and to the community' (quoted in Pearson 1973: 49). *Captain Confusius* drew on Interaction's *Moonmen* and Interplay's *Apollo 15*; *Jack Russell's Circus* on Interaction's *Make a Circus*.

By 2001, Buchanan imagined that the whole area would be redeveloped (Buchanan, Vol. 6, Paper 21: 5). But Topaz Street is still occupied. On Clifton Street: 'No more Patrice's grill though: the place you used to be able to drink all night long as you ordered a portion of chips had finally bitten the dust' (Williams 2000: 37). And the lettering on the Tredegar Hotel reads 'gar'.

proto-Cardiff Laboratory for Theatrical Research, *Image*, June 1973

3. Ruby Street

The stone reads: 'To the glory of God and in honour of Saint Lawrence the Martyr. This foundation was laid All Saints Day 1908. To the poor the gospel is preached.'

St Lawrence's Mission, an annex of St German's Church, was planned for a converted, end-of-terrace house and adjoining triangle of land – the coal yard of Jasper Oram – at 56 Ruby Street; Lord Tredegar himself donated Nos. 52 and 54 for its extension. For fifty-five years, it housed the Sisters of the Society of Saint Margaret who were dedicated to the care of the sick and poor, helping mothers and the victims of domestic violence, rescuing neglected children, and running a free refectory amongst the rapidly expanding population of Adamsdown. The nuns lived on the first floor where there was also a small chapel; the downstairs hall accommodated parish events – Sunday schools, sit-down suppers, Boy Scout and Girl Guide meetings, Christmas pantomime. By repute, it had the best dance-floor in the parish.

With improving post-war social standards, the mission fell into disuse; the remaining three sisters left in 1963 – the statue of Our Lady (now lost) went to St Saviour's in Splott and the oak crucifix to St German's – and the building was purchased by the Welsh Arts Council. Rented to the Welsh Theatre Company, initially for storage and set construction, it opened in 1968 as the Casson Studio Theatre – named for Sir Lewis Casson, husband of actress Sybil Thorndyke, and key figure in the establishment of the actors' trade union movement.

A small rake of fifty former cinema seats (with planning permission for eighty) was installed facing a flat floor stage area, its walls painted black; offices and changing rooms were on the floor above. With no internal access to the stage, actors descended the fire escape and entered via the Nora Street door. In 1971, the company mounted its own productions including Frank Marcus's *The Killing of Sister George* (1964) fittingly with Jessie Matthews, star of BBC radio soap opera *Mrs Dale's Diary*. But size always limited revenue: 'I shall be a Casson activist, and persuade or bring at least ten people to each play', read the theatre club's membership card.

In the early 1970s, it became a receiving venue for touring companies. The autumn programmes of 1971 and 1972 included comedic and physical theatre groups: the Ken Campbell Roadshow, Low Moan Spectacular, Keith Johnstone's Theatremachine, The New Fol De Rols, Triple Action Theatre Group and Steven Berkoff's company.

Campbell's show featured the exploits of Sylvester McCoy, later the seventh Dr Who in the long-running BBC television science fiction series. In sketches resembling variety theatre turns, McCoy hammered nails up his nose, put live ferrets in his trousers, and invited audience members to strangle him by hauling on a thick rope round his neck. In the interval, we were invited to witness 'Sylvester McCoy:

the Human Bomb' – the actor on his back in the rear yard with small pyramidal fireworks on his chest.

In October 1972, Low Moan Spectacular presented *The Adventures of Bullshot Crummond* – 'an extravaganza' based upon the exploits of literary hero Bulldog Drummond – in which the shadowy biplane that flew across the stage was effected by the manipulation of a model in a spotlight at the rear of the rake.

In November 1972, The New Fol De Rols – their name a parody of the seaside song-and-dance company – appeared: 'Twice Nightly at 7.00 & 10.30 p.m. N.B. These performances will be given as "added extras" to the main performance of the evening, i.e. FREE!'

There is here a changing relationship between stage and audience: performances are in close proximity and plain view, with implications for both the nature of production, and styles and registers of delivery. The converted hall lacks the appendages of the auditorium, with neither 'tower' for flying scenery nor 'wings' for entrances and exists.

Little can be hidden: stage artifice is revealed and sophisticated illusion difficult to contrive. The techniques and expressive capacities of actors are open for scrutiny, often for the duration. In response, they may turn and address the audience directly, though in unfamiliar tones and registers.

A new mobility was facilitated by cheap transport – the ubiquitous Ford Transit van from which, as an aspiration, Theatre in Transit derived its name – but limited capacity and the varying conditions of staging, in venues of varying scale and proportion, militated against the use of elaborate settings and technologies. A general lack of money – despite the Arts Council of Great Britain increasing subsidy – fostered theatrical aesthetics with an economy of means.

This did not however preclude scenic devices, notably three-dimensional and architectural in design. Steven Berkoff performed his adaptation of Kafka's *Metamorphosis* (1969) on a scaffolding frame; and Triple Action's *Hamlet* – 'An unusual interpretation on a spider's web of rope' – used the setting as an extended metaphor. For ninety minutes, actors traversed its mesh: in Hamlet's meeting with the ghost he was hung head down; for the famous soliloquy, he was suspended by wrists and ankles.

> In a spectacular finale Laertes and Hamlet dive out of the rope net onto the stage floor, to duel with rope-whips. As they fight deaths succeed each other, two bodies falling into the side-rigging – the King and Queen. And afterwards Laertes and Hamlet. (Cohn 1975: 60)

Sandy Craig (1980: 9) identifies three common ambitions amongst these diverse groups: to create a new language for theatre, to extend its social basis, and to reveal the potential of collective creation. John Ashford (in Craig: 101–2) lists shared and characteristic markers: creating work 'from the particular performance abilities, interests and obsessions of individual members', rather than the exposition of dramatic literature; abandoning dramatic conventions 'for the construction of elliptical, speedy and pivotal images borrowed from the techniques of film and television'; challenging existing approaches to plot, narrative and character; and integrating a diversity of styles, genres and media.

Of *Image* (1973), by a provisional group with three members of Llanover Hall Theatre Workshop that will become Cardiff Laboratory for Theatrical Research, three rolls of black-and-white film survive. In the first, four performers in white t-shirts and trousers are confined to the chambers of two upturned rostra; in succeeding images, they change position though their impulsive adjustments are lost between photographic frames. Sitting on chairs, the two men and two women next mirror each other. As they march back and forth and up and down the side aisles, the timber-planked interior and seating rake are registered. They pose singly in the light cast by the wall lamps. They snarl at each other; the men fight with naked torsos; all embrace. The work is redolent of the Living Theatre's *Mysteries and Smaller Pieces* (1964); the actions resemble the sound-and-movement exercises of Joe Chaikin's Open Theatre. Inaudible is the recorded slide-guitar soundtrack inspired by Ry Cooder's work on Roeg and Cammell's *Performance* (1968); unacknowledged is the film's influence on the posturing and references to cosmetic self-image in the performance.

And in a single frame, the auditorium is glimpsed.

In 1980, the Casson was leased to the Cardiff Community Dance Project; Rubicon Dance was officially opened in 1982 by Diana Princess of Wales.

In the hall, there are now mirrors and a sprung maple-wood floor. The empty niche for a small statue remains high on an outside wall.

Transitions, rehearsing *Dracula's Castle*, August 1972

4. Metal Street

In the sheaf of papers and document files that is the Transitions archive are the scripts for *Captain Confusius* (1971) and *Jack Russell's Circus* (1972): potentially restage-able, though lacking details of the participatory games. But to invoke a world in which cardboard boxes became space helmets and paper potato sacks clown suits will doubtless be difficult. Here too the charitable trust deed:

(A) To promote, maintain, improve, and advance education, particularly by the promotion of educational drama and other Fine Arts, including the arts of drama, mime, dramatic improvisation, literature, dance, singing and music, and to formulate, prepare and establish schemes therefore.

(B) In the interests of social welfare to provide, or assist in the provision of, facilities for recreation or other leisure-time occupation with the object of improving the conditions of life of the persons for whom such facilities are primarily intended, being persons who have need of such facilities by reason of their youth, age, infirmity or disablement, poverty or social and economic circumstances, provided that nevertheless such facilities shall be available to members of the public at large.

(C) In furtherance of the above-mentioned objects but not otherwise (i) to present, promote, organize, provide, manage, and produce such plays, dramas, comedies, dramatic and literary improvisations, operas, operettas, burlesques, films, broadcasts, concerts, musical pieces, puppet shows, ballets, entertainments, exhibitions and literary publications, whether on any premises of the Charity or elsewhere, as shall further the promotion, maintenance, improvement and advancement of education or encouragement of the Arts (ii) to all such other things as shall further the above objects.

'All such other things': a proviso barely conscionable today.

In the winter of 1971, in furtherance of its social and educational mission, Transitions began weekly group sessions for pre-teenage boys and girls in a non-denominational youth club run by the local curate at the church hall of St. German's on Metal Street.

Sessions employed games and improvisational exercises drawing upon Interaction antecedents: formats that the group used in educational, therapeutic and community situations and that required and instilled self-discipline – whilst eliciting self-assertion – for successful functioning. Though non-competitive, they involved complexities of risk-taking, strategic operation, decision-making, commitment to action and to response, and the contribution and inclusion of personal feelings, ideas and statements. The aim was to make pleasurable participation possible through inclusive structures that lessened inhibitions: empowering the insecure and restraining the over-zealous. No value judgments were offered; spectatorship was discouraged and the accent was shifted from display. The essential task for the leader was to sustain the arc of the session and maintain the flow of exercises.

Many games were based on the circle as an ostensibly democratic form in which individuals were equally invested with a parity of viewpoint and potential for involvement; and it defined an area for activity, with an inside, an outside and a linked circumference. Such games – with consecutive contributions around the circle – were fundamental to the methodology: each individual was aware of an approaching opportunity, of the possibility of making a personal statement and of the necessary responsibility – though without forfeit – to ensure continuity. At a basic level, this might serve to introduce participants; later, it could be used to compose collective stories.

Sessions commenced with an explicit and public 'contracting in': a verbal agreement to participate fully and to respect others. They then continued with a clapping game:

> The workshop leader commences a rhythm, usually two claps, two spaces, two claps. Then moving round the circle each individual is asked in turn to complete a task in the spaces. Initially, this simply involves saying something such as one's name, or one's favourite food, television programme or colour. Subsequently, animal noises or horrible faces can be substituted…. Eventually the games may be used to build group stories with one or several words being said … in the spaces. (Pearson 1973: 114)

Games were both physical and verbal, requiring the simultaneous, sequential or random involvement of members: each was given a title. In 'Crossing the circle', members of the circle were numbered off '1, 2, 3, 1, 2, 3'; then assigned a role – 'All ones are cats, all twos are policemen'; and then charged with traversing the space. Much hilarity could ensue as instructions became more abstract –'plates of soup'– and the differing types began to interact. In 'Monkey', one member left the room, and upon return had to identify the leader of a series of claps, stamps and noises established in their absence. In 'Ghost Train', a narrator would tell a story and as characters, animals and objects appeared so members were chosen to enact them – the narrative often modified in response to their antics – until everyone was involved.

Some were instructional: in 'Robots', two standing members were directed how to move by consecutive commands from members of the circle. Others involved observation: in the 'IBM Computer Game' [sic] an individual was invited to identify and stand in front of someone with a named particular trait who then changed places and issued a further instruction, often straying into the world of fantasy.

Some verbal games were instigated by the leader: in 'Policeman', the whole group was charged with a misdemeanour that had happened at a particular place and time; as collective suspect each individual had to remember all the preceding details revealed through questioning until a mistake occurred. Others, such as 'Passing the buck', enabled individuals to participate at a level and for a period they desired or felt able in contributing to a theme or building a story. In an Adamsdown variation, the member not only told part of a story whilst holding the buck, but also drew it on the floor in chalk as a cumulative cartoon; others then chose a section of the image, standing on it and making commensurate sound effects.

Such games can be of vital importance for the participants as a forum for examining, reinforcing and challenging the behaviours, relationships, and conventions of everyday life, with real changes in status possible. They offer new experiences: a context where identities might be created, contested and changed, allowing the child 'to rationalise absurdities, reconcile himself to not getting his own way, assimilate reality, act heroically without being in danger' (Opie and Opie 1969 3–4). They involve the dynamic interplay of strategy and tactics: of planning and execution. They are framed by explicit or implicit *rules* – albeit fluid, constantly renegotiated understandings in the form of contracts, agreements, taboos and prohibitions, that mark off the activity and ensure coherence, direction and momentum, as well as outlining the parameters to be adhered to – and potentially transgressed, though not perhaps without consequence. They give purpose to the release of energy, and once understood can help communicate intention and inform planning towards achieving desired outcomes. The rules of games offer a balance between freedom and restraint. They require self and group regulation and although there may be division and contest, there may be no attempt to keep the score or move to resolution. There may be sequence or pattern, if not plot.

The girls in the photograph – preparing a scene for the *Dracula's Castle* horror film – we know from St German's, though our weekly sessions have not survived the energy cuts and restricted openings of early 1972.

East Moors Youth Centre, March 2013

5. Sanquhar Street

The Calvinistic Methodist/Presbyterian Church of Wales Forward Movement hall on Sanquhar Street opened in 1892 at 'the darkest spot in Cardiff' (Childs 2012: 116) – beside the saw-mills and just prior to the building of the slaughterhouses of the Monmouthshire Hide, Skin, Fat and Wool Co. Ltd. Vacated in 1928, a floor was inserted at balcony level, giving the upstairs room the appearance of a roller-skating rink surrounded by five tiers of benches; between the two world wars, it was noted for its magic lantern shows.

On 8 January 1977, at the renamed East Moors Youth Centre, Cardiff Laboratory Theatre presented *Roundabout and Circular*:

> A bus-trip from the theatre to a converted chapel, with many rooms, in the shadow of Cardiff steelworks. A different action in each room. A box full of shadows. The birth of a clown.

> The audience sat in tight rows behind a curtain. As the curtain was drawn back, a large room was revealed. Only then did they realise that they were sitting on a stage. And who was watching whom? This section was more tightly structured, with a musical framework and action giving hints of cabaret, clowns and pantomime. It allowed the introduction of objects which were to recur throughout the Guizer Project – umbrellas and deckchairs, both of which are functional objects but which cause man so many difficulties in operation, and they have endless improvisational possibilities. A game of bowls. Strange actions with the tuba. A man/woman on roller skates. A rowdy supper of biscuits and milk. (Pearson 1980: 34)

This was the first episode in the *Guizer Project*, a programme of outings and performances conceived by Richard Gough: 'I think it may have been from reading TDR [*The Drama Review*], from Meredith Monk certainly and from the early productions of Robert Wilson. I just got very excited by the idea of taking the audience on a journey, literally' (Gough 2006a: 248).

Partly inspired by Alan Garner's compendium *The Guizer* (1975), it featured Gough's wistful white-faced, bowler-hatted trickster figure:

> … wandering through strange worlds, confronting unusual objects, in his own idiosyncratic way … as mystified as the audience by the curious events, and reacting, sometimes with innocence, sometimes with knowledge, to the prearranged sequence of music and action. He is a free agent, an intermediary reacting with gentle humour and likely to improvise with the audience. (Pearson: 32)

Guizer is the fool, the advocate of uncertainty, creator and destroyer. He has a child-like sense of wonder and enquiry. He encounters the world as if for the first time, a perfect analogy for the performer in an improvised situation (Pearson: 33).

Its ambitions were threefold: to relocate audiences, so challenging their expectations; to employ a subtlety of delivery *contra* the vigorous physicality of other Cardiff Laboratory productions; and to employ musical sequences as structuring devices.

It was prepared over four weeks: 'This time was divided between working with a selection of objects gathered from attics, antique shops and junkyards and the construction of a musical repertoire' (Gough 1977: 4). The various rooms suggested the form of a conducted tour, the site's history a parish supper: 'Certain actions arose in response to the peculiar qualities of each space and in collaboration with objects found there' (ibid.).

It featured the music of John Hardy who, in a revelatory exercise, had played and sung an entire collection of nursery rhymes at a piano: 'The rendition lasted for more than an hour; a very personal statement and a powerful image. There was something disturbing in the relentlessness of his playing, something funny and yet frighteningly absorbing in the world of the rhymes themselves, full of creatures suffering sad and peculiar fortunes' (p.2).

It began as a mystery outing: 'The meeting at Chapter, the embarking, the journey, the disembarking, the arrival, the leading and guiding were all celebrated' (p.5). A trip to a place prepared:

> John leads the audience up the stairs and into a long narrow room and seats them facing a curtain. After a short pause the curtain opens. They find themselves looking out into a large area. It is a drab muddle of browns and greens. There is tiered bench seating on three sides and the audience is seated on an old and dilapidated stage on the fourth side. (p.10)

The beginnings of a recurring and transferable signature style: a theatrical 'look' and demeanour; live music of an elegiac quality, with settings of Thomas Hardy's poetry; a particular range of materials – 'the same set of objects was seen in different contexts' (Pearson: 33); a responsive, improvised quality, creating a sense of informality and immediacy.

> Richard becomes waiter and raises the sheets to reveal buckets of milk and gingerbread men.
>
> Richard serves a feast giving generous helpings with a rough and intimidating service. (Gough: 21)

Silent clowning, unruly instruments, long held poses, Victorian surroundings: a black-and-white pastoral – 'as if a group of old photographs had come to life' (Pearson: 33).

On 26 February, *Death of a Naturalist* followed: Guizer 'in mourning' in a corrugated-iron church hall on King's Road, Canton.

The audience met by a white chauffeur on a white tricycle. To each spectator he presented an open umbrella. Even though the evening was dry, he led them on a solemn march across city streets to a small hall in a wooded churchyard. They became the event, glimpsing their unity in shop-windows and commented upon by passers-by. The hall was cold and sombre. A tape recording of Tibetan Buddhist chants echoed from an adjoining room. The audience sat at small tables as if they were at a wake. The action was slow moving and filled with sterile experiments – trying to feed a dead hare with lettuce, playing with mechanical flies, a man trying to fly with crutches for wings, a man painting out his own eyes. There were moments of relief – a tiny black rabbit was conjured from a hat-box – but this was an event for quiet observance. There was a feast, a meal of uncooked fish and bread, but nobody ate …

There were also smells, principally the smell of coffee being ground which would never be drunk. (Pearson: 36)

The company termed these one-off works *special events*: fleeting occupations of locations off the beaten track, created quickly, barely rehearsed, that celebrated places, dates, people and past events. They sought novel places for performance, using prevailing conditions and ambience as inspiration: 'to allow the work to embrace collaboration with, and response to, objects, buildings, and environments'; though 'occasionally, we change the building, but in sympathy with it' (p.32). They precipitated relationships with audiences that included proximity and touch, offering experiences of smell and taste. They entailed distinctive structures: performance as excursion, procession, supper. They involved extemporization within agreed sequences of action – the 'what' might be prescribed but not the 'how' – demanding that performers maintain coherence of exposition whilst accommodating chance occurrences and diversions.

Their scenarios are described in *Dream Train: a photographic record of the Guizer Project* (Gough 1977): combinations of texts, photographs, cartoons and maps in a self-published document – part guidebook, part souvenir, part promotional brochure.

The Centre's exterior is relatively unchanged since the 1970s (see Pountney 2012). Inside, its Victorian auras persist, if faintly. With *Dream Train* in hand, it is possible to position and plot *Roundabout and Circular*: holding it at eye level, to transfer past event onto present scene.

Julie Andree-Trembley, *Unexpected Thought*, February 2002

6. Moira Place

Beyond the metals and the heavenly bodies – Sun, Star, Comet, Planet and Constellation, Eclipse, Orbit and System: on Moira Place.

The small, oval enamel plaque on the front door, European in style, reads: 'Prof André Stitt. 26 Study – Learn – Leave'; below it, a second in polished brass bears the word _trace:_ – 'the house's hidden identity' (Roms 2006: 16).

Inside, to the left, is a double glass door leading into a double-sized room; the lathe-and-plaster dividing wall Stitt demolished to create a single space, though the floorboards of the rear and concrete of the front betray the previous layout. The entrance to the back room – in which the previous owner had played snooker and that he blocked off – is still evident in the corridor in winter, as the cladding expands differentially in the central heating; or sonorously when tapped with fingertips. Two rustic 'Western style' stonework-and-cement fireplaces Stitt removed, bricking up the rear but leaving a small rectangular opening in the front chimneybreast. The walls he painted white, the floor grey.

Stitt was aware that the remains and residues of his own performances – a consequential aftermath of the event – were often cleared quickly. What if one could return to the detritus with the memory of performance, prompted to recall the 'live' through the inanimate: or to the room, the present suffused with recollections of previous times and events?

Between 2000 and 2007, he curated an annual programme of performance events in the newly named _trace: installaction space_: 'A "safehouse" for like-minded artists to push the envelope' (Stitt 2006: 8). Each month a practitioner from an extended international network was invited to live in the house with him and to create time-based work in response to the characteristics and qualities of the gallery and its immediate environs: trace-making as an artistic imperative, in a play of presence and absence, current manifestation and future evidence. This included both short-term interventions and longer engagements.

> There are few traces left of the living room it once was. But the house around it is very manifestly still home to someone. Its functioning as an art space and its role as a domestic space are deeply interwoven, and it is this interpenetration that creates a unique context for the performance work presented here. (Roms: 28)

Towards 6pm on a given Saturday, a small audience would gather – standing; sitting on the floor; occasionally moving to see better or to avoid the action; sometimes remaining outside, peering through the glass doors. Over the succeeding hour, artists either presented autonomous events, though sometimes a reconfiguration of existing work; or brought the processes of durational endeavours to conclusion. The outcome – objects and marks – of the performance, intentionally arranged or casually created, remained in the gallery – either as planned installation or inadvertent emission – for the following month: 'offered up for contemplation and reflection' (Stitt 2011: 9).

The concept he termed *installactions*: frequently extreme happenings in a sequestered setting.

> The exhibition is installed through live performance and once this is completed the installation remains as a documentation and reminder of what has taken place in the room. The art space becomes a container for traces of previous lives, a ghost ship carrying the people and events that have occupied it. (Debbie Savage in Stitt: 8)

Some artists intervened directly and purposefully into the fabric of the house. The hole that Brian Connolly (2002) hacked in the concrete to bury a time capsule and the crack cut with hammer and masonry chisel by Roddy Hunter (2004) are still visible from certain angles, in certain light, beneath the layers of paint that have become smoother as they accumulate and are repeatedly washed: '[g]ently mocking the concept of the "white cube" gallery as a neutral space with no particular past' (Roms: 34).

Other artists inscribed surfaces, strategically and coincidentally. Marilyn Arsem covered the walls in pencilled text, completing circuit after circuit during twenty-four hours of continuous 'automatic' writing; Morgan O'Hara (2002) drew perfect circles with sweeps of her arm. Julie Andree-Trembley (2002) listed objects, proposed actions and tasks both everyday and poetic for her performance in charcoal. Valentin Torrens (2003) invited the audience to write instructions for him to enact ('Kick the book'). Istvan Kantor (2002) wrote in his own blood with a syringe, whilst Kira O'Reilly (2000) dripped carelessly as she cut precise diagonal nicks on her legs that were gridded in masking tape, leaving behind heaps of red-stained cotton wool, bowls of tinted water, and scalpels.

Each artist was invited to address the same space. In *My Niche* (2000), Eve Dent was nowhere to be seen as the audience entered. Only gradually were we aware of a tiny fall of soot in the opening that was once the fireplace; Dent was standing vertically in the chimney in 'an interplay between hiding and being seen, mimicry and merging the body with the environment' (Dent, in Trace Gallery 2013); 'In the creation of my body/architecture hybrids I seek to animate the hidden poetic life of a space' (Dent, in Rees 2003: 27). Gradually she descended, depositing her black, sooty dress on the floor in an action evocative of Victorian child labour and more traumatically of women's bodies confined and built into houses: giving 'expression to the house's capacity and effort to remember' (Roms: 28). The filthy mattress, dirty suit and other objects found locally – 'containing, the visible traces of someone else's past actions' (p. 34) – in Hunter's *[The Noise Of] The Street Enters The House;*

[The Noise Of] The House Enters The Street (2004) brought the immediate vicinity into the space: though his dead crow became impossible to live with and had to be removed.

In her use of paints and pigments – red and black – and repeated, protracted actions, both Tremblay and the gallery became increasingly patinated – body, space and locale inseparable:

> When actions such as walking, talking and making sound are performed within a context where a clear imprint of action is left within a space in which it was produced, one can see a real cohesive relationship between action and matter. As if the echoing of human gesture possesses a valuable and sensitive continuum, even within the smallest of traces. (Tremblay, in Trace Gallery 2013)

Accumulations of objects, smears, stains and spillages, purposefully displayed and randomly dispersed and always adjacent to the domestic: resembling considered artwork or scene of crime or illegal squat, with no chance of it returning to 'order'. 'Performance as ENTROPY, as the creation of an energy that is chaotic and unsettling' (Roms: 33). Enigmatic marks tracing trails of footsteps and arcs of movement, occasioning forensic contemplation: 'What happened here?' And sometimes disappearing without a physical trace, as when Peter Baren (2005) filled the room with smoke.

At the conclusion of each installation Stitt restored the gallery: plastering and repainting the walls and sometimes the floor too, sealing traces but not totally erasing them. Most difficult was the greasy graphite that Tremblay used: it had to be first sealed with PVA.

Residing in memory: successive performances in the same space existing as scratchy overlaying filters or echoing background resonances, intermittently brought to mind when viewing current works.

The thinnest of archaeological strata: preserved in an interior now reverting to living space. And when Stitt leaves, they become part of the spectral history of 26 Moira Place.

What lurks in the domestic, unrecognized?

Transitions, building *Dracula's Castle*, August 1972

7. Adamsdown Cemetery

The twelve-minute, silent Super-8 colour horror film is lost.

Picture then a vampire rising from a disused motor inspection pit; the pet monster of several witches – fashioned from a fallen tree trunk, a papier-mâché head on one end and triangular fins nailed down its spine – consuming a small boy; terror-stricken children fainting and scattering their dandelion posies over the ground at the sight of a cardboard werewolf; boys running on the spot as if in flight; and a giant spider attacking three young girls. The creature, of rolled newspaper, is suspended in a rope web between two conifers: in handmade bonnets the girls skip, unaware. Cut to trembling spider, to girls looking up and screaming in horror, to descended spider, girls writhing beneath. There are bats, vampires and ghouls at work in a graveyard, and in an enchanted forest. A screenplay untroubled by glaring inconsistencies.

During the summer of 1972, Cardiff Student Community Action (SCA) – a student-led charity founded in 1971 to work with the disadvantaged (the homeless, mentally ill, elderly) and with children, and springing from the growth of university courses in social sciences and administration – ran an *adventure playground* on the disused railway sidings and embankment above Adamsdown Cemetery. The supervised, though risk-taking, 'free play' and a do-it-yourself ethos of these sites gave children access to tools to build shacks, walkways, ladders and platforms from railway sleepers, pallets and scrap metal. Collaborative, improvised and potentially transgressive endeavours to design and construct environments: archaeologically enigmatic shanties wrought through play rather than the exigencies of profitable production; self-built domains in which to accommodate and test their own sociabilities and to enact their imaginaries.

Cardiff Voluntary Community Services (VCS) ran six further sites in the city that summer: temporary appropriations of vacant, marginal, semi-abandoned, interstitial but adaptable spaces, such as the derelict barrage balloon hangers in south Ely; obsolete, unproductive, *terrains vagues* where other worlds might be envisaged and created. Frequently in edgelands:

> Children and teenagers, as well as lawbreakers, have seemed to feel especially at home in them, the former because they have yet to establish a sense of taste and boundaries, and have instinctively treated their jungle spaces as a vast playground; the latter because nobody is looking. (Farley and Roberts 2011: 8)

In August, at the Adamsdown site, Transitions organized a *dramascape* – 'an abbreviation of "dramatic landscape"' (Pearson 1973: 97) – a term coined by Interaction to describe its urban outdoor play projects of an extended nature, based around a single theme, such as its own *Gulliver's Travels* (1968) and Interplay's

Apollo 15 (1971). They involved large-scale construction, and interventions into –
and sculpting of – the topography and fabric of the site: 'Taking a central theme and
using basic materials (timber, sacking etc.) an area of land is transformed by local
young people into a different environment' (Transitions application for Urban Aid).

Central to each project was the building of a structure (a fifty-foot high figure
of Gulliver over Lilliput) or the modelling of a landscape (heaped rubble formed
into lunar craters) around which craft, dramatic and media activities were focused.
The onus was on the need for self and peer group discipline; for collective and
co-operative decision-making regarding the trajectory of activities over time; and
for the orderly completion of cycles of work and achievement of tasks towards the
fulfilment of identified ambitions and goals that might require training in the use
of tools, technologies and creative approaches, from carpentry to photography, from
singing to tape-recording. The overall objective was to enhance communal and inter-
generational relationships, and belief and confidence in the capacities of an ad-hoc
group of individuals of different ages, engaged in diverse pursuits with varying levels
of achievement, through the establishment of durable frameworks of, for instance,
consultation, and recurrent recall of, and recourse to, the established theme.

By 1972, the Adamsdown Cemetery was semi-derelict – a mass of leaning and
fallen gravestones, over-grown and abused: 'Graveyards seem to have the power to
unleash a particular anger, a particular contempt, among vandalistic youth' (Bonnett
2000b: 92). A place too of childish make-believe, offering vicarious pleasures. 'The
modern imagination has learned to be unnerved by physical signs of mortality. They
are "creepy", "eerie", the stuff of "horror"' (ibid.): an ideal place in which to make
a horror film.

Transitions's *Dracula's Castle* commenced with the arrival and procession
through neighbouring streets of costumed characters – suave film director Wilbur
J. Haycock with megaphone, his assistant Ethel with clipboard, and two of his actors
in heavy, grotesque make-up. They had supposedly come to Adamsdown to make
a horror film:

> We're gonna make a film, a creepy scary horror film
> With Wilbur J. here today
> We are the film crew, we're gonna film you
> Do what you wanna do.

As the procession reached the site, the theme was announced and the timetable
outlined: without set, props, costumes and script, with only two incompetent actors,
the children would need to help make the film.

For one week, activities that could be given a horror twist were encouraged: each
morning a meeting was held in a specially arranged circle in order to elicit ideas
and to embrace ambitions, however tenuous or apparently beyond the scope of the
theme; and to plan the goals for the day within the strict demands of making a film.

A large wooden 'Dracula's castle' was built around an old railway wagon, acting as potential film location, climbing frame and grandstand:

> The older children set to with boards and planks and hammers and nails to create their own version of the castle they had seen on films and on TV. A few old pieces of scenery that were donated helped provide the battlements and turrets, and though possibly not looking quite as it had in those other films this Dracula's castle was built with no less energy and imagination. (Transitions internal report)

The short episodes devised and rehearsed by children were filmed mainly by a group of youths living rough on the site; it was premiered in September 1972 at St German's church hall.

The Victorian cemetery – increasingly regarded as 'unhealthily morbid' in 'showing an excessive concern for the status of the deceased' (Penrose 2007: 82) – is now transformed: the gravestones are ordered, levelled and set in arcs; half-buried to secure them, names obscured. The stones record the drowning of Lum Andenken, Captain J. N. Bradhering and John Scudamore in West Bute Dock, of William Thompson master of the schooner Jessy of Exeter in Bute Dock Lock: events wrought from the dangers of rapid expansion.

The rich and famous though are elsewhere, in Cathays: boxer Peerless Jim Driscoll, balloonists Louisa Maud Evans and Ernest Willows – who flew Willows I over Splott in 1905 – and shipping magnates John Cory, William Tatem, William Reardon Smith, William Henry Seagar.

> For the Victorians the urban cemetery was a place of contemplation, a place to wander through and picnic in. When Cardiff's Cathays Cemetery opened in 1859 the *Cardiff Times* opined that it "would form the principal walk of the inhabitants of Cardiff". (Bonnett: 92)

At Cathays, a world of meaningful materials and forms, and complex symbolism, in a concern to signal the status of the dead: up-turned urns, broken column, ivy-entwined boughs. Difficult now to decipher.

At Adamsdown, a world before the Health and Safety Executive and Criminal Records Bureau checks: groups of children on the street; youths with hammers; young children caring for younger siblings. Difficult now to contemplate.

Keith Wood Group, *The Philosopher's Stone*, May 1974

8. Howard Gardens

Built in 1966, it is by city architect John Dryburgh. The north-facing windows high up betray its function: Cardiff College of Art, Howard Gardens, where in the late 1960s lecturer John Gingell fostered conceptual and performance art.

Here sculptor Frank Triggs proposed selecting, by chance, a one-kilometre grid square on the one-inch Ordnance Survey map of the Brecon Beacons, and then painting the land the same colours – brown contour lines, green trees, blue streams. Here too Newport-born Keith Wood created his first explosive event:

> I'd got all these fireworks and ended up blowing this hole in the car park which kind of created a little bit of a furore ...; people were ... really looking at me sideways – what the hell is this guy doing? Is it art? Or is it a hole in the ground? Of course it was both. (Wood, in Roms 2013)

Wood's performance practice had a fundamental graphic element: the happenings in his early *Coyote Saloon* (1971) series were based on 'huge drawings, long drawings of many sheets which was (sic) like a score'; with a soundtrack – 'very primitive rockabilly and other things' – played on a reel-to-reel Revox tape-recorder and mixed 'sometimes in a random way' (ibid.).

On graduation, he created two formal theatre works with the Keith Wood Group before founding Highway Shoes in the mid-1970s as a vehicle for his own writing: an adaptation of Antonin Artaud's *The Philosopher's Stone* (May 1974) in the Sherman Arena – 'I was very interested in alchemy, a very sixties kind of thing, the idea of change and all these things'; and *The Nighthawk* (December 1974) in Chapter – 'Will you be the first to crack!' (production publicity).

Of *The Philosopher's Stone* – which 'indicated in many respects Artaud's feelings of dismemberment: his desire for wholeness, the constant torment caused by the unreconciled polarities within his own personality – the sexual and spiritual, the healthy and the sick, the ugly and the beautiful' (Knapp 1980: 108) – five rolls of black-and-white film survive, shot in the white-walled Sherman rehearsal room consumed during the refurbishment of 2010–12.

A row of white posts bisects the space: I stand on one leg, in the pose of a North American shaman at a waterfall in an image suggested by Wood; I am wearing a one-piece suit made from over two hundred diamonds of coloured jockey silk, indistinguishable in monochrome. Finnish dancer Ritva Lehtinen's abstracted, fractured movements echo the dismembered limbs scattered around. Artist Andrew Walton mimics his mannequins. Much mirroring and manipulating and mutated movement as Dr Pale sadistically experiments on Harlequin – his own grotesque creation, and object of desire of his young wife Isabelle. Later, I appear in the large gold carnival head of a baby.

To accompany the performance, Wood's paintings – 'Dr Pale's Trophies' – were exhibited on the Arena balcony: 'They depict the heads of his famous and infamous forebears, alchemical mandalas and records of psychic encounters etc., they are like the shrivelled heads hanging from the head-hunter's belt, the pictures with moving eyes in the haunted house': 'Count Dracula'; 'Mr Crowley'; 'Kenneth Anger as he is'; 'The eyes of Castenada at midnight' (production programme).

In the precise arrangement of bodies and objects, the scenic composition of the work is informed by visual art sensibilities. The scenario is variously novella, play-script, screenplay, choreographic instruction: it includes technical and stage directions, musical cues and projections in a single pro-active, utopian document that effectively sketches and outlines the performance, drawing no distinction between elements. The stage picture and its animation is imagined precisely and *in toto*, in a single document that attempts a form of notation in order to communicate intentions to performers from different fields: 'The Philosopher's Stone has few words and communicates by the use of intoned sounds, outcries and hieroglyphic gesticulation' (Wood, in Roms 2013).

> 1. Isabelle enters from the laboratory with two buckets of smoke (dry ice).
> She circles and weaves her way through the set/this is done silently and slowly/she is careful not to touch anything/the effect is that of a sleepwalker gracefully walking a tightrope.
> Lights dim on Isabelle.
> Lights up on Harlequin.
>
> 2. Harlequin leaps out onto the balcony/he thunders around/cartwheels/long jumps/ head-stands/this is a continuous sequence/suddenly he stumbles and stops as if caught in an invisible net/he fights it silently …
>
> 29. A sound of Dr Pale snoring comes from the laboratory. The lights slowly come up. Harlequin is dragging himself along he has a babies [sic] head/he slowly rises/feels his head/he sways drops gets up again/Harlequin advances on Isabelle he picks like a doll and holds him to her/she wakes and slowly pulls him to the ground. (Wood 1974)

The Nighthawk was inspired by American comic books and the B-movies of Ed Wood: as The Nighthawk, dressed in black silk cloak lined in red, I resembled Bela Lugosi. The style mixed schlock horror with formal design: a world of rubber skeletons and blood capsules and contemporary jazz, in the search for prankster Ace Mime. The set was a large rectangle of artificial grass: at the back, a city skyline painted in red; above this, a line of black-and-white painted skulls. The programme was a scurrilous newspaper, sold outside the auditorium by John Gingell, amongst dustbins and litter.

Again the scenario incorporates the diverse components of a hybrid practice in schematic though evocative renderings, poetic enough to excite contemporary imaginaries:

12. Music. Scarlet Woman – Weather Report.

… Nighthawk enters carrying a lighted torch – his cloak is pulled around him 'classic Dracula' style – he carries a long vicious looking dagger – he advances on the unsuspecting back of Ace still happily playing in the bath – Nighthawk raises the knife – as he stabs with the knife the torch is extinguished – there is the sound of water running over the edge of the bath onto the floor. The lights come slowly up there is a skeleton in Ace's place. […]

13. The Nighthawk rises to his feet – he mimes to the tape of his last speech – his actions are grotesque – at times his body is light then unbearably heavy – he staggers – falls – gets up again etc. – he circles in the performance area as if in an arena – he is like a bear being attacked by dogs – as his monologue unfolds he is getting cut to pieces.

Ace follows him around – he mimes walls which start to enclose the Nighthawk more and more walls which he pushes from the limits of the stage down and into the Nighthawk until at the end of the Nighthawk's words Ace has made a coffin in which the Nighthawk is trapped and dies.

Nighthawk – Watch out boy – there's a black dog here – he has a cold cold crow in his eyes and his tongue licks sharp teeth – there are angels in the sea – they're coming to get you – out of the blue and into that green grey – hold – listen and pour paint in your ears/paint this Ace and Joker with your eyes – the sky is full of laughing horses – their iron hooves pound in my heart so fast – so fast – but I will not fail in my life's purpose and I spit into the oncoming wave (Wood 1974).

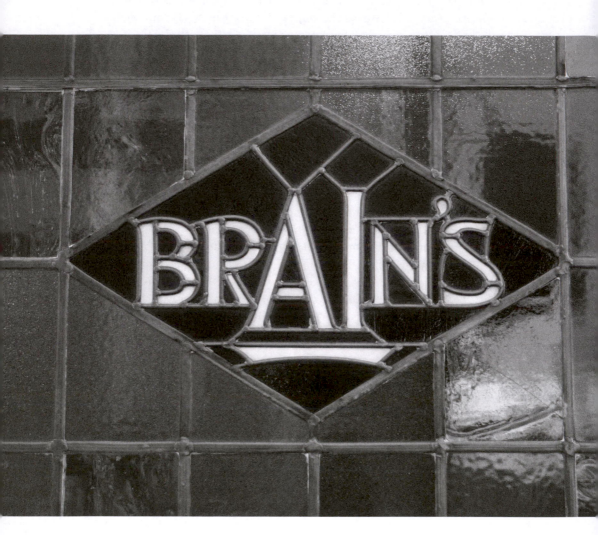

Window detail, 'The Golden Cross', March 2013

9. 'The Vulcan'

'So, a vampire walks into 'The Vulcan'; or 'So, a ghost stands in the Coal Exchange'. Not the beginning of a stand-up comedy routine but scenes from television series *Being Human*, previously shot in Bristol but with the move of BBC Drama production to Cardiff, an increasingly frequent local phenomenon: the use of existing locations to stage fictive, indeed fantasy, scenarios, notably in *Doctor Who* and *Torchwood*. An overlay through which the city appears, spectrally: places distinguishable through momentary glimpses of odd features, details and materials.

The blue glass diamonds in the windows mark 'The Vulcan' as a public house of Cardiff brewers S. A. Brain & Co. Ltd., whose former premises off Caroline Street are now designated the Brewery Quarter. Its tile-work is cream, green and brown though not as extravagant as either the nearby 'Golden Cross' with its L-shaped ceramic bar featuring grotesque heads by Craven Dunnill (1903) and panels showing Cardiff Castle, the second town hall and Bute's statue in St Mary Street in 1863, and Brain's brewery around 1890; or 'The Queen's Vaults' on Westgate Street, 'Ind Coope and Co. Entire' in faience on its exterior.

> It had good pubs, real pubs, Brains pubs, the Salutation, the Vulcan, the Oak, the Cottage, the Arcade, the Greyhound – all of them gone or changed utterly except the Vulcan. (Williams 2003b: 89)

Cardiff author John Williams spoke too soon. As adjacent industrial units were demolished, it had become increasingly stranded amongst car parks and building plots: its world gone. Then it too disappeared. In 2012, 'The Vulcan' was dismantled and its parts taken to St Fagans: National History Museum, where it will eventually join the collection of reconstructed Welsh buildings.

Formerly the Welsh Folk Museum, St Fagans was inaugurated in 1948 to collect and preserve domestic, agricultural and industrial buildings in an open-air setting: church, chapel, school, Workmen's Institute, row of ironworkers' houses – 'dismantled, transported and rebuilt here, brick by authentic brick' (Finch 2004: 123). Occupying a hundred-acre site adjacent to St Fagans Castle, at the bequest of Lord Robert Windsor-Clive, and inspired by models in Scandinavia, it was the brainchild of first curator Iorwerth Peate: 'It's Baudrillard at the Eisteddfod' (Hatherley 2010: 279).

The process of dismemberment is precise. First, all significant architectural features are identified by means of a letter code and each major stone then given a specific number; different colours distinguish interior and exterior elements. Next, two horizontal datum lines are laid out at right angles with a vertical line at their intersection: any point in the building can be measured off against these lines. Photographs, sketches and notes augment the numbering: 'Any discrepancies or original mistakes in the structure have to be reproduced in the re-erected building' (Butler and Davis 2006: 110). The stripping of surface render can reveal earlier, hidden components, blocked up and painted over: 'The process of dismantling the building can be viewed as a form of above-ground archaeology' (p.108).

Erection of 'The Vulcan' may take five years. It will then be 'dressed' with enough material to 'set the scene', though in relatively expendable items: the presence and passage of visitors – the greasy deposits from handling and high humidity – along with the acidic soot from open fires are 'a recipe for decay' (p.9). There is a play of authenticity and purposeful illusion here, in a simulacrum, a replica of something that never quite existed in the first place – 'The Vulcan' without the fug of cigarette smoke, the drunken banter of its regulars. And when exactly was 'The Vulcan'? On the gable end, the lettering once read: 'Guinness Is Good For You'. How will it be depicted at St Fagans: in bright tones or in the weather-beaten outlines of its final moments?

Removed from its original context, it will find a place in a new community – a virtual Wales – where like and unalike, from here and there, adjoins.

St Fagans houses relics of performance: the Mari Lwyd – a horse's skull and white sheet worn in a house-visiting tradition; the wren house, decorated with ribbons, in which men paraded their captured bird on St Stephen's Day. With settings that suggest period stagings lacking only characters, it also has a tradition of performance: story-tellers sit in cottages; the Sealed Knot re-enacts the English Civil War Battle of St Fagans; and craftsmen – baker, clog-maker, weaver – go about their business under the gaze of visitors. To contemporary practice, it offers architectures, spatial configurations and some nebulous sense of the past; though lacking the auras that transplantation inevitably forfeits, its buildings can conspire and enhance spatial and temporal dislocations.

Brith Gof's *Boris* (1985) was created in Hendre-wen, a barn of cruck-timber construction built around 1600. Two large opposing doors assisted the passage of air during flailing, and the open-fronted hayloft at one end provided a cow byre beneath. *Boris* was performed in Welsh, in a translation of the drama John Berger developed from his own short story (Berger 1983): 'a love-story, a tragedy, a depiction of pain and destruction'. From his corpus of works on peasant life in the Haute-Savoie in France, it tells of the fate of a shepherd who falls for the wife of the local driving instructor: his life-story is supplemented by the gossip and memories of villagers.

The audience sit on two tiers of straw bales arranged along the long walls in an echo of the *noson lawen*, a Welsh rural get-together: at one end, the elaborate kitchen of his female neighbour; at the other, Boris's spartan dwelling with pony in the byre, sheep dog on a rope. Scenes alternate between settings, and actions occur between the inward-facing audiences: actors in close proximity, speaking directly to individual spectators. Boris carries bales down from the loft, and unbolting the door, lets four sheep into the space – that leap in rehearsal but that amble in in performance, regard the audience disinterestedly, and amble out. As Boris dies in the doorway, dead leaves fall to cover him; in the barn it is always cold, colder still in that moment.

A death in the family (1992) – a personal reflection on childhood, on people and places now gone – was presented in the seventeenth-century thatched cockpit, the interior of which was re-imagined as the original had not survived. I sit together with the audience on the circular terracing; occasionally, I step on to the cock-fighting stage, turning, circling, and squatting as I deliver the intimate monologue.

Elsewhere, on the site of the Channel Dry Dock, the 'Dr Who Experience' recently opened. The website announces: 'The world's most extensive collection of original Doctor Who props and artifacts includes the entire collection of Doctors' iconic costumes from 1963 to the present day; the David Tennant TARDIS set and the Doctor's arch foes through the ages.' The fabricated properties of performance – all that created illusion – become authentic artifacts: 'It's Baudrillard ... '.

Elsewhere too, as small audiences drift across the city videoing performers in Pearson/Brookes's *Polis* (2001), they find photographer Paul Jeff in 'The Golden Cross' inviting couples to show how they embrace, in a lesbian pub his motives open to question; and at a telephone kiosk on The Hayes, Richard Morgan, returning to a city altered beyond his character's comprehension, seeking numbers from directory enquiries, for the demolished – 'The Salutation', 'The Greyhound', 'The Lifeboat'.

'The Big Sleep', March 2013

10. 'The Big Sleep'

> I'd expected it to be different here: made-over, brand-new.
> Not the Gas Board with a lick of paint.
> (*Who are you looking at?* 2004)

Currently the 'The Big Sleep' hotel, it was once the British Gas headquarters. A nondescript tower of glass and green panels, part owned by Hollywood actor John Malkovich. The conference suite is named for him, though, unlike in the film *Being John Malkovich* (1999), there is no floor 7½ with a portal into his mind.

> R2 It's not the reason I came here.
> R3 I just like the name. I needed a sleep.
> (Thomas, *Stone City Blue* 2004)

Inevitably in the name, there are Chandler-esque connotations.

The camera outside catches her at a lighted window; a second, as she paces the room; a third, as she looks into a mirror. On this night in 2004, she is one of five young women each asked to perform alone for ten minutes, largely in the public domain: on a platform at the Central Station; in a taxi; in a sandwich bar in St Mary Street; on St Mary Street itself; in a hotel room. These covert interventions, drained of dramatic rhetoric, are videoed simultaneously and surreptitiously from three viewpoints: the performer wears a small camera, as does a second operator close by; a distant third camera provides a long shot.

At 'The Big Sleep', she records herself looking nervously at her own reflection, whilst tracked on hidden CCTV, and glimpsed from the front entrance. The women are recording *Who are you looking at?*, the second performance by Pearson/Brookes with playwright Ed Thomas.

Thomas and I had begun a conversation in June 2001: for eighteen months, we met every Friday afternoon at 4.30pm in Canton. Initially our talk rambled: it was the *schedule* of discussion that was as significant as content. Our meetings were set against preparations for Cardiff's bid to become European City of Culture 2008: the slogan 'Take me somewhere good' was taken from Thomas's play *Song from a Forgotten City* (1995), which is 'firmly located in a real, existing topography: the text mentions famous landmarks in Cardiff, from the Hayes Island public toilets to the Angel Hotel' (Roms 2008: 117). How might the bid, in its extravagant, politically driven espousal of the role of art, provide the context and set a timetable for performative pursuits? Could it provide a platform, an officially sanctioned platform, whilst in its inherent myopia admitting the critical and the dystopian? Our estimation of the city was orientated around several increasing concerns: the intrusion of surveillance into civic space; the surrender of such space to specific constituencies, particularly at night with the emergence of cultures of profligate alcoholic consumption; and municipal amnesia. As Cardiff pursued a post-industrial/commercial identity, it appeared to be hurriedly dismantling and disguising its past.

Our stratagems for creative projects were manifold: we would book a room in the new waterfront St David's Hotel every Friday for seven years for a local resident or celebrity and then record their dreams of Cardiff. The city as a terrain of passion 'endlessly nuanced' (Sadler 2001: 93).

Finally – and in attempting to address the problematic of writing for 'post-dramatic' theatre, theatre not predicated upon the routine staging of dramatic literature – we challenged each other, initially at least, to write ten one-minute texts, as a pretext for the shooting of a series of videos of men in the city. These became the components of the multi-media performance *Raindogs* (2002) in which we ourselves appeared, voicing our own writings.

Who are you looking at? (2004) extended this dramaturgical form: in Chapter's 'black box' studio, sequences of projections appeared on three similar, perfectly painted, white rectangular screens above head height, to enhance the clarity and vividness of the images. Through multiple and juxtaposed images, it gradually became apparent that these were different views of the same event that conspired in their conjunctions simultaneously to evoke the city and to render it disconcerting: resisting both the pedagogical impulse to indicate, authoritatively – 'Behold this thing' – and the dramatic urge to annex urban facades as filmic backdrops. Performance barely enacted, quickly disguised.

A collage of recorded texts was edited from interviews with the performers, registered both before and after the episode, expressing, as young women alone, their expectations and fears. Thomas and I spoke of them in the city, attempting neither to ventriloquize them nor to prefigure their personal experiences. Again, we were the only live performers, speaking texts over, in reference to, on behalf of the figures on video.

John Hardy created the pre-recorded soundtrack and played trumpet and Hammond organ live. All technical apparatus – DVD players, sound equipment – was present and in view on the tables at which Thomas and I sat, with the audiences gathered informally around. Mike Brookes, as designer and technical director, was now to be found at the centre of the room rather than hidden in the lighting box. The theatre machine was in full view, in the immediate exposition of an *assemblage* and *mix* of fragments, rather than unidirectional narrative.

The effect is of a camera obscura, with pictures of the city, documents of ephemeral events, entering the studio: 'a series of panoptic visions, offering us a recognisable view of the world (our world) that lay just outside of the theatre walls, and yet locating us firmly outside of its frame, thus making us share the performers' sense of displacement from it' (Roms 2008: 120). But they do not pretend to completeness: these are moments in an event or narrative or set of relationships of indeterminate extent that may be continuing off camera. The studio resembles rather an *oligopticon*: 'the opposite of panoptica: they see much *too little* to feed the megalomania of the inspector or the paranoia of the inspected, but what they see, they *see it well*'; 'From oligoptica, sturdy but extremely narrow views of the (connected) whole are made possible – as long as connections hold' (Latour 2005: 181). The scene Henri Lefebvre sees from his window (Lefebvre 1996: 219–27; 2004: 27ff).

With hindsight, these were prophetic views of a city increasingly en fête, later observed by photographer Maciej Dakowicz: 'When last orders are called in Cardiff, the party is just beginning. Out on the street the full pantomime is both engaging and revealing and these images give us a ring side view' (Martin Parr in Dakowicz 2012, cover). They dress up, and pose draped: making an impression, performing feats, already on screen. But 'normal rules of behaviour start to dissolve into a more fluid kind of human interaction' (p.106): falling, brawling, groping. The domestic become public: lounging, eating, chatting, sprawling. Sometimes stilled: leaning, slumped, passed out, asleep. Sometimes caught in compositions with various moods, focuses and rhythms in a single image. Unbound relationships with others and with surfaces: 'a certain collective doggedness in this wild pursuit of pleasure and abandonment, a doggedness that suggests much deeper discontent' (p.92).

> But every loose paving, rolling bottle, is a hazard
> Waiting to send them sprawling, pancaked.
> They struggle to regain balance, composure,
> A footing, a posture, a moment of poise,
> Tilting their heads, lifting their chins
> In small shows of stylish defiance.
> These are new creatures, with new strategies of survival,
> Already looking away, before 'Who are you looking at?'
> Becomes a threat.
> (*Who are you looking at?* 2004)

1 Windsor Esplanade

2 44-46 James Street

3 Mount Stuart Square

4 7 James Street

5 Wales Millennium Centre

6 Senedd/Welsh Assembly Government

7 126 Bute Street

8 Butetown

9 St Mary's Church

10 Callaghan Square

SOUTH

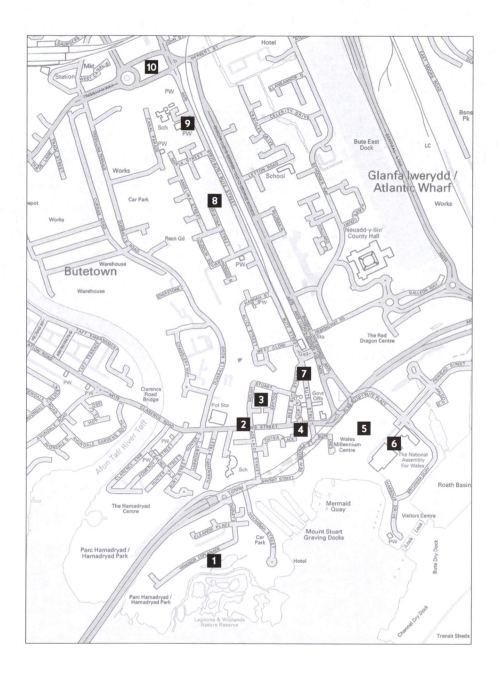

Mike Pearson in *Dark Sounds for a City*, 2004

1. Windsor Esplanade

I stand shirtless on the roof of a council-owned tower block, scanning the sky and looking out over the city and over the bay as 'Water Torture (58")' provides the soundtrack; close by, a trembling, elderly woman fails to drink a cup of tea in a new show apartment against 'Eerie Wind (1'00")'. Scenes from John Rowley's video *Dark Sounds for a City* (2004).

In his series of short films *The Lost Sounds of Wales* (2004), Rowley returned documentary recordings from the BBC sound archive to their places of registration – to Aberystwyth station as the last ever train to Carmarthen is announced. In *Sounds Effects of Death and Disaster* (2000), made with filmmaker Robert Hardy, he himself improvises short choreographies on the streets of Sheffield against which are set sound effects from the BBC recordings of that name. At site, in *Dark Sounds for a City* (2004), performers follow instructions without knowing their eventual soundtrack.

The Severn estuary has one of the largest tidal ranges in the world: at high tide water once lapped the wall here at Windsor Esplanade where Rowley lived in the early 1990s, as did John Williams whilst writing *Bloody Valentine* (1995), in houses originally built for pilots, dock-masters and tugboat owners; at low, a grassy foreshore and extensive mudflats were exposed. But Cardiff is no longer a tidal city; the main legacy of the Cardiff Bay Development Corporation (CBDC) is the barrage, forming the lagoon foreseen as a catalyst to attract investors, employers and tourists.

CBDC was inaugurated in 1987 in order 'to promote property-led regeneration using land acquisition powers, a large capital fund for infrastructure, specific development incentives and direct subsidies to flagship projects' (Punter 2006: 149); it had an annual budget of £60 million. In revamping a waterfront city – as an attraction for affluent residents and visitors even if this meant 'the erasure of local identities and place meanings' (ibid.) – Baltimore provided the exemplar.

The statutory authority planned a huge work of transformation for two thousand seven hundred acres of semi-derelict commercial and industrial estates and working-class housing; the Regeneration Strategy (1988) imagined three million square feet of office space, six thousand new homes and a 'complex of leisure facilities of national significance' (Thomas 1999: 181), with a target of two million tourists: 'How everything will be knitted together is at the time of writing hard to envisage, for the area due for regeneration is formidably extensive' (Newman 2004: 187). The principal objectives were to reunite city centre with waterfront; to create an attractive environment for housing, work and leisure; to ensure high standards of design and quality; to guarantee mixed, sympathetic development in order to enhance local opportunities; to stimulate residential development at a number of scales of affordability; 'and to establish the area as a recognized centre of excellence and innovation in the field of urban regeneration' (see Punter: 151) – Cardiff 'boosting' as ever.

The radical restructuring of the area had the twin objects of 'creating a pattern of infrastructure and land ownership which will facilitate profitable development', and 'recasting the image of the area, the old Tiger Bay and Docks, by reshaping its spaces' (Thomas: 183). The key component was a tree-lined dual carriageway named Bute Avenue, as a safe corridor to the waterfront; Bute Street – the 2nd Marquess's thoroughfare – would become a service road for the potentially embarrassing Tiger Bay, where the population could not be moved but could be segregated, hidden, 'othered': the negative connotations of the area quietly left to dissipate behind the curtain wall of the old West Dock. In delineating new routes and locations with non-contentious names – even Bute Avenue becomes Lloyd George Avenue, 'a one-sided road to nowhere, leaving its new housing as a piece of literal stage scenery' (Punter: 164) – CBDC orientated visitation, and re-ordered dwelling. But such planning imperatives fail to create the localities that are 'constructions out of the intersections and interactions of concrete social relations and social processes in a situation of copresence' (Massey 1991: 277).

The waterfront was designated an arc of entertainment – the first incoming occupant was Harry Ramsden's fish and chip shop in the converted Landsea House. Swept away were 'the North Star club and other down-at-heel establishments of dubious repute' in order to cater for a change 'in the kinds of people for whom the Bay is to be a place of leisure' (Thomas: 183). The drivers would be flagship buildings and an on-going programme of spectacular events, but CBDC had no mandate to build and it missed the property boom. John Punter (pp.149–72) identifies five factors militating against its success: the size and fragmentation of the designated area; the unfavourable property market in 1989–94; the historically modest rates of commercial development in Cardiff; the delay on the construction of the barrage; and its cost, which precluded more pressing investment in a rational transport infrastructure. Overall, the vanity and absurdity of ambitions for a city the size of Cardiff.

At the outset, there was a situation made for site-specific performance, as large buildings fell vacant, though who owned what, who could capitalize on what, was never entirely clear.

> [s]o complete and so extensive was the spectacle of industrial desolation, and all of it wrapped in a serene and death-like stillness, that, like any other perfect landscape, it could only fill one with a sense of wonder. (Briggs 2002: 64)

In December 1988, Brith Gof rented the former Rover car factory to create *Gododdin*, even as it was being illegally stripped; yet in 1990, Associated British Ports – which had already filled the West Dock in 1986 – allowed the company to rehearse *PAX* gratis at Channel Dry Dock.

The outcome of CBDC's tenure is a jumbled concatenation of piecemeal and uncoordinated development incorporating the new, the appropriated, the occupied, the converted: the inauspicious low-rise Mermaid Quay with shops, bars and restaurants, and St David's Hotel with its ocean liner design; Techniquest housed in the skeleton of an engineering shop from the 1880s; and a brasserie in the Pilotage House. And the relic: Mountstuart Dry Docks Ltd. No. 1, 2 and 3 remain undeveloped watery slots.

In *The Poppy-Seed Affair* (1981), a video by Matchbox Purveyors conceived by G. F. Fitz-Gerald with an improvised score by saxophonist Lol Coxhill, People Show actor Mark Long climbs over the wall with spade and bread-loaf; John Batchelor's Mountstuart Dry Dock appears in the background as artist Ian Hinchcliffe, playing a private investigator, looks on. The absurd plot moves through the Central Station, Chapter Bar and Queen Alexandra Dock; it is in the vaudevillian style – with the parodying of television soap operas and amateur dramatics through domestic disorder and pantomimic make-up – that marked British performance of the period. Long is eventually drowned in a bath. The saltmarsh onto which he ventures is now a compensatory freshwater wetland.

Butes and Windsors still haunt the streets of the Docks: Adelaide, Dudley, George, Louisa, William. And the foundation on which this rests results from their enterprise. At Rat Island to the west, there was a ridge of ship's ballast quarter of a mile long; it provided the hardcore for a city sitting on alluvium: 'Down in the foundations of cities are other cities' (Manaugh 2009: 229). On Charles Street, Ebenezer Chapel (1854–5) – Batchelor's chapel – is reputedly of variegated rocky imports.

44-46 James Street, early 1990s

2. 44-46 James Street

44 and 46 James Street adjoined the rear car park of Baltic House, then headquarters of the Cardiff Bay Development Corporation. Vacated in August 1989, the former shops were protected from vandalism by a painted mural showing an Edwardian street scene, erected to disguise their abandonment during a visit by the Prince of Wales.

Entering in 1994, archaeologist Julian Thomas, artist Emma Lawton and I found the remains of previous occupants, the 'ghostly cast' (Edensor 2005: 154): things purposefully discarded, casually forgotten, and thereafter sealed – fittings, utensils, possessions. And traces: wear patterns that attested to their presence, and their passing – 'Evidence of the passage of life is there in the traces' (Lawton 1997: 38). Scatters and accumulations of detritus and marks: revealing configurations of usage; indicating, in concert, how human activity had shaped the place. Passages and locales charting the human/environment interface, the performance of everyday life: 'circuits of routine movement faintly inscribed' (Edensor: 154); 'The floorboards were bent and cracked next to the enamel sink where I presumed he had washed every day' (Sinclair 1999: 27).

The life-story of these places didn't cease when they were removed from the histories of the people who worked there: 'These spaces are dis-ordered by the agency of non-human life forms which seek out opportunities for spreading and colonising, and by the contingencies of climate' (Edensor: 73). They began to decompose, to fall apart of their own volition: slates became dislodged, paint peeled, a veneer of dust settled – 'a collage of time, built up in layers of mould and pigeon shit' (Farley and Roberts 2011: 157). Places and things constantly, if slowly, in motion: mingling, melding, changing in ways that condition how we observe and interpret them.

Perhaps we were drawn by aesthetics of dereliction; to uncanny atmospheres occasioned by dilapidation and neglect.

> For a gothic sensibility, ruins possess the attraction of decay and death, and to enter them is to venture into darkness and the possibilities of confronting that which is repressed. (Edensor: 13)

Even the most mundane set of circumstances has a density: micro-landscapes apparent in close-up. But recognizing this depends upon looking at them in oblique ways. What is banal at one scale of viewing may be minutely detailed: complex layers of decoration and structural alteration lurking in the domestic and the ordinary. Tools and utensils – some familiar, others specific to context and period – bear chips and abrasions that attest to their usage, to events they have witnessed, things that had happened to them, signs of aging, time and use – the carving knife ground thin on the doorstep, a much-loved mug cracked and handle-less.

Our aim was to reflect upon and critique conventional archaeological approaches in a place rendered worthless and due for demolition; to suggest playful and conjectural approaches to observation, recording and retrieval and new forms for the display and reconstitution of the recovered data, artifacts and operational processes. Without the need to provide an authoritative record for future re-interpretation: 'free from the constraining effects of norms surrounding their value and function' (p.123). An opportunity to construct narratives out of fragments: 'to make up stories that seem plausible or fantastic but are not contained by form or convention' (p.163).

Our findings presented as alternative guidebook or installation rather than museum exhibition: recovered 'finds' re-contextualized and animated in performance. And this prior to Buchli and Lucas's 'excavation' of an abandoned council flat in 1997 (2001), a foundational moment in contemporary archaeology.

The remnants appeared to evidence a single act of desertion. The task was to disaggregate the patchwork of short and long-term events and processes, intentional, inadvertent, ephemeral. Renovation and repair, redecoration and adaptation, rot and decay: the scars of both human action and natural process evidenced by surface and deposit, texture and tone.

In the shops, functions had changed and their identity had been recurrently renegotiated and re-evaluated; and we too made a sensual encounter, and changed them, as they became a resource of data and of inspiration in our various projects.

Julian Thomas planned a 'Harris matrix' – a technique to view stratigraphic sequences in diagram form – of a large patch of mould; and to undertake a typology of marks. Following *Interior Cutting*, a work undertaken in her Chapter studio which she referred to as 'an archaeology' (Lawton 1997: 39), Emma Lawton intended to hack into the fabric: to cut, hammer, slice; and then sift and sort, order and reorder the fragments of brick and mortar by shape, size and colour. Together, we envisaged removing fixtures and objects, integrating them into artworks elsewhere: to contest conventional curatorial arrangements based on age, authorship, nationality, material and ownership and demonstrate how the ordinary is transformed when segregated museologically.

Additionally, performance – as both spatial practice and analytic – might demonstrate how the organization of space and the built environment not only reflects but actively generates social structures and practices; site as mise-en-scène of quotidian choreographies:

> In the old bank manager's office, through a heavy oak door behind the counters, what looks like a wooden desk opens up to reveal a washbasin. We think of the manager, ushering out another disappointed would-be entrepreneur, shutting the door and washing away the sweat of a nervous handshake. (Farley and Roberts: 154–55)

But 'do we want to make a drama out of loss, abandonment, inattention, forgetfulness?' (Schofield 2009: 4). And:

> What could be the plot to this mise-en-scène? The remains, conceived as evidence, make us think we might be able to say something of what happened, colluding somehow with the material. But really, there is only the retelling of a search, rummagings, incitements, connections engendered through the insinuating detritus. (Shanks 2004: 173)

Performance rather then as an account of encounter: as a vehicle for conjoining artifact and experience, as a vehicle for describing places for those who were absent.

Detached from former usage or assignation, things form heterogeneous assemblages: 'Inside ruins, objects, textures and fragments fall out of their previously assigned contexts to recombine like elements in dreams, a random re-ordering which is determined by where things land or are thrown' (Edensor 2005: 115). In the Polaroid photographs shot in the attic: a man's suit lies beside three Coca-Cola cans; a tray of cutlery spills across floor. Can we ever be sure that human agency was involved in what appears now as the outcome of a performative event? Was the chair knocked over and the knives scattered in an emotional outburst; or as an incident during evacuation; or later in an un-witnessed moment as the result of perching birds? Suggestive arrangements of objects, particularly when framed in the viewfinder of the camera, to an eye adjusted by the forensic 'turn'. Conjecture leading to narrative: conjuring 'uncanny and bizarre scenarios, fantastic happenings through which monstrous forces have inverted the order of things' (p.116).

So, we removed things. Out of context – away from the plenitude of setting – they became so much rubbish, already left as surplus to requirements by their owners. We threw them away.

Then without warning, the buildings were demolished: to provide parking bays 12–14 at Baltic House.

What remains are a few ambiguous images, and the stories we – and any surviving ghostly cast – might tell.

Former National Westminster Bank, January 2013

3. Mount Stuart Square

There are ambulances and fire engines on West Bute Street: on the National Westminster Bank, once the largest outside London, scaffolding has collapsed catastrophically. But all is not what it initially appears: the logos on the vehicles read 'Wyvern', the fictional county in the BBC television series *Casualty*. The old commercial district of Cardiff become set: in its relative desertion become standing set, recurrently used.

At the heart is Mount Stuart Square is Edwin Seward's massive Coal and Shipping Exchange (1884–88) – 'that huge and ponderous ideology in Bath stone' (Williams 1985: 223) – extended in 1912 to include restaurant, wine merchant, tailor, barber and refitted throughout in mahogany. Here daily between 11.00am and 1.00pm world steam coal prices were fixed; here the first one million pound cheque was signed; here, on the trading floor, 'you could reach out in any direction and touch the shoulder of a millionaire' (Lee 1999: 47). And here in 2012 Patti Smith sang 'Gloria', 'Redondo Beach' and 'Land' from her 1975 album 'Horses', and John Cale showed no diminishing of his musical powers. Intended as the accommodation for a Welsh parliament – before rejection of devolution in the 1979 referendum – it is now a concert and events venue, though shrouded in scaffolding to guard against falling masonry.

Around the square and in adjoining streets are the former headquarters of Cardiff's principal companies, with panelled board-rooms intact and a mixed iconography in the moldings on their exteriors – phoenixes, dragons and sea monsters; steam ships, pit heads and railway wagons. Corys' Buildings, John Cory's Building: 'showpiece developments whereby coal and shipping companies, banks and other financial institutions on which the prosperity of the Docks depended competed with one another to present an image of dynamism and success' (Newman 2004: 268). Not that construction was easy: the subsoil is sticky clay; Merthyr House is built on concrete piers to a depth of thirty feet and a concrete raft to support its bulk.

Bethel Chapel was built in 1858; its site is now a car park. In the 1970s and 1980s, with twisted columns painted black and white, it was the infamous Casablanca Club, housing 'a tension free mingling of different races' (Briggs 2002: 109, 161). The 'Casa B' was where suspects in the murder of Lynette White congregated; it is a locale in John Williams's *Five Pubs, Two Bars and a Nightclub* (1999). Here in 1981, as the snooker and drinking continued unabated, theatre company Moving Being presented *Decade* to celebrate the tenth anniversary of Chapter: 'A nostalgic though unromantic look back at hippies and flower power, Charles Manson, drugs, Patty Hearst, social therapy, the Women's Movement, Vietnam, Ulster, Gary Gilmore, ecology, racism, punk. It's all told in raw rough terms, explicit in word and action'

(Moore 1982). Moving Being had been resident in Chapter since 1971, developing a style of mixed media production integrating theatre, dance, design, film and video (see Dixon 2007: 131); *Decade* was the first step towards relocation.

'This stone was laid April 15 AD 1909' – all else is too weathered to read. St Stephen's Church was designed by E. M. Bruce Vaughan, in classic Cardiff Gothic style; at least one stained-glass window is from the studio of William Morris. The last service was held in 1975. Here in December 1982 Moving Being created *The City Trilogy* – 'A three part drama of urban civilisation from Babylon, to Belfast, to a city of the Future, set within the framework of Greek tragedy'– which had its origins in the company's *Brecht in 1984* (1981) that was itself set against the backdrop of inner city riots and the wedding of Charles and Diana. Further inspired by Peter Stein's version of *The Oresteia* (1980), its overall theme was the death of the city. The production saved the church from further dereliction, though its dark oppressive interior seemed to mirror the disquiet of the times: 'At the time both inner and outer space were seemingly innocent unpolluted frontiers. It was as if we had the privilege of starting a new journey'; 'The space theatre offers is a human space, a societal space, a political space. Theatre's job is to keep that space relevant, and to keep it always open to question' (Moore 1997: 156).

Shortly after, Moving Being moved to St Stephen's permanently; Moore's aim in a politically inauspicious period was to stress the wider implications of their work 'in and for society'; 'It is sincerely hoped that St Stephen's will be fully used in the service of such essential debate' (Moore 1982).

> The conversion of the church into theatre is an appropriate one, the interior spaces of the building being left as open as possible so that actors and audience can assemble together in different ways. (Moore 1989: 33)

It allowed the company to replicate the auditorium of the Elizabethan playhouse; and for a work about the Austrian satirist Karl Kraus, to convert it into a turn-of-the-century Viennese café, 'with the audience sitting at tables attended by waiters serving coffee and strudel, as the action progressed outside, visible through the walls' (ibid.). Amongst Moore's conceptual concerns were 'a space between things, at the edges of objects, the space that defines one thing from another, one form of expression from another' (Moore 1997: 153).

Tiger! Tiger! Burning Bright (1985) with a cast of over fifty actors, singers, dancers and musicians presented scenes and stories of the rise of Cardiff. The space became 'a kind of industrial cathedral' (Moore 1989: 33), though the narrow nave with immovable pillars posed problems for the installation of a large setting, and the floor had to be strengthened. Tramlines were laid back to front for mobile coal drums; at the rear, a cutaway mineshaft showed several strata in full working operation. Temporary washing lines created a sense of depth and perspective; a temporary boxing ring was formed with a single rope. A key scenic component was a large wooden cube that could be rotated, opening on each side to show different scenes.

Against the loss of populace and the need for regeneration in an area of industrial dereliction, an HTV documentary (Stokes 1985) recommends the production as a possible stimulus for a re-establishment of local confidence and enthusiasm. Cardiff Bay Development Corporation has yet to appear, though the projected move of South Glamorgan County Hall to the East Dock is seen as a potential catalyst.

On Friday 2 October 1998 Mike Brookes and I meet a small audience close to the site of the Casablanca Club. We arrive in a red Series 3 Mercedes saloon; I am wearing a radio microphone. As I begin to move around the vicinity, out of earshot – pointing out places, naming names, committing inadvisable acts of speculation, fifty yards from Butetown police station, one hundred yards from 7 James Street – the audience clustering around the car hear my voice on its stereo system. Here they are at the heart of the matter. I speak urgently: 'For time has not healed here. It's still raw.' A monologue to tell Lynette White's story: to disentangle an event in which so many were implicated, the text including details from family memories, character testimony, media articles, eyewitness accounts, police interviews, pathologist's reports, scene-of-crime reconstructions: *Body of Evidence*.

Then the radio is switched off and we drive away: the most ephemeral of performances vanishes.

7 James Street, early 2000s

4. 7 James Street

Flat 1, 7 James Street is, as often, for rent. No one stays long: disturbed by stories, or by presentiments.

> It was a cold and forbidding place and she was known to hate it. She kept no possessions there but simply used it to earn money from her clients. The small first floor flat above a betting shop had no electricity and very little furniture. In the sitting room was a dirty, soiled bed. (*Body of Evidence* 1997)

In the early hours of 14 February 1988, Lynette White was murdered in Flat 1, above Kingsport bookmakers (see Williams 1995). She had been stabbed fifty-one times and her head was all but severed.

It was a killing on the cusp, a crime redolent of old ways, old Cardiff: 'For eight weeks the redevelopment of Butetown was stopped in its tracks. The crime had to be cleared up quickly' (Sekar 1997: 10). Although witnesses saw a single, white male with bloodied hands on James Street, the event became infamous for the wrongful arrest and trial of the Cardiff Three. In the ensuing furore, Lynette all but disappeared.

In *Body of Evidence*, these are some of the words I spoke:

> There's a performance I've struggled to make. And failed. Why? Perhaps because I am not separate from it. It happened on my landscape, the place that BBC's *Panorama* made look like *Naked City* – 'The past still clings stubbornly to these damp streets.' Perhaps because Marianne Faithful is right: after a certain age every artist does work with injury. And Walter Benjamin too: 'Death is the sanction of everything that the storyteller can tell. He has borrowed his authority from death. In other words, it is natural history to which his stories refer back.' Perhaps because no one deserved to die like this, and the only real memorial is one that has to be rebuilt – or at least retold – every day …

> The headlines in the press were as predictable as they were banal: 'young prostitute; wretched trade; semi-derelict flat; gruesome discovery; savagely murdered; hacked to death; horrific crime; mutilated remains; a frenzy of violence.' For others, it began with the rosiness of memory: 'She was a little gem. I remember we used to fight over who would do her curls. She had lovely skin, and a fantastic personality. I used to call her my protégé. We used to say she would be a model. That was the dream we used to giggle over in the kitchen.' And even: 'She was really a good worker out there. She had a lot of nice gentlemen friends, a lot of regulars.' Then a need to make sense of it: 'She wanted to please people. She would do anything for you. She was easily led.' 'We look in the mirror and we never see how we are. We only see the faults. She always felt insecure because she never felt as good as the rest of us.' But no one in Butetown really seemed to know anything: 'Prostitute murders are often difficult to solve – too many casual contacts, too much furtive behavior.'

'There were theories, stories, hunches and Chinese whispers' (Sekar: 17).

> Then in November three key witnesses all came forward at the same time, admitted they'd lied in their original statements, and the two women admitted some involvement in the killing. And they named five black men: Stephen Miller, Tony Paris, Yusef Abdullahi, John Actie, and Ron Actie. And so the fictions begin: 'Every answer and statement was filled with half-truths, half-lies, and self-justifications.' 'The truth about how she died is shrouded by the murky gloom of the world in which she lived. In a world of secrecy and deceit, questions from outside go unanswered'.

At the scene of crime, body and things are out of kilter, in a place haunted by absent presences – of victim and perpetrator. Forensic enquiry seeks to establish choreography and dramaturgy – who did what, when, in what sequence; but it is riven by conjecture – 'a classic narrative locale' (Shanks 2004: 162).

> Certainly there were traces, terrible traces – arcs of blood, quantities of semen. But no forensic evidence ever linked those eventually charged to that scene – no fingerprint, no single hair, no drop of blood …
> This scene was so pitifully, desperately bare: body, shoe, bed. No weapon....
> a red divan with small, white flowers – the only item of furniture.
> There was an unused condom and money on the bed.

Perhaps it was the very emptiness of the scene that inspired such fervid speculation. Eyewitnesses did it. Defendants did it. Police did it. I do it too …

> At first, it was as if everyone was trying out stories to see if they would stick to other stories – editing, trimming, rewriting. But then it moved on and James Street became a stage-set upon which everyone was free to choreograph and direct the behaviours, actions, and motives of the protagonists: to create the scenario; to write the dialogue; to give oneself a starring role; to use scenes and characters from other times, other places: 'I heard a man say, "Give it to me. You've got what I want. I know you've got it and I want it." I heard another male voice say, "Give the man what he wants or he'll fuck you up real good". I heard a female voice say "I haven't got it." And then the first male said: "I know you've got it. I fucking want it. Give it to me".'

At various stages in one version of the crime there were between five and eight people in the small room.

> The computer simulation on *Panorama* shows an airbrushed room, a shape on the floor and standing figures. But in the animation, it is the room that moves not the aggressors. They stand passive, mute, turned to stone. They are observers, not murderers. And perhaps this is how it was. Perhaps in those twenty hours, many people came to look at her, fascinated, entranced, hypnotized by her stillness. It was in that gaze – that confusion – that the stories began.

In April 1991, following the murder of Geraldine Palk, I gave a sample of blood backstage at Butetown police station. Four of us had sat in the waiting room: each suspecting the others, rehearsing our stories in nervous chat.

Early in 2003, a section of skirting board was removed in Flat 1: after several layers of paint were stripped, blood from the injured assailant was recovered. Advances in mitocondrial DNA analysis indicated it resembled that of a fourteen year-old boy listed on the national crime register: his uncle Geoffrey Gafoor was subsequently convicted of Lynette White's murder. It had been an argument over money he said. Every contact really does leave a trace.

Kingsport is now Ladbrookes; the 'North Star' where 'Lynette and Stephen played out their lives' (Williams 1995 54) long gone; a fish bar occupies Babs' Bistro, from where Lynette would call a cab, and where I noted: 'Men came in, men went out, singly and in groups. And in their laughter, and in their silence, I began to realize that in familiar places, other maps are being drawn, other stories are unfolding.'

The case rumbles on: in the trials of those who told tales and perjured.

Wales Millennium Centre, February 2013

5. Wales Millennium Centre

The brief: to design a place for performance, a landmark building with visual impact akin to the Sydney Opera House. To terminate the new Bute Avenue: uniting city centre with this peripheral, though rapidly developing and culturally desirable, location.

The competition for Cardiff Bay Opera House was announced in 1994. Amongst the short-listed world-leading architects who were invited to submit maquettes was Rem Koolhaas, whose three white boxes – one small to sell tickets, one medium to make opera, one large to present opera – was, after his signature formulation (Koolhaas and Mau 2002), an exact XXXS version of the full-scale building.

It was won by Iraqi-born Zaha Hadid: 'The proposed design aims to embody two often mutually exclusive paradigms of urban design: monumentality and space' (Hadid in Betsky 2009: 80). Her concept was to dissolve into a single continuum two types of architectural and spatial configuration: an exterior perimeter block and an enclosed interior.

> This is achieved through three compensatory tactics: the raising of the perimeter, the opening up of the perimeter at the corner pointing at the pier head to reveal the volume of the auditorium as the main solid figure within the delineated site, and finally, the continuation of the public space by extending the piazza within a gentle slope into the site, establishing a new ground plane over the main foyer areas. (ibid.)

In Hadid's design, the auditorium and other semi-public spaces are hung 'like jewels from a band' which is then wrapped around the perimeter like 'an inverted necklace' (p.83), creating an accessible public space at the centre and allowing the servicing of individual rooms from the rear.

The overarching themes are of openness, invitation, accessibility and revelation, in a construction primarily of glass and fairface concrete. The raised, glazed outer wall draws visitors into the open courtyard – itself an addition to the open spaces of the city, 'a more explicitly-charged space taking its cue from the drama of the Operatic performance' (Hadid 2000: 213), and incidentally for outdoor performances – whilst retaining views into the bay: 'This is what Zaha Hadid described as a "living room" for the city' (Crickhowell 1997: 102). It also makes apparent the mechanisms of the creative process: the orchestra rehearsal rooms and the main auditorium are distinct entities on the necklace. The effect was to be both impactful and magnetic: 'a building alive with practice and performance' (ibid.), that might even afford glimpses of artists at work.

Crickhowell imagines the effect of the various planes and spaces, 'in terms of the drama they create as you move through foyers and upstairs towards the auditorium;

and in the theatricality of the auditorium that helps create the mood for the performance that is to follow' (p.101). He foresees 'the intensely dramatic views into the great sheet of glass, the grand staircase, the foyers of the auditorium, with its soaring prow, and out from those foyers to the sea beyond' (p.102).

In Hadid's work, the key conceptual relationship is between ground and plan:

> The Ground organizes spaces, which in turn organizes social relations, political structures and the very fabric of everyday life. It is at once mundane and sublime. The Plan is the architectural vehicle for the manipulating of the ground, its multiplying, renewing, intensifying and re-naming. (Hadid 2000: 211)

This involves a concern with the topography of the site, whereby the fundamental organizational patterns are rendered as emerging from the very strata of the existing ground condition: giving rise to 'an architectural order consisting of the interaction between synthetic plate tectonics or artificial and expansive landforms reminiscent of geological effects' (ibid.). But the strata in the resulting architectures are fractured and faulted as if rather by volcanic intrusion and eruption than sedimentation.

The ground constitutes a continuum – 'an ideological plane of open and continuous space' (ibid.) – as a potential field for fluid architectural forms, segueing from exterior to interior. But the spatial narrative is itself incomplete: it contains gaps, elisions and interstitial occlusions, un-programmed or even half-demolished moments that leave open the possibility of dialogue with the surroundings. The overall effect is of a terrain upon which there is an asymmetrical play of space and surface that provides manifold and diverse experiences for spectators, visitors, workers and tourists.

'This all looks extremely promising, a building of great visual force which will do much to integrate the various structures at the head of Cardiff Bay. It is due for completion in the year 2000', posits Newman, before the fact (1995: 265). As chair of the Opera House trustees, Crickhowell attests to the subsequent debacle in a forthright account of the negotiations and machinations, the conflicts of ambition and opinion, the rancour and failure of civic will that prevented its construction.

In the Millennium Centre, constructed in its stead, there is a significant shift from articulations of space to the manipulation of materials, from performance to semiology. The design concepts are inspired by the landscape and industrial heritage of Wales: in the reference to the layered strata of sea cliffs and the slate quarries of North Wales, and in the application of the texture and shades of steel and hardwood. The appeal is to Welsh traditions – to ersatz symbolism rooted in native-soil materials – versus intrusive modernity, in the desire for a 'national icon for Wales'. The slate strata are even-bedded, enshrining nostalgia for permanence and authority. It is all front – running to red-brick and 'what looks like creosoted lap-wood fencing' (Finch 2004: 148) at the rear – a brooding, monstrous carapace on a building designed from the inside out. Architecture as stolid, sculptural manifestation: materials rendered political, as meaningful and readily intelligible in this geological assemblage; and text too as the building is badged in large illuminated letters by poet Gwenith Lewis – 'In these stones horizons sing. Creu gwir fel gwydr o ffwrnais awaen'.

> In the public eye, architecture is about comfort, about shelter, about bricks and mortar … but it is also about advancing society and its development, the device of shock may be an indispensable tool. (Tschumi 2000: 170)

The Millennium Centre takes its place amongst the architectural mélange of Cardiff Bay. There is no 'boost' here, no re-thinking, no seeking after those unfamiliar solutions that brought Portland stone to Cathays Park – architecture as incitement, to make things happen. No 'intensifying and accelerating urban experience through clash and disjunction' (ibid.) or creating 'a place of invention of ourselves' (p.176) in the dynamic articulation of concept, use, image, structure and experience.

'Architecture at its most potent is performative: it is the concrete manifestation or deployment of a design matrix or servo-mechanical diagram' (Kwinter 2010: 19). Difficult to appreciate what is being performed, when an acoustically sound auditorium is hidden behind a foyer resembling an airport departure lounge.

In front of the Millennium Centre, the elliptical Roath Basin was filled in 1970; it is now Roald Dahl Plass, named for the Cardiff-born author christened at the Norwegian Church. It is still edged with large granite blocks – eroded, worn, chipped, patched, plugged, tied with metal clamps; with redundant bollards, rings, studs – inconsequential survivors of development.

The entrance to Torchwood's underground monitoring station is somewhere here, though shielded from view by a 'perception filter'.

Brith Gof rehearsing *PAX*, Channel Dry Dock, 1990

6. Senedd/Welsh Assembly Government

The brief: to design a seat for the National Assembly for Wales that meets a number of constitutional stipulations for sustainable development: a design-life of one hundred years; the use of indigenous materials; the minimizing of energy consumption and waste; the application of renewable technologies. In addition: to be an exemplar for access, and to symbolize open democracy.

Richard Rogers's Senedd Building which opened on 1 March 2006 is in essence all roof: an undulating lightweight canopy clad below in resilient Western Red Cedar, set on a massive concrete plinth that has substantial thermal properties, with curtain walls that are in the main of louvred glass.

> The glass facade is representative of the transparent nature of the Senedd and envelops the building. The indigenous slate used on the external walls and the floors internally and externally cleverly brings the Bay up and into the building, attempting to draw people into the building and to engage them in the democratic process. (National Assembly for Wales brochure, 2006)

Outside, the tiered frontal steps lead down to the former entrance of the West Dock, where granite blocks are scored by the passages of metal hawsers. The resulting risers are intended to evoke the image of exposed indigenous slate cutting. Inside, the circular debating chamber – set deep in the building's core as both the physical and metaphorical centre of the design – can be viewed panoptically by visitors looking down through glass from a circular gallery; they also have video screens on which to view the main speakers and events. Above the chamber is a curving wooden funnel rising through the building and topped by a rotating cowl and lantern structure that creates natural ventilation and admits daylight.

Rogers's design attempts to enshrine openness, transparency and participation in its architectural form: a place to witness the performance of democracy in action. From the foyer, even the committee rooms set in two incisions in the plinth can be viewed. It is acoustically hermetic, and often hushed. It is 'decidedly low-voltage for its site' (Hatherley 2010: 274).

The slate-floored foyer looks out onto the lagoon. Here in October 2011, National Theatre Wales's production of Shakespeare's *Coriolan/us* was given a preliminary reading. The arrangement aped chamber and gallery: actors sat facing inwards on a closed circle of chairs; permanent and temporary audiences, and passers-by, were seated on concentric rings of seating, effectively eavesdropping on a conversation that was often heated and politically charged. Yet the actors never directly referred either to audience or to the location: any additional dramatic meanings or implications resulting from 'this act in this place' were coincidental, in a purposeful ambivalence. But the effect of being party to public and private conversations informed the eventual production staged in August 2012 in a disused hangar at RAF St Athan for the World Shakespeare Festival/London 2012. Here the actors wore radio-microphones, and the audience radio headsets as they followed the debates and 'breaking news', often standing in transient circles around dramatic encounters and events in the perambulatory performance.

Looking out from the Senedd: to the right, William Frame's Pierhead Building (1896–97) for the Bute Docks Company. In elaborate French Gothic style and hot red brick and terracotta – with dragon gargoyles and the company motto in relief 'Wrth Ddŵr a Thân' ('By Water and Fire') – it was both a land-mark for incoming shipping and a mark of commercial confidence and profligacy. To the left: the white wooden Norwegian Church – a relic of trade links when Norway provided pit props for Welsh mines – that once stood closer to the dock entrance off Bute Street, new-build as much as reconstruction. In the lagoon: the wooden 'dolphin' towers to which boats under repair were attached.

Gone now is the Wil Alsop's Visitor's Centre – an elliptical plywood tube covered in PVC fabric – that gave a view onto the bay through its glass-walled end and that contained a wooden model of south Cardiff, regularly updated to show the latest achievements in redevelopment: ever 'boosting'.

Gone too is the Channel Dry Dock where Scott's *Terra Nova* was overhauled in June 1913, and where in June 1991 Brith Gof prepared *PAX*, for its premiere in St David's Hall. Its large, semi-derelict sheds were amongst the few buildings offering sufficient height to suspend performers – in a production featuring a descent of angels into an ecologically imperilled world, intended for presentation in cathedrals.

Here designer Cliff McLucas first developed his architectonic conceptualization of site-specific performance:

> The breakthrough that enabled me to get to grips with the themes in scenographic terms occurred when we began to focus on angels, in particular, the notion of angels leaving heaven and visiting the earth became a source of useful ideas that have developed into the built installations and moving vehicles you will see in the performance.
>
> ... the notion of two entirely different worlds coming together remains a powerful and potentially traumatic idea, and it is from that trauma that I have tried to develop the scenography – or rather two scenographies – one for the angels and one for the humans – one for the visitors and one for the visited – one the ghost and the other the host.
>
> The Angels are beings of the heavens and therefore operate the vertical dimension, on an elegant flying system of pulleys and counterweights designed for us by Steve Crawley – the specialist who designed the systems that enabled both Superman and Batman to fly in their films. The humans (including us, the audience) are earthbound and operate in the horizontal dimension within the host building – in this case, a concert hall.

> The ghost building is a full-size section of the cathedral made of scaffolding, and is the angels' means of entry into our world. Like all ghosts, the cathedral is invisible, like all ghosts, it walks through walls, like all ghosts, its relationship with our world (the host) is a tenuous one.
>
> My decision to build a cathedral did not come from a love of Gothic architecture or of cathedrals themselves – places that I find oppressive and strangely dismissive of the 'human'. Instead, the idea of 'hi-jacking' the image of the cathedral and then shifting its identity in some way interested me greatly.
>
> By building a cathedral in a humble material such as scaffolding or bamboo; by building our cathedral in a factory, in the street, in the docks; by building it overnight, we may alter its meaning. As a ghost, the cathedral may become a shadow of its former self. (McLucas in production programme for *PAX*, 1991)

At Channel Dock, McLucas constructed a single Gothic arch, its curves intimated in tubing cut to length and intricately bolted, within which angel performers could be lowered, hoisted and swung. Although he was able to install an aisle of arches across the stage and into the auditorium at St David's Hall, the scenography never achieved the lucidity apparent when standing in free space in the dry dock. In subsequent stagings, angels hung from roof-beams.

The cleared site now houses the 'Dr Who Experience', in a blue, pupa-like edifice. Slightly to the north is the new BBC Drama Centre. The city will provide both setting and back-story for future programmes: in *Torchwood*, the time-rift apparently particular to Cardiff leads to a plethora of alien presences.

Scott Memorial, Cardiff Bay, February 2013

7. 126 Bute Street

He was on his hands and knees
    and they were trying to leave him –
Titus, Birdie, Uncle Bill, the Owner.
Not that he'd ever called them that.
He'd dragged them there and now they were running away,
Not that you could call *this* running.
Only later did they turn, from guilt or fear.
'We stuck to our companions to the last.'
And he … laughed.
He'd seen the dog-shit first.
Birdie said it was a flag.
The Owner wrote, 'It was a flag'.
But he knew dog-shit –
    had scraped it off his fingers, on his knees, dead drunk, in Bute Street.
Nature displays nothing black here.
And it was so black.
Dog eat dog.
Dog eat dog-shit.
Dog eat man-shit.
Man eat dog.
'They licked their cracked lips, unable to take their eyes off the delicate cutlets
spread on the snow.'
And his hand … pulsed.
(*Dead Men's Shoes*, 1997)

The lettering on the exterior reads – 'Provision Curers Bonded Store Merchants'. 126 Bute Street is part of a block built in the 1840s by Hemingway and Pearson, who constructed Bute East Dock, for Joseph Frazer and Company, Cardiff's main ships' chandlers. Frazers supplied everything from biscuits to anchors. In the 1980s, it became an annex of the National Marine and Industrial Museum whose main building was demolished to make way for Mermaid Quay. The frontage is narrow; the offices of 'Business in Focus' now occupy the long storeroom that once extended to the rear. Here in 1997, Pearson/Brookes presented *Dead Men's Shoes*, the story of Welsh seaman Edgar Evans and Robert Falcon Scott's fateful expedition to the South Pole.

In 1909, Edward 'Teddy' Evans, a member of Scott's *Discovery* (1901–1904) expedition and later Lord Mountevans, used his Cardiff connections to garner support for his own polar assault. Learning of Scott's renewed ambitions, he persuaded *Western Mail* editor W. E. Davies and ship owners including Daniel

Ratcliffe and William Tatem to transfer their backing: Scott aspirations and cause provided an attractive and practicable vehicle for civic promotion.

In June 1910, Scott's *Terra Nova* arrived in Cardiff: all docking fees and routine repair costs were waived and she was painted and checked for leaks in Channel Dry Docks. On 11 June, she took on three hundred tons of briquettes – made by mixing and heating waste small coal with pitch – donated by the Crown Preserved Coal Company and later one hundred tons of Insole's steam coal *gratis*: 'everything was done with an open-hearted generosity' (Evans 1921: 13). Such was the level of support that Scott designated Cardiff homeport of the re-registered vessel.

Scott, Teddy Evans and their wives stayed at the Mansion House. On Monday 13 June, Cardiff Chamber of Commerce organized a seven-and-sixpenny dinner for the officers at the Royal Hotel on St Mary Street that added £1,000 to the £26,000 already pledged in the city: the menu included beef *Terra Nova*, soufflé *Captain Scott* and *South Pole* ice pudding. The men ate at Barry's Hotel before joining the officers for a smoking concert at which the expedition was presented with flags bearing Cardiff's mottoes: 'I have no hesitation in entrusting this magnificent emblem into the safe-keeping of Petty Officer Evans, our "Taff", a true son of Wales and the companion of my earlier voyage', announced Scott (see Williams 2012). Edgar Evans, seated between him and the Lord Mayor – gave an impromptu speech:

> Every man has confidence in Captain Scott. I know him and he knows me very well … As regards the Welsh flag, if Captain Scott wants to know the English translation of the Welsh mottoes, here it is, 'Awake it is day' and 'The Welsh dragon leads the van' … Of course that depends on Captain Scott bringing back the Pole … If we do bring it back I hope you will let it go to Swansea (loud cheers and laughter).

The inebriated Evans had to be carried back to the ship.

The room at the Royal Hotel was later named 'The Captain Scott Room'; in the refurbishment of 1998, the wood panelling was removed and installed one floor above.

Monuments to Scott abound in the city: the lighthouse-shaped clock tower in Roath Park lake – where *Terra Nova*'s figurehead stood until 1932 – dedicated to 'Britons all and very gallant men'; Jonathan Williams's sculptural group of men hauling a sledge in a blizzard – their figures covered in a mosaic of broken white tile – at the entrance to Roath Dock, ironically next to the Norwegian Church; the bronze plaque in City Hall by W. Wheatley Wagstaff that reads 'Victory for him was swallowed up in death. This tablet was erected to commemorate the memory of one who sacrificed his life to obtain glory for his beloved country'. No mention here of vaunted scientific ambitions. The penguins appear modelled by someone who had never seen one and again ironically there are six dogs, which Scott disliked and which ensured Amundsen's success.

Dead Men's Shoes was scenically arranged by Mike Brookes as a series of parallel zones of equal length in the narrow store room: against the wall, a suspended canvas projection screen fifty feet in length; against this, five evenly spaced, identical chairs, and between the chairs, twelve low-wattage halogen lamps at the foot of the screen – focused down on the floor, flooding the room forward of the projections with low-level reflected light; a performance strip twelve feet wide; a single row of chairs for the audience; seven computer-controlled slide projectors on stands; two high-wattage halogen lamps focused on the top edge of the wall opposite the screen, illuminating the performance area, and two audio speakers.

Dead Men's Shoes attempted to recover Edgar Evans: the only non-officer in the polar party; the man who died first, whom they blamed for failure. Relating Evans's story and the fateful journey to the South Pole in a text combining new writing with first-hand accounts, I travelled the length of the screen over eighty minutes. I wore a radio microphone, my voice amplified and distributed evenly throughout the body of the room. I was ever approaching, pausing in front of, or departing from individual spectators.

On the screens were two image groups: four abutting full-screen projections with three small picture window insets across the junctions. The controlled transitions and movements of similar and unlike images – details reshot from documentary photographs of the expedition – created complex collages, juxtapositions and superimpositions. But closeness to the screen meant that it was impossible for the audience to view the whole panorama, reinforcing the impression of being lost in whiteness. The floor lighting was structured across the duration through ten consecutive fades, the lamps on stands through six hundred and twelve regular pulses representing days en route.

Scott's departure from Cardiff is recorded in the documentary film *90 Degrees South*: the 1933 version with sound is introduced by cinematographer Herbert 'Ponko' Ponting and Teddy Evans, who both wear dinner suits. In *Dead Men's Shoes*, I wore a similar suit, in acknowledgement of the lecture tours of expeditionary leaders through which they financed their exploits, though in white, to avoid compromising the projections.

> I want to say he died of disappointment.
> I think he died of going quiet.
> Of having nothing left to say.
> Of being lost for words.

When Teddy Evans returned *Terra Nova* to Cardiff on 14 June 1913, 60,000 Cardiff citizens greeted her.

Pavement detail, Bute Street, March 2013

8. Butetown

Bute Street is the original link between city and docks. To the east runs the perimeter wall of the West Dock; to the west, the 2nd Marquess's first plot of residential housing, centred on Loudoun Square, in 1853 already described as 'increasingly vile and abominable' (Newman 2004: 185).

By 1911, Cardiff had the second highest proportion of foreign-born men after London – Somalis, West Africans, West Indians – arrived as stokehold crews or drawn to a source of work and gathered mainly in Butetown. In his 1947 study of Cardiff's docklands, anthropologist Kenneth Little observed that: 'It was in the "rooming house quarters" that the great metropolitan centers had their "racial colonies"' (Mort: 2008: 334).

On 22 April 1950, *Picture Post* published a photo-essay by Bert Hardy, with a text by socialist and folklorist A. L. Lloyd. It is the first portrait of a multi-racial community in Britain: a scene of crowded occupancies, of men congregating outdoors, of Joe Erskine standing next to, if not leaning against, a lamp-post on the corner of Angelina and Sophia Streets. 'The subject matter is *faces, gestures, action, encounters* – in a particular time and place' (Jordan 2001: 13); 'The pictures are immensely *eventful* – they are faces, groupings, moments of action "frozen in time" by the intervention of the camera' (Hall 1972: 79). And they record too an intimate and vernacular landscape of interiors – domestic, social and religious – and street scenes, in photographs that 'insist on their content – on the what of the events and subjects they document' (Jordan: 12).

Lloyd never uses the pejorative Tiger Bay – with its connotations of the animal and violent – but he does characterize it as a ghetto: 'They live marked off from the rest of the city by social barriers, by race prejudice, and by the old Great Western Railway bridge. They live in a community bound together by under-privilege, where the grocer's an Arab, the boot maker a Greek, where a sailor takes a drink in a Somali milk-bar or an Irish pub' (Lloyd 1947: 17). He does not refrain from describing the housing conditions and resulting deprivations nor the social realities of transient populations, drug use and prostitution: 'Even so, the area is not the heart-rending desolation of the usual industrial slum' (p.23). His aim is to show the community as functional and routine, with glimpses inside Berlin's Milk Bar and the Peel Street Mosque.

A world if not of social harmony, then at least rubbing along, but liable to disturbance. And with external perceptions based 'on "stories" of the city' (Holloway and Hubbard 2001:109): fictive narratives of dark underworlds and rapacious appetites.

Three people died and dozens were injured in the disturbances of 1919, ignited primarily by post-war frustrations at the lack of employment opportunities for demobilized white troops (see Evans 1980). As a result of manning shortages in the First World War, merchant sailors had been recruited in the colonies; demobilized West Indian soldiers further increased the immigrant population. There was resentment against a community regarded as having benefited from the war, as affluent and marked by intermarriage: 'Such consorting is ill-assorting; it exhibits either a depravity or squalid infatuation; it is repugnant to our finer instincts in which pride of race occupies a just and inevitable place' (*Western Mail*, 13 June 1919). The body of black men on the streets was regarded as profligate and dangerous. And as the coal trade slumped, unemployment became more widespread.

Events unfolded on a terrain partly extant, partly now turned into access alleyways, partly erased by later commercial and infrastructural development: a performative landscape possible to imagine on a map or in the field, but unmarked – lacking those displays that on heritage battlefield sites help visitors to imagine deployments and the course of events, as they move from station to station.

Trouble flared on 11 June near Custom House Street when a group of disaffected former soldiers attacked a brake containing immigrant soldiers and their white wives, assuming them to be pimps and prostitutes. Groups of blacks and whites quickly assembled on Canal Parade, throwing stones and firing blanks. Some whites broke the police cordon and entered Bute Street, smashing property; blacks sought cover in Hope Street and Homfray Street, where a house was set on fire. The police tried to keep the rolling incident on the move. A white man died on Caroline Street from a cut throat; Arab lodging houses on Bute Street became a target. Three days of rioting followed.

At 7pm on 12 June, a crowd of former servicemen, youths and women gathered on the corner of Custom House Street. Around 8pm, allegedly following an altercation between a black man and a prostitute, they surged down Bute Street. They attacked an Arab restaurant and boarding house at 264 Bute Street, smashing windows. Following shots from upstairs, the mob and the police entered. Mohamed Abdulla was badly beaten and later died of a fractured skull. A mob then roamed Tredegar Street and Millicent Street looking for black men; at the Princess Royal Hotel on Millicent Street two white men were shot, one fatally; on Caroline Street, a black man had to be rescued.

On Friday 13 June, large crowds of sightseers gathered in St Mary Street, Custom House Street, the Hayes and at the top of Bute Street. Police ringed Bute Street Post Office; they then cleared Butetown in a baton charge that removed the sentries and barricades erected for self-protection. On Saturday, the party escorting prisoners was rushed at Mill Lane and Bridge Street, but as it reached the Royal Arcade, police dispersed the crowd.

Blacks and whites were charged with riotous assembly. One effect was for Butetown to withdraw further into itself: resilient, poor – the community that Bert Hardy witnessed.

Demolition began in the mid-1960s. As the ensuing development was itself recently redeveloped, a mural – part-decoration, part-protestation – appeared on the fencing around the site. Here were familiar faces and places: Joe Erskine, 'The Quebec', the Rastas. Also moments of rupture, events that still rankle: the violent dockers' strike of 1911 against Chinese labour when laundries were destroyed; the 1919 race riots; the hanging of Mahmood Mattan in 1952 for the murder of Bute Street shopkeeper Lily Volpert; the case of the Cardiff Three.

Butetown is now an area of low-rise housing with twin central tower blocks – Loudoun House and Nelson (Mandela) House. But its essential footprint survives, and Bute names too: Alice, Angelina, Christina, Hannah, Maria.

Bute Street is calmed by chicanes and parking bays. Along the pavement are a series of regularly spaced, silver metal pillars one metre high, marking the locations of noted businesses and organizations that stood opposite at various times in the twentieth century: 219 Bute St (1920) Somali Boarding House; 206 Bute St (1932) M. Monterio Gramophone Repairs; 167 Bute St (1920) Wah Lee Chinese Laundry; 130 Bute St (1910) Ecuadorian Venezuelan Consulate; 29 Bute St (1920) Speiro Lambadares Tobacconist. On the faces of the pillars are the names of former residents – singer Shirley Bassey, guitarist Victor Parker; and places off Bute Street – the Ghana Café, the Cairo Café, Manuela Ice Creams. As much as laying a trail for tourists, they attest to disappearance: their references as enigmatic as inscriptions on the gravestones of a community long passed. Tiger Bay.

National Theatre Wales *De Gabay*, in front of St Mary's Church, March 2013

9. St Mary's Church

St Mary's Church (1840–45) on Bute Street – 'Big and ambitious, but a foolish design' (Newman 2004: 265) – has an imposing facade but no front door. As Butetown developed, the 2nd Marquess demanded an appearance fitting for the location, but the church faces east, and, after convention, the altar sits directly behind the blocked frontage.

It is here that Gillie Evans sings in the choir in J. Lee Thompson's crime drama film *Tiger Bay* (1959), the story of the killing of a woman and the relationship between murderer and child.

Tiger Bay was shot mainly in south Cardiff – 'Watch the film Tiger Bay and you'll see dark little alleyways, threatening, exciting, raw and dishevelled' (Palfrey 2006: 26). But curiously, also elsewhere: as Polish sailor Korchinsky (Horst Buchholz) is paid off from his ship, he exits the docks onto the transporter bridge with its suspended roadway in Newport; his escape attempt was filmed in Avonmouth near Bristol. Nevertheless, there are many recognizable locations: Korchinsky walks across Loudoun Square where the original town houses survive here in multiple occupancy; his sometime girlfriend and victim lives in rented rooms, with the communal toilet on the landing. And scenes of a multi-racial community: men squatting on the pavement throw dice; children play in the central gardens, under the eye of adults who sit and talk on the perimeter wall. There is a poor Welsh population – inhabitants and police force cheek by jowl – played by well-known actors of the period: Megs Jenkins, Kenneth Griffiths, Glyn Houston, Meredith Edwards and Rachel Thomas, though there is little hint of 'Kairdiff' in their accents, more an all-purpose 'stage-Welsh'.

We first meet Gillie (Hayley Mills) as she plays on the slipway in front of the present Mermaid Quay, with glimpses of the Pierhead Building, Channel Dry Dock and 'dolphins' in the background, a paddle steamer to the fore. The granite block wall is currently visible, though the slipway is built over. This is the site where the vernacular shrine to the late Ianto Jones, a bisexual character in *Torchwood*, has been created by fans: an array of photographs, messages, plastic flowers pinned to a wooden barrier. Part campaign for his return, part remorse for the loss of a sexual, albeit fictional, exemplar, it is close to the tourist office in which he worked and which provided a second entrance to Torchwood's underground headquarters.

In Thompson's film places in Cardiff are named – Loudoun Square, Bute Street, St Mary's – and police Superintendent Graham, played by Hayley Mills's father John Mills, has a map of the docks on his office wall. But scenic constraints often confound actual geographical layout and orientation – dockside cranes appear in the distance as Gillie walks northwards to her home.

On site today, one scene is easy to locate, for little has changed: the West Indian wedding ceremony in St Mary's at which Gillie reveals to a fellow chorister a bullet taken from the murder weapon hidden in the communal toilet she has recovered, and where she fails to complete her solo as she recognizes Korchinsky in the congregation. Another is more difficult to place. The wedding party and calypso band appear in a dramatically lit street, in the landscape of bridges, pubs, steps and canal at the top of Bute Street erased by Callaghan Square. The houses that cluster close in *Tiger Bay* are gone: St Mary's stands apart – next to a sports field, in front of the grassed strip that was once the Glamorganshire Canal.

The argument leading to the crime-of-passion is in Polish. The event is redolent of the murder of Lynette White and its aftermath – a single white man with a prostitute; stories building on stories. And Gillie is an unreliable witness, well known for lying, for mixing fantasy and reality: her account of the murder is an extraordinary combination of physical re-enactment and quoted dialogue. Her confrontation with Korchinsky in the loft of St Mary's – though surely shot in a studio – mixes filmic references and their adoption in children's games:

> Stick 'em up. Drop that gun. Don't move. I've got you covered. It's loaded. Come any nearer and I'll shoot. I mean it. Put your 'ands up. Go on, go on, put 'em up. Now turn round; Now what's the big idea.

Gillie and Korchinsky escape to a rural idyll before the final arrest is staged on a ship in the Bristol Channel. Throughout the film, Tiger Bay is never once mentioned.

Cardiff appears in Jules Verne's *Around the World in Eighty Days* (1873), Phineas Fogg departing by ship from the docks; Eugene O'Neill's *Eastward Bound for Cardiff* (1914) is set on an inbound tramp steamer. As a ground, it features in works from Dannie Abse's *Ash on a Young Man's Sleeve* (1954), relating Jewish experiences, to Trezza Azzopardi's *The Hiding Place* (2001), on the Maltese in Butetown. Canton author Howard Spring is shockingly forthright in his description of Tiger Bay:

> Chinks and Dagoes, Lascars and Levantines, slippered about the faintly evil by-ways that ran off from Bute Street.

> It was a dirty, smelly, rotten and romantic district, an offence and an inspiration, and I loved it. (Spring 1956: 51)

John Williams's approach is subtler – 'formed from strata of recollected events and ascribed stories' (Donald 2000b: 150).

> The Cardiff that appears in this book is an imaginary place that should not be confused with the actual city of the same name. Anyone who knows the city may be surprised to encounter assorted landmarks – The North Star, The Custom House, and so on – that no longer exist in Cardiff today. (Williams 1999: frontispiece)

Williams's *Bloody Valentine: A Killing in Cardiff* (1995) recounts the murder of Lynette White, an event he weaves into the eradication of a landscape and of a community's old ways. His subsequent trilogy – *Five Pubs, Two Bars and a Nightclub* (1999), *Cardiff Dead* (2000) and *The Prince of Wales* (2003a) – emerge almost seamlessly from the same ambience. They inhabit a familiar landscape, part actual, part fictional: 'This novel is set in a city called Cardiff that broadly resembles the real one, but it isn't a guidebook; now and again history and geography are played around with for fictional purposes' (Williams 2003a: frontispiece). His characters speak a familiar argot, have familiar points of social reference – in local history, in contemporary events, in musical preference – and move through a familiar circuit of locales, present and recently past: Spillers's Records, Les Croupiers, the Taurus Steak Bar. And they perform as we once did: buying records at Spillers; eating 'the cheapest greasiest breakfast left in captivity' (2000: 81) upstairs in the market. His stories describe real though unnamed individuals, such as guitarist Victor Parker, and occurrences that could conceivably have happened – the establishment of an illegal radio station atop the Loudoun Square flats. The space of the city conjured 'through the projection of these narrative images' (Donald 1999: 183).

For Williams, 'Tiger Bay's landmarks were its pubs' (Williams 1995: 22): he is repeatedly drawn to the now demolished 'Custom House'. Yet he resists nostalgic tristesse: '"No, butt," he said finally, "I don't remember the Capitol or the bloody trolley buses or the sodding Kardomah, or the bloody Casablanca, come to that".' (Williams 1999: 179). Cardiff noir: with a farcical twist.

Site of 'The Custom House', Callaghan Square, March 2013

10. Callaghan Square

It is a paved traffic island, named for the late Labour MP and Prime Minister, deserted even by the skate-boarders who have left their skid-marks on the seating blocks.

It was a warren of back streets, of small workshops and railway arches, of disreputable public houses such as 'The Custom House' – 'a legendary dump' (Williams 2000: 13) – and 'The Quebec': a zone of nefarious activities and deals.

In December 1993, in a disused warehouse on West Canal Wharf later demolished during road realignment, Brith Gof staged *Camlann*, one of a series of productions with limited scenic emplacements that encouraged audience participation and that mixed languages. The four works of the *Arturius Rex* project – *D.O.A.* (1993), *Camlann* (1993), *Cusanu Esgyrn* (1994) and *Arturius Rex* (1994) – mirrored events in Yugoslavia following the death of Tito, and the ensuing internecine strife, with the collapse of Roman rule and authority in Britain, and the exploits and demise of the semi-mythical King Arthur. Both precipitated a vacuum for internal chaos: factional fighting, the rise of warlords, invasion, the redrawing of the map, the creation of independent nations.

Audiences were segregated and directly implicated in the dramaturgy; Welsh and English were used in concert and in conflict. In Cardiff, audiences include Welsh-speakers, non Welsh-speakers, and learners of varying abilities. Performance as a potential site of misunderstanding: of purposefully misinterpreting what others are saying; of not listening; of attempting to translate; of trying to communicate; of speaking a second language. Who is one to believe here? Is it natural to have greater faith in those who speak 'our' language most fluently?

In *D.O.A.*, performers struggled to speak Welsh in a desperate attempt to convey the horrors of war, scrawling in chalk on the black walls of a ten-foot cubic room constructed in Chapter's backyard – the Black Chapel of Arthurian myth – in which fifteen spectators were enclosed with them, as a further forty-five looked down into the roofless space.

In *Camlann*, the audience was divided into Welsh-speakers and English-speakers, each group following different performers in different areas of the empty warehouse, and only gradually coming together: both languages were constantly heard over and through each other. Audiences took part in tugs-of-war and processions, and created soundtracks by rhythmically beating sheets of paper. Name-calling across the room eventually developed into the physical confrontation of the two groups, that had previously been united around the dead body of Arthur. Amongst the few objects used were oil drums that performers mounted for orations, and that formed a temporary frontier. Midway through the performance, spectators were invited to change sides if they wished: occasionally some English-speakers did so.

Cusanu Esgyrn – performed in a barn during the National Eisteddfod in Neath and based upon a Welsh translation of Euripides's *The Trojan Women* – gave voice to women in war: the performers sometimes speaking with, sometimes creating corporeal sequences against, their own amplified recording of the text. Female spectators joined the performers on the barn floor, whilst men watched from raised scaffolding galleries to either side.

In *Arturius Rex*, performed in an industrial unit in east Cardiff, there were no formal divisions between performers and spectators. Welsh and English were spoken at the same time; each spectator was free to find and follow the voice of her choice, whether on the factory floor, or from flanking galleries atop high wooden walls.

In *Prydain: The Impossibility of Britishness* (1996) both languages were again present but half-heard, over-heard, heard in fragments – to match the theme of revolution. The spectator had to negotiate her presence, moment by moment, deciding whether to participate: 'Who is who?', 'Whom do I listen to?', 'What's going on here?' Standing, moving, running with, running away from …

The city rubbish dump was being bulldozed, allegedly cleansed of its heavy metals; the days of the reclamation yard, home of the vernacular detail of the city, were numbered. Ferry Road was changing and men who lived in caravans were scavenging the detritus. At the time the British economy seemed to be comprised of three elements: negative equity, the National Lottery and three workers in a rusty Transit. But Asda and Ikea were waiting in the wings. The only building we could find was a leaky shed close to 'The Red House' pub, last refuge of the marginalized and disaffected.

We should have known better: the time for this kind of work was already passed. The building was insecure, full of holes. People were obviously entering over night, leaving graffiti and worse. So we hired a container, locked all our tools and amplification equipment in it. On the second day we arrived back and it had been opened with car jacks, everything stolen. So we re-equipped and hired a truck with a tail lift – we'd take everything back to Chapter each night, back it against a wall and lock the yard. Next day that too was gone: we had been followed; somehow the amplifiers had been squeezed out.

Prydain was part building site, part performance, part gig – a hybrid of action, soundtrack, architecture – for five performers, ten technicians, two music groups, forty participants who nightly volunteered to work with us, and a standing audience. The main artistic conceit was that the whole show arrived on vehicles and was built during the performance in a makeshift manner: stage managers, directors, performers, participants working to devise the scenic and performative effects and events as they happened. The work was always in process of being built and falling to pieces, in and around the audience. It utilized small generators, megaphones, battery amplifiers, portable lighting and a repertoire of crude materials – scaffolding frames, plastic sheeting. It proclaimed itself a theatre-in-the-making, a work of construction with nothing to watch and everything to do. Within the maelstrom of activity, self-selected participants were choreographed and taught actions only minutes before they were presented, as the previous section unfolded.

In Forced Entertainment's production *The Travels* (2002) performers recount memories prompted by visiting places in Britain with unusual names. On Scar Lane in Barnsley, John Rowley reflects on his 'performance-related scar'. How he jumped out of the van and began to shred his suit with a Stanley knife; how he was the focus of attention; how the knife jammed; how he forced it, as his colleagues were already moving on to the next part of the show; how he stood, blood dripping from his hand, the words of William Blake emblazoned on his naked torso:

> and everyone's looking, and somebody's going to put some books into my hands and set them on fire. So I just carry on.

Perhaps performers always recall the bad times best: the moments of failure, when the plan stalled, when the dramaturgy was compromised. What Rowley doesn't mention is that from his ripped shirt he would make a blindfold and walk – arms extended, holding the blazing books, in an extraordinary apocalyptic image – into the crowd; that here he would speak one of Blake's most ecstatic and accusatory texts: 'What is the price of Experience?' – memory of experience for the performer seemingly outweighing memory of image and effect. *Prydain* he never names.

In the video of *Camlann*, Rowley's head appears to be on fire as he makes an ultra-nationalist speech standing on an oil-drum: steaming in the effort of performance, and the cold of the warehouse.

1 House
2 Street
3 School
4 Llanover Hall Youth Arts Centre
5 Chapter Arts Centre
6 Chapter yard
7 Chapter Theatre
8 The Gym, Chapter
9 Cowbridge Road
10 'Llwyn yr Eos'

WEST

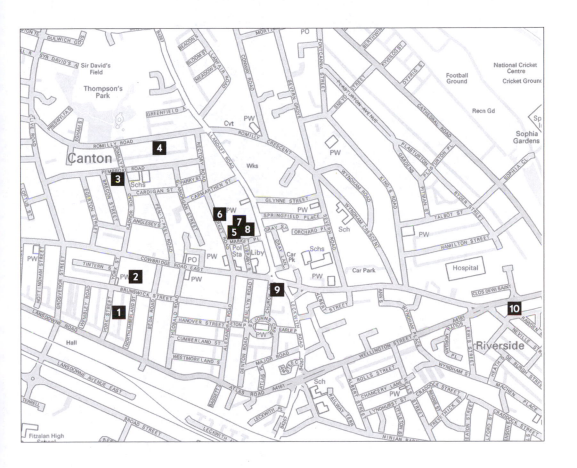

Tiled entrance porch, Canton, March 2013

1. House

For several years in the 1990s, we lived in the area of streets named for Welsh shires – Caermarthen [sic], Cardigan, Glamorgan, Pembroke, Radnor. Without foundations and sitting on low brick walls, the house was thrown up quickly in 1909: lift the floorboards and there is the bare earth. Cardiff terraces were often constructed from either end, so that the middle house is somewhat larger or smaller than the others, and insurance is higher on the terminals that support the whole structure. In the garden wall were rounded boulders, scavenged from the streams that once crossed this alluvial plain. When the rendering – a later addition to improve appearance – fractured and fell, there too were boulders in the jerry-built fabric: 'The city as a geological deposit and a quarry' (Schlögel 2005: 18).

The original Schedule of Restrictive Covenants proscribed activities: 'Not to use or suffer to be used the property hereby conveyed for any illegal or immoral purpose'. But what might go on behind closed doors, on the side of 'me and *my place*' (Perec 1997: 28), when 'the border is drawn which allows us to shut off temporarily the stream of proposals of the outside world' (Kittlausz 2006: 197); in 'the multiplicity of functions and practices of which private space is at once the effective décor and the theatre of operation' (Certeau et al 1998: 146)? Whilst layout may prescribe diurnal rhythms of activities and relationship (Perec: 28), Bernard Tschumi's axiom remains salutary: 'Imagine children playing ice hockey in the living room. The relationship proposes the performance of an architectural transgression, exactly like when you say, "I cook in the bathroom"' (Tschumi 2012: 185). Yet despite personal freedoms of dwelling, social impacts may accrue when types of living are 'realised in similar buildings – *mass* and *density*', resulting in 'a certain homogeneity of living' (Rossi 1982: 65). However opulent the interiors, many of Cardiff's inhabitants occupy similar spatial conditions.

'Many original features' the advertisement to our current house read: in the porch, ceramic tiles in pinks and greens with floral motifs in relief; in the hallway, earthenware tiles – diamonds, stripes and chevrons of white, blue, red and brown; in the lounge, cornices with flowers and grapes; in the bedroom, tiles showing daisies and lilies. Burges's influence echoing through the inner suburbs.

Those who have lived here in the interim have left their mark – refurbishing, patching, botching, exorcising relic auras under the pretence of modernization, or of making a personal statement: removing fire-places; covering a blue-and-red tiled floor with laminated wood; stripping pine doors. With each new layer of wallpaper, each lick of paint, change of surface, colour, texture, a stratigraphy is created: each repair or decoration – professionally undertaken or 'done yourself' – a horizon in the house's history, recording a crucial moment – for better or worse – of aspiration, discussion, argument and action. Accretions of the past, operating on various time-scales of preservation and decay: layers of decoration and structural alterations, complex sequences revealed in the domestic and the ordinary – in the patinas of dwelling.

And we too do it: painting surfaces white throughout; restoring the cement scar where central heating piping was laid with commissioned tiles; stripping accumulations of paint on the exterior Bath stone linings in the contemporary urge to return it to how it once was. 'But you had to take care. This was old Cardiff. Press hard, he told me, and you could push your hand through the plaster into next door' (Finch 2002: 32).

Here too are the symptoms of dwelling: the erosion and deposit of materials and matter through the passage of bodies that maps activities both customary and inadvertent. And quietly the house itself changes, of its own volition – shifting, leaking, cracking: 'Wallpaper comes off. Skirtings need replacing. There's salt in the mortar' (Finch 2004: 90).

Occupancy has biographical and curatorial aspects, albeit it as 'variations on a fundamental theme' (Bachelard 1969: 15): in 'the game of exclusions and preferences', in all that 'already composes a "life narrative" before the master of the house has said the slightest' (Certeau et al: 145). The multi-temporality of the house is attended by the multi-temporality of the objects it contains, also decaying at different rates: the fortuitously gathered, the purposefully collected, the intrusively tolerated – selected, hoarded, retained, preserved. Heirlooms, gifts, tools, paraphernalia, mementos, 'comforts': 'The passage of time (my History) leaves behind a residue that accumulates' (Perec 1997: 24). All that constitutes the domestic: 'a space overfilled with my possessions' (p.37). As Daniel Miller surmises this is not a random collection: 'They have been gradually accumulated as an expression of that person or household. Surely if we can learn to listen to these things we have access to an authentic other voice' (Miller 2008: 2). A manifestation of the 'constitutive coingredience' (Casey 2001: 684) of self and place: though missing those peripheral places within which anxieties dwell – 'the night side of the house' (Troutman 1997: 145).

Things may be informally scattered, differentially stockpiled, conveniently distributed or typologically ordered – all knives in the knife drawer; or aesthetically arranged in a 'desire for harmony, order and balance that may be discerned in certain cases – also dissonance, contradiction and irony in others' (Miller: 5); or confined to the margins of the domestic – lingering, stashed in the attic. Concentrations and densities, attenuations and vacancies: with degrees of agency in memory.

The house also as repository for transient objects: that which is just passing through, on the way to disposal or reuse – today's newspaper, a week old tomato, a second-world-war bomb discovered under a garden shed. Leftovers: indexical of scales of consumption.

And always ancient dust – the sloughed skin of former inhabitants: 'To live with dust, to admit that it will continue to fall, continue to settle, suggests an ability, a desire, to live with the irrational, with history' (Bonnett 2000a: 63). In the Welsh counties, we were never able to save seagull chicks that fell annually down chimneys with blocked fireplaces and that died increasingly less noisily in the sooty darkness.

On the walls are the things that display and profess choice, taste, preference and allegiance: a pair of wooden wings doubtless hacked from a nineteenth-century Italian religious sculpture; a photograph of Tomi and Eddie Davies leaning against derelict wagons at their farm Hyde Park in Patagonia; an artwork – an A4 sheet of drawings, instructions, lists of materials – created by André Stitt in preparation for his performance *akshun* entitled *Pilgrim*; three black-and-white posters issued during the evenements in Paris in 1968 by Conseil Pour le Maintien des Occupations – 'Occupation des Usines', 'Abolition de la Société de Classe', 'Fin de l'Université'.

In a study, portrait photographs of my parents, fossil trilobites, an inherited eighteenth-century bird book in Dutch. Relics too of performance, that which goes 'before' and that rarely appears in documentary accounts: a library relating to research on individual productions, or that are recurrent sources of inspiration such as the photographs of Don McCullin, the etchings of Francisco Goya. And things from 'during' performance – the bird skulls from *Whose Idea Was the Wind* (1978): objects in which investment was made during the rehearsal process, that became 'familiars' – fetishes even – and co-participants.

And a brass trophy found in the attic of the late Pete Sykes's son, awarded to *Hunchback* at the Zagreb Festival in September 1971, the only evidence amongst his possessions of Sykes's early work: 'The body, naked or dressed, I can state was absolutely truthful' (*Bulletin*, Zagreb 1971).

Scenic aggregations and assemblages: in a 'design for life'.

Pavement detail, street, Canton, March 2013

2. Street

In the bid to become European City of Culture 2008, the 'square mile' – the immediate neighbourhood to which we feel alliance, and that we know in some detail – provided an attractive concept to describe the conjunction of architectural continuity and traditions of habitation in Cardiff's inner suburbs: 'The neighbourhood is a palimpsest, textured and animated by layers of history and memory' (Donald 1999: 182).

In south Canton, the terraces date from the early twentieth century, the Pennant and Bath stone designs infused with varying amounts of brick: bordering streets are differentiated by distinct patterns of ceramic porch tile. Pebble-dashed, clad, coated and stone-painted, its houses are now further individuated.

In the pavement: the covers of utility companies of successive periods giving access to underground connectors – drains, pipes and cables; 'Cardiff Sewers Patent Landaf'. And vernacular impressions: each patch of cement bears crude inscriptions – initials, hearts, a mouse – and the footprints of passers-by, both human and animal, in a consuming urge to leave a mark.

In the gutter: foil packets, cigarette filters, fast-food menu, sock, can opener, plastic bottles, beer cans, vomit, paper bags, cup, broken umbrella, bottle tops, phlegm, dog faeces, leaked oil.

A series of interstitial zones in which the past is caught:

> This is the city of lost things, thrown away,
> caught in the space between Sunday afternoon
> and the rest of time. (Lewis 2005: 128)

On this day, against the low wall that demarcates the small front garden, now paved, are a black bag, a green bag, and a brown, handled box. Each bears a bilingual list, with attendant images, of what they might contain, in the categorization and ejection of materials from the domestic.

The black for landfill waste reads: 'No medical waste. No poisons such as pesticides and household chemicals. No syringes. Push lid inside can [with image of a cat]. Wrap in paper [a broken bottle].'

The green is for recyclables: 'Yes, put them in! Food tins, drink cans, aerosols, plastic bottles, yogurt pots, margarine tubs, plastic punnets/ready meal trays, glass bottles and jars, jam jar lids, newspapers, phone directories, magazines, junk mail/flyers (remove plastic wraps), office paper, catalogues, all cards'; 'No, keep them out! Plastic bags, shredded paper (use green bin/white bio bag), wallpaper, paint tins, clothes or shoes, broken glass, plastic toys, kitchen foil, fake foil (e.g. crisp packets/cat food pouches), polystyrene packing/takeaway trays, coat hangers, kitchenware, electrical items, video cassettes, CDs/DVDs.'

The brown box contains a disposable white 'bio-bag' for organic materials: 'Yes, put them in! Food waste, grass cuttings, shredded paper, hedge and tree cuttings (no thicker than your wrist), flowers and plants, leaves, clean wood shavings (no animal bedding)'; 'No, keep them out! Animal waste, plastic, metal, or glass (put into your green bag and place on pavement), plastic bags, soil or rubble, juice cartons, plant pots, certain harmful weeds (common ragwort, spear thistle, creeping thistle, curled dock, broad leaved dock and Japanese knotweed).'

The box guards against the scavenging of herring gulls for which Cardiff's rooftops have become cliffs, its streets the foreshore: they can shred a plastic bag in seconds. The admonition against Japanese knotweed is to prevent the spread of a pernicious alien plant that can sprout through concrete: though infertile, any fragment can reproduce vegetatively. Locally, it is red valerian that causes problems: an attractive fleshy plant, with flowers on top of the wall disguising a thick, woody stem that can pressurize brickwork and dislodge capstones. Buddleia – spread in the UK along railway lines – sprouts wherever a niche appears in unattended wall or roof. Plants occupying 'meeting points of the urban framework's organizational elements: in the gap where boundary wall meets sidewalk, where sidewalk meets street, in the cracks in the asphalt. These are the interstitial spaces where human control fails. This is where life/nature/creativity prevails' (Jahangeer 2010: 3).

Items such as beds, cookers, refrigerators, and washing machines are collected *gratis*; a fee of £5 is charged for toilets, doors, radiators etc. Non-collectables include pianos, garden sheds and car batteries. The council will also recover 'small quantities of asbestos which arise from the on-going wear and tear of household living.' In 'Nasty nappy facts', it warns: 'Around 200 million disposables are taken to Welsh landfill sites every year; 'once on a landfill site a disposable nappy will take around 300 years to decompose.'

At the Cardiff Council Civic Amenity Site on Bessemer Close, where rubbish can be disposed of by householders, there is further disaggregation into dedicated containers, colour-coded and symbolically badged: used engine oil, fluorescent tubes, books, clothing and shoes, small electrical goods, televisions, paint, cardboard, metals, hardcore rubble. The site does not accept waste from large-scale renovations: 'However, small quantities of building and demolition waste from small scale DIY projects carried out by members of the public to their own properties may be accepted.'

In the surrounding area are silver metal standpipes capped with spinning cowls to disperse escaping methane. This has always been a municipal dump, the repercussions of less guarded disposal returned.

Angela Piccini's video *Guttersnipe* (2009) tracks a gutter in Bristol from a camera lashed to a pushchair, with attendant commentary on objects and materials seen in passing as an entrée into an exegesis on the history of the city.

Cardiff buses passing through Canton show similar shots: from multiple cameras both inside and outside the vehicle on monitors that intercut views of the city with BBC News.

The streets of Cardiff appear too *en passant* in several Pearson/Brookes productions. In *Raindogs* (2002) an older bearded man is videoed in the rear of a car, regarding the moving scene. For him, I write:

> The dog sniffed, pissed, moved on; he turned.
> It left its mark – stinging, stinking –
> He didn't care.
> At least he was acknowledged
> Brought low, ignored, invisible.
> By others he was unmarked, unremarked.
> By passers-by
> Who just passed by …

In *Who Are You Looking At?* (2004), one of five young women alone in the city appears in the back of a taxi, witnessing the nightly choreography:

> Without fur on flesh, their teeth chatter, their skin pimples,
> Without goose-grease, their lips crack, their joints stiffen.
> Yet they stay naked, skinny dipping,
> All dressed up with nothing on.

Be Music, Night (2004) was an homage to American poet Kenneth Patchen: a live reading of several of the author's love poems with the free jazz of The Peter Brötzmann Chicago Tentet, performed at The Chicago Humanities Festival. Behind the band was a pre-recorded, projected video triptych of a male and female performer. In the first section of the performance, she is alone on the left screen in a white room, he on the right, completing precisely timed, one-minute solo improvised choreographies to the same instructions; they perform a similarly constrained duet in the centre. In the second half, they again appear to left and right but seated in the back of a Cardiff taxi and recorded from two rear-facing drop-down seats diagonally opposite. They now intrude into each other's image, as the city is glimpsed through steamy windows.

It snowed heavily, and the snow turned to ice. The tenor of the city altered: sounds became both muted and more acute. A new urban choreography commenced: pedestrians walking gingerly, vehicles driving slowly and occasionally moving unpredictably. And uncollected rubbish bags became a new hilly topography.

Street marking, school, Canton, March 2013

3. School

The school (1887) in Pennant and Bath stones is by E. M. Bruce Vaughan in his preferred Gothic style, 'or as close to Gothic as board school formulae would allow' (Newman 2004: 280). Its name appears in incised letters across the width of the building.

In the playground is the paraphernalia of early childhood, to exercise bodies and minds: on the ground, lines that delineate the boundaries and dividers of games and activities, including road layouts to rehearse traffic safety. Here, Canton author Howard Spring played 'Bumberino':

> Sides were chosen, and about six boys made a team. A boy, tucking his head well down would grasp a waterpipe. The next would grasp this bending boy around the waist, the third would grasp the second, and so on, till the whole team made a line of bent backs and had the appearance of a strange and rather tall caterpillar. Then No. 1 of the opposing team, taking a run of 10 yards, would make a leapfrog jump, landing as far as possible along the line of backs. No. 2 would follow, and soon the whole team was astride its opponents, and as each leap was made, the leaper would yell: "Bumberino!". (Spring 1956: 36)

The leapers would then struggle to bring down the team below, who shouted 'Strong horses! Strong horses!' as long as they could stay upright. As they inevitably collapsed, the riders exclaimed: 'Weak horses! Weak horses!'. 'A strange game which I have never seen played elsewhere' (ibid.).

It takes time to distinguish and disentangle games occurring simultaneously in the playground and to acknowledge how quickly desires, proposals and decisions are translated into action: 'Speed is essential. If they argue about the rules they argue rapidly and agree without much delay, knowing that prolonged argument means that the game may not be played at all' (Opie 1993: 4). Games may involve contest, display, companionability, exhibitionism, recklessness, sentimentality and sexuality, but they are as quickly abandoned as they are ignited: 'A game is a microcosm, more powerful and important than any individual player; yet when it is finished it is finished, and nothing depends on the outcome' (p.15).

But there are individuals in the meleé 'apparently just "mucking about"', who are 'conducting serious (if minor) experiments on themselves and their environment' (p.2). They are engaged in play – an essentially solo activity in which energy is expended for reasons other than material gain. It is governed by implicit, self-defined rules: as a child plays, she creates a world under her own control, with its own internal logics. She is the event: she makes and breaks rules, devises self-protective control mechanisms and determines the amount of commitment, exertion and assertion required from time to time. She decides on durations; she tests her own courage, stamina and endurance; she engages in imitative, quasi-theatrical role-playing without necessarily making an appeal to the outside. There is opportunity for exaggerated emotions, for experiment that may test the norms of the socialisation and conditioning of everyday life – examining ideas and relationships, making a critical stand. Yet there may be no concept of total form at the outset.

There is no plot, script or even prearranged sequences. She just begins. She creates a situation but doesn't necessarily know the outcome. There is a dynamic flow of activity that may have an occasional pattern. There may be sudden shifts in direction or emphasis, irrelevancies, repetition of the pleasurable sections, random activity, mistakes – although these are rarely identified. There may be no concept of climax, completion, goal-orientation or finished creation. There may be stylistic diversity and discontinuous engagement: she is deciding on the 'what' and the 'how'. This flow is connected to the life rhythms of the player: tactical, improvised but informed by previous experience and memories, and described by personally acknowledged thresholds.

Of particular note is the dialogue between environment and play: the former may suggest the nature, type and quality of play. Conversely, play may alter the environment in real and in fantasy terms, in the mind's eye. And this is reflected in the activity: 'I walk this way because this is a desert. And I wear this bucket because I am a Crusader'; 'I'm blowing out my cheeks and slowly waving my arms because this is the bottom of the ocean.' In addition, objects have an enhanced – even arbitrary – value, beyond their material worth; transmogrifying 'this' into 'that' in the mind's eye, and through application.

Play and improvisation are cognate activities. In *Improvisation: Its Nature and Practice in Music* (1980), guitarist Derek Bailey effectively outlines a mission statement for musics free from 'stylistic or idiomatic commitment' (p.99): 'The skill and intellect required is whatever is available. It can be an activity of enormous complexity and sophistication or the simplest and most direct action: a lifetime's study and work or a casual dilettante activity' (ibid.).

Bailey elaborates potential approaches in improvisation: from producing exactly what the player wants, to 'letting the instrument have its say' (p.118); to including both accidents and clichés; to imposing tonal or technical restrictions or conditions on the activity. But Bailey is also realistic about the desirability of building a personal vocabulary, and extending it in both preparation and performance: 'At such times, when other more aesthetically acceptable resources such as invention and imagination appear to be absent, the vocabulary becomes the sole means of support. It has to provide everything needed to sustain continuity and impetus in the musical performance' (p.127). Once a vocabulary – a signature – is working, material can be included from any source: 'Its subsequent rejection or retention is decided by its ability to be absorbed by the language' (p.128).

Percussionist Jamie Muir extols the virtues of the junk shop and the rubbish dump as 'undiscovered/unidentified/unclaimed/unexplored territory' (p.113).

Bailey's text and the experimental music magazine *Musics* – a mix of polemic, conceptual ideas and technical approaches to which he contributed – were significant influences in distinguishing principles for improvisation in theatre: in using pitch, rhythm, silence in corporeal interactions, and in the inclusion of objects. The theatre performer might resemble the child totally absorbed in play without ever appearing childish; or be akin to the free jazz musician, engrossed but aware of his audience.

In Cardiff Laboratory Theatre's *Notes on Physical Preparation* (1978) the onus is on flexibility, isolation (of individual body parts), equilibrium, impulse, spontaneity, motivation, reactivity, intuition, precision, sensitivity, visualization (objectifying the absent), concentration; upon destroying the cosmetic image and developing an internal body image; upon conceptualization – 'A chair is a chair. The performer can see it and feel it. But depending on his imagination and his actions it can be castle, prison or submarine. The action must define the intent. It is play.' All that might inform the nascence of a personal vocabulary.

But when two play together, and theatre is an essentially collective activity, then mutual understandings if not rules intervene to communicate intent and direction: what saxophonist Steve Lacy calls a 'brotherhood of language' (Bailey 1980: 126), without this necessarily giving rise to stylistic traits. Indeed, it may include determined 'mutual subversion' (p.113): 'The thing is to maintain some kind of balance between the positive aspects of the relationship and the possible repetitive ones' (p.146).

'Strong horses! Weak horses!'

Llanover Hall Theatre Workshop, *The Ancient Mariner*, 'Summerthing', August 1973

4. Llanover Hall Youth Arts Centre

The large villa at 17 Romilly Road was built by William Symonds from Longbredy, Dorset, who established his construction business in 1880 as Cardiff's expansion was at its peak. In 1938, it was acquired by the city corporation and renamed Llanover Hall: with the addition of a wooden hall and workshops at the rear, it became the Juvenile Employment Centre for Girls. In 1971, the disused premises were re-launched as a youth arts centre offering evening classes and vacation schools for fifteen to twenty-three year olds in drama, music, art, photography and ceramics.

In an HTV documentary of 1974 (see Mainwaring), a student cycles from Splott, passing East Moors steelworks where he works; Dek Leverton of Pauper's Carnival runs a physical theatre workshop that includes Janek Alexander, later director of Chapter; and on the site of a former air-raid shelter in the garden, artist John Gingell constructs a tower with ramps and steps using materials recovered from demolition work on Wellington Street: 'I'm committing myself at the level of being the labourer in the work as a social thing'. Local inhabitants are curious and confused: 'They think I'm digging it up or revealing it.' Its remains may yet lie beneath the current car park.

The theatre workshop that met weekly in the hall in 1972–73 became a test-bed for assessing the pedagogical potential of exercises and approaches developed elsewhere: in Theatre in Transit, in RAT Theatre, and in their Polish and American antecedents. In the photographs, students in tank top pullovers, flared trousers and sweatbands lift and carry; in the background are the wooden walls and radiators still extant today.

During the 'Summerthing' course directed by Keith Wood in August 1974, the workshop produced a version of *The Ancient Mariner*; the earliest manifestation of Cardiff Laboratory for Theatrical Research would include several of its members.

In 1975, Richard Gough and I presented the first of two iterations of *Bricolage* – an extended improvisation with objects – in the hall. Over the preceding week, we gathered portable items and natural substances, arranging them formally on a large tarpaulin as distinct elements in a performance landscape: earth, flour, fish, conical cat baskets, functional tools and utensils, Victorian bric-a-brac, junk shop curios. Things purposefully selected for their intrinsic qualities and attributes – appearance, age, quiddity; for their roles in quotidian activities that might be challenged in performance; and for their innate properties – elasticity, friability, odour. In combining antiques and rubbish, the work entailed a re-evaluation of that ejected from the domestic: objects taken out of context and ascribed usage, confounding normative assessments of their value and function. Objects accumulated, rather than being functions of prescribed design.

As the audience entered, I was buried in soil, then gradually revealed as Richard burst balloons in the mound with a spiked pole. Of a second staging, Janek Alexander's diary relates: 'Sarah and others gasped when P came out of the earth.... The show was great, and more horrific the 2nd time around. Richard fried steak which was worse for vegetarian P.'

We worked singly and in concert to create images and sequences suggested by the objects, partly through a conscious emulation of, and allusion to, other iconographies – religious, sculptural, photographic; partly through working with the repercussions of 'this' brought to 'that'. Seeking allegorical potentialities for the 'congealed life in discarded things' (Edensor 2005: 104).

There is a shift here from Grotowski's poor theatre, reliant upon the mutability and multi-valence of a restricted repertoire of objects – 'sufficient to handle any of the play's situations' (Grotowski 1969: 75) – that through repeated revisiting and change in context reveals metaphors, anachronisms and ambiguities, within a frame bound by Polish nationalism, Communism and Catholicism. Whilst everything in *Bricolage* was present at the beginning, these items were not necessarily indispensable to a dramatic action, and only partly controllable, in their material and symbolic viscosities.

Objects lacking natural affinities of origin, provenance and type were brought into extra-daily juxtapositions, into heterogeneous assemblages, into new and contingent taxonomies only feasible within the (at least partially) fictive conditions of performative exposition; subject to idiosyncratic, implicitly agreed – though constantly negotiable – principles of association, and confounding normative typological ordering, of 'like' with 'like'. Significantly, no pre-judgment was made about the suitability of objects for performance; anything might slip its boundary – tools, toys, foodstuffs, art works. We characterized the approach – after Claude Levi-Strauss – as *bricolage*: improvised responses to an environment of disparate though limited resources; a way of existing and making meaning in a hypothetical world with the tools to hand where dissimilar objects might combine and clash. Anything present might be called into play or ignored: at once a 'Chekhov's gun' ('If present, it will inevitably be used') or a 'Macguffin', an object whose presence is unexplained and that may never be employed.

Performance may even question the habits of thought that separate objects and create a flow or slippage between classes and types of things normally kept apart, dissolving parameters, interpenetrating their zones of operation to reveal other, potentially rich, even paradoxical relationships and continuities, outside their conventionally assigned identities. With objects always potentially at a point of slippage: in play, in activities that may – as Edensor notes of objects in ruins – 'free them from epistemological moorings' (p.123).

Richard used a brass garden spray: 'with me as some strange gardener tending a desolate landscape' (Gough 2006a: 274). He made dough, modelling it into grotesque facial masks on the upturned cat basket on his head. At one point, unbeknown to me, he dressed the audience in party hats, whilst I was otherwise engaged in attempting to resuscitate a mackerel.

In examining the nature of the relationship between performers and object in improvisation, Bruno Latour's description of social interaction is instructive – with his proviso to heed the nature of the site, here the particular conditions of performance. Latour suggests that no interaction is isotopic – what is acting in any moment is coming from several places; that no interaction is synchronic – time is always folded; that interactions are not synoptic – few participants are simultaneously visible; that interactions are not homogeneous – material is included from different sources; and that interactions are not isobaric – they do not have equal pressure throughout (Latour 2005: 200–02). Improvisation in performance as informed and qualified by experience, ability and interest; by the presence of audience; and by operational exigencies.

In 'Perfect Time: Imperfect Tense. An Object Exercise in Conditional Remembrance' (Gough 2006a: 266–83) – a text springing from a performed lecture entitled *Fifth Column, Fourth Wall, Third Theatre (or Thirty-one Objects to Aid a Forgetting)* – Richard proposes a series of objects as aides-memoire for moments in Cardiff Laboratory Theatre's history: an egg; a metal bucket; 'Martin the polecat … animated by hand and two walking sticks; me, the master puppeteer of a great aunt's fur wrap' (p.273); and The Hay Cutter (p.282), a heavy, right-angled blade:

> The streets of Canton were to be our world – go forth and discover – and this is what Mike came back with. I am sure he did a strange sort of dance with it. I am sure I felt this could lead to a bloody end. It was never used. And I include it for all the objects that never appeared in a show but that desperately wanted to.

André Stitt, *The Institution*, May 2005

5. Chapter Arts Centre

It was the showpiece Higher Grade School, opened on 21 October 1907, and later Canton High School; it is Chapter, longest surviving of the multi-disciplinary arts centres that appeared in the late 1960s.

Built in hard red Ruabon brick, the girls' school was on the ground floor, the boys' on the first, with matching assembly halls around which classrooms were ranged, and from which corridors led.

Vacated in 1963, it became Chapter in 1971, following a campaign – primarily to provide studio space – orchestrated by artists Chris Kinsey and Brian Jones who made the character masks for *Under Milk Wood*, and Mik Flood, who appeared in the production. The drive included a benefit concert featuring Pink Floyd in Sophia Gardens Pavilion – the Earls Court of South Wales – that collapsed under the weight of snow in February 1982; the occupation of an empty shop on Queen Street as a platform for free art events; and a screening of the Bob Dylan documentary film *Don't Look Back* (1967) at the Globe Cinema, demolished in 1987.

> The building itself is in very good repair. Its total area is 29,000 square feet and has two large halls and two playground areas. Some internal walls will have to be removed, the whole place must be decorated. (*Cardiff Cake* No 1, October 1970)

Tenancy and conversion were initially piecemeal, akin to squatting in rooms that had forfeited their ascription but that provided suitable accommodation for diverse groups: the Radha Krishna Temple next to Transitions's storeroom; the Workers' Education Association close to the cinema created by Cardiff Cine Club in the washrooms. Early, Moving Being installed a sprung dance floor in an upstairs classroom to facilitate daily exercise.

At first, performances were presented in what is now part of the restaurant and bar: Keith Wood's *The Nighthawk* (1974); Cardiff Laboratory for Theatrical Research's *Mariner* (1974); and Moving Being's *The Idea, the Image and the Space In Between* (1974), an homage to influences including Artaud, Brecht and Cage that was structured as a multi-media theatre company's attempt to make a television documentary about multi-media theatre. Only gradually did the upper hall become the theatre: shuttered, painted black, regularly improved though always invariably the same size.

Over time, Chapter has been substantially remodelled and reconfigured. In the major refurbishment of 2010–11, walls and fittings were removed; the bar extended over the small garden; and the heavily worn parquet floor lifted. But it is taking time for Chapter not to be a school. It never totally sheds its former identity – still apparent in the glass-panelled doors in back corridors; in the five-foot-high brown tiling on walls in the foyer.

Rooms have changed in use: artist Paul Brewer's studio in which he built a large camera to create long-exposure bitumen prints is now a meeting room. But here and there are marks of practice: the faint outlines left as the tape that marked out stage placements was lifted from the floors of rehearsal spaces – two-dimensional shapes that in performance would transmogrify into three-dimensional scenography, requiring a leap of imagination and faith for performers.

And occasionally, the school reappears. Between 8 April and 8 May 2005, André Stitt created *The Institution* in Chapter Gallery (Stitt 2005): a series of durational *akshuns* each lasting several hours that advanced an on-going installation – 'a lengthy process of archaeology, transformation and liberation in which the very nature and structure of what constitutes an art gallery were rigorously challenged' (Babot 2010: 288). In preparation, Stitt intervened in the fabric – stripping away plasterboard fascias and accumulated layers of renovation to reveal classroom doors, walls and windows – 'the all too familiar sickly green pallor' (ibid.) – the school as proxy for experiences of institutional repression in Northern Ireland during 'The Troubles': a place of memory and reclamation; of nightmare and disorder.

Stitt's *akshuns* involve generative actions that draw materials and objects into configurations that range between the illusive, the allusive and the allegorical: intimations of incarceration, interrogation and internment. Some everyday objects are present *en masse*, disquieting in their plenitude: stacks of boxes mutely recalling information storage and the threat of the archive; scattered heaps of enamel mugs and plates and plastic toothbrushes evocative of concentration camps; piles of children's vests; jars and bottles containing bodily fluids. Others have personal connotations: his wife Eddie Ladd's child's tricycle carefully housed in a recess cut into the wall. Others are the artist's familiars: a personal vocabulary of things recurrently re-addressed over time.

Some actions and images are punctually effective: Stitt dips white underpants into thick brown molasses and hangs them dripping in rows from meat hooks. And he performs rhetorically – crying at an imagined photograph of a woman in Srebrenica; sitting passively after carving the word 'informer' on his forearm. That he is a painter is evident in 'the countless soakings, drippings and spillings, the spraying, coating and covering of solid forms with liquid alterations' (p.293). It is the accumulating aftermath of these actions that causes disquiet in the interim – dog muzzle, a totem with teeth, an axe in the wall, chicken's feet; pools of molasses and tracks of salt – traces suggesting a scene of terrible events, in scenarios barely imaginable.

Of installed elements, the most striking was a cast iron lamp-post – made in Llandaff and retrieved from Cardiff Reclamation Yard – suspended diagonally at a point of equilibrium on a steel hawser and pulley. Beneath the lamp-post, the parquet flooring was removed and a rectangular pit dug; in *Akshun V*, it was lowered into the ground and cemented over by Stitt, recalling his own past as a builder's labourer. As the floor was made good, it created an archaeological enigma, though perhaps evocative of the German bombing of 2 January 1941 that destroyed Chapter's bell tower and blew a similar post from Market Road through the window. In *Akshun III*, the massive timber upright – a stanchion impregnated with the oils and grease of ships from Cardiff docks – set opposite the lamp-post in a patch of lifted floor, was studded with rows of human teeth by Stitt, wearing the outsized muzzle purchased in Poland.

Stitt also erected false walls to create three adjacent areas: in *Akshun I*, he hacked through the end wall with an axe, tarring and feathering the frames, to create apertures suggestive of custodial scrutiny and rough justice.

Stitt's *akshuns* are planned graphically: as instructions to self, as inventories of materials as much as detailed score – 'Cut open bundle – feather – honey'. Each document – 'a dense palimpsest of diagrams and verbal directions' – is 'anticipatory, utopian even – it is the promise of an event yet to be realised, and it proposes strategies for its realisation'; 'Between the ideation and intentionality of the score and its performative realisation a space opens which allows for things to happen that are as yet unpredicted and unpredictable' (Roms 2010: 13). Roms regards early examples as programmatic: annotated lists of actions, objects, sounds and images against a time line, though actions themselves are rarely described; unreliable as evidence of what actually happened.

The totem has been relocated to Coed Hills Rural Artspace where it quietly rots in the woods; the Gallery is reconfigured again; and the child's bloody handprint, discovered by Stitt on a glass pane, concealed once more.

IOU, *The House*, May 1982

6. Chapter yard

> Bewildered residents peered through their bedroom windows last night to witness the strangest spectacle a Cardiff back-yard has ever seen. (Brian Jarman, unprovenanced newspaper cutting)

Imagine this: sitting huddled on a temporary seating rake at the rear of Chapter, in the place now occupied by outdoor drinkers and smokers; facing west towards the unoccupied red brick house in which Mik Flood had initially lived, and that is now a halfway house.

> For a long time nothing happened, then slowly the household began its nightly ritual of going to bed; And then the audience was plunged into the most marvellous dream sequences you could witness in waking hours (ibid.).

An angel appears from behind a chimney. The sleep-walking family emerges to beat carpets hanging in the garden, the patterns in chalk disappearing with every stroke and filling the air with multi-coloured dust.

From behind the main building come the blaring sounds of rock music, a revving engine and the crash of metal on brick. Suddenly a car lurches into view, painted entirely matt black except for a narrow strip in the windscreen that emits blue light from the interior. Driving erratically towards us, it stops just short of striking the seating. The music continues; the situation is ominous. Then the doors fly open and out climb two giant bees, both smoking – 'who plunder the pantry of the house and have a picnic on the lawn' (ibid.).

A wooden monoplane, after the style of Louis Bleriot – suspended from a crane hidden in the car park behind the high perimeter wall – circles the chimney stack; silhouetted against the Canton skyline, it delivers a parcel to a man who wakes from his slumbers on the roof and crawls towards it.

Scenes from *The House*: conceived in 1982 by Yorkshire-based company IOU (see Burt and Barker 1980), that included former members of Welfare State, during a residency in which they lived in the house itself, though with the converted coach in which they toured always parked close by. Their aim was to make work not reproducible elsewhere; their concept to show the building's other life, after dark.

Performer David Wheeler kept a photo-diary of the devising process, taking one image every day. They show vertiginous ladder runs, the construction of platforms on the roof, the painting of the car as a baby looks on, and the demolition and partial restoration of the wall to the house's small back garden to improve sightlines. And artists sitting and joking in the camaraderie that sometimes accompanies collective creation.

The performance was site-specific in all but name: the term was not widely applied to theatre until the late 1980s. When asked in a public discussion how IOU made performances, co-founder Lou Glandfield offered, if memory serves: 'Someone says – "I want to do this"; another – "I think we should do this"; another – "We need to do this". And that's what we do. And well, meaning usually comes along.'

In 1978, IOU had devised *Between the Floods – the Churning of the Milky Ocean* over a three-week period in Chapter. In the yard, 'The company built a landscape of a sunken silted up village – rooftops and the tops of towers poking up through the sand; a pool; a boat with oars stranded high up a telegraph pole' (Burt and Barker 1980: 78). This was one of a series of projects, beginning in the late 1970s, in which companies were in residence for several weeks: the People Show, Dutch group Waste of Time and Pip Simmons. Each residency began with the presentation of existing work – in 1982 IOU showed *The Trumpet Rat* and *A Musical Meal* – and culminated in a performance particular to Chapter that frequently occupied and moved through different rooms and spaces in the building.

For *Woyzeck* (1977), Pip Simmons fabricated eight separate scene settings: 'you had a narrative progression through the rooms' (Simmons in Barker 1979: 18), including the bar where the tavern scene occurred.

> Two specific advantages were thereby gained. Each setting could be developed with far greater sophistication and detail than would have been possible with conventional sets and properties, and it made the audience, to a far more conscious extent, voyeur participants in Woyzeck's tragic fate …
> The audience became fully implicated in the scenes which it so dutifully observed. (*Audience*, Issue 10, January 1978: 5)

Most spectacular was the skull-shaped artificial lake constructed in the yard for the episode in which the persecuted Woyzeck kills his unfaithful wife Marie. In indoor sequences, actors and audience jostled together:

> A number of vivid moments stand out in the memory: of Woyzeck clawing his way through the crowds of drinkers in the tavern in a desperate attempt to find Marie; of four seated doctors closing their chairs in on Woyzeck in unison as he is forced to eat endless plates of peas; of Woyzeck clutching a teddy bear and gazing fearfully into outer space after discovering Marie's infidelity; of the ragged old aunt's story of the boy who travelled to the stars, only to find that they were tiny golden gnats stuck to a solid sky. (ibid.)

To increase their scale and scope, these works often included local performers for whom they were pedagogically and experientially noteworthy: in Waste of Time's concluding performance, and inspired by the precision of a style stemming from the 'new Dutch mime' movement, Richard Gough and I attempted a sequence backstage in Chapter Theatre using umbrellas and ladders, that we could present with the same precision both forwards and in reverse.

In-house companies also constructed unique scenographies in Chapter's range of spaces, placing audiences in unexpected relationships with performers. For *Dark*

Corners: a fantasy for grown-ups (1979), Pauper's Carnival created a woodland glade that filled their studio and that featured growing grass and trees, live rabbits and birds. Their aim was 'to create for the audience both a place, and a set of events which, when added together, would afford a glimpse, perhaps, into the real world of faerie, the Middle Kingdom.' The audience of twenty-five sat in a single row, their backs against one wall. The opening scene was enchanting. Only when a small door in a tree stump was opened to reveal a protruding naked backside was an elfin world of darker shades revealed.

Imagine this too: a handleless door flies open and two men rush in carrying a third who is writhing and screaming; the scene is chaotic – three grimy and frightened men in a frightening situation, wearing the distressed remnants of dirty and reeking uniforms.

The fatally wounded King Arthur is portrayed by disabled actor Dave Levett, lifted, carried, supported, restrained and manipulated in a sequence of thirty actions each lasting two minutes and inspired by images of hospitals in Sarajevo: 'seeking in its overcharged (but highly disciplined) physicality, to create a kind of hyper-naturalism, and in its deliberate refusal of easily framed images, a challenge to television pictures of the Bosnian conflict' (Taylor 1994: 74).

The dynamic is most intense in the opening moments: it concludes with the exhausted Levett's vivid story of a horse on fire. In the room, fifteen standing spectators in proximity to the thrashing, spasmodic actions of the dying king witness events in close-up; from above, a further forty-five see Levett performing prone on a bed and on the floor, as well as the shifting relationship of audience and action in the room.

Effects conspired in the black cube erected in the yard for Brith Gof's *D.O.A.* (1993). The physical techniques were developed in an outhouse against the perimeter wall; next-door, the trapezoid-shaped shadows of incisions made by Emma Lawton in *Interior Cutting* are still evident.

Brith Gof, *In Black and White*, 1992

7. Chapter Theatre

Although Chapter Theatre has been repeatedly revamped, expansion is constrained by the width of supporting walls: it always maintains the same dimensions – those of the boys' assembly hall.

Gone is the roller door at the rear that Janek Alexander threw up abruptly as he exited from *Howard Hughes* (1976); gone too the fixed rake of former cinema seats from which we watched Pip Simmons's *An Die Musik* (1975), the naked concentration camp orchestra gradually disappearing in smoke, and the Wooster Group's *L.S.D. (... Just the High Points ...)* (1984) crushed onto the stage that defined the spatial parameters of their performances for in-house companies. Before touring, productions were premiered at – and at a maximum had to fit – Chapter Theatre. Relatively limited scenic resources were, however, sufficient to fill its confined area and manage its restricted aspect.

From its earliest conversion, it has been that quintessential and ubiquitous 'empty space' of the late 1960s – a black box: 'the form that responded best to the complex of aesthetic demands made by Brook in 1967/8' (Wiles 2003: 254); a phenomenon that purports to be 'a neutral environment, allowing any desired configuration of seating. Its walls being invisible, lighting could make the space seem as tiny or expansive as the director might desire' (ibid.). David Wiles regards the period appeal for flexibility and the possibility of adopting multiple modes of organizing the theatrical microcosm as utopian. But this is no anonymous scene of representation: 'There is nothing neutral about blackness' (ibid.). As a cloistered space, it is cut off from 'an implicitly corrupt and false social world outside' (p.257). For Wiles, in 'isolating it from other social practices' (p.258), it encourages abstraction and aestheticism flourishes, ruling out styles such as the naturalism of the conventional auditorium – 'for any stage set framed by a black wall is revealed to be mere stage artifice' (ibid.). It constitutes: 'a depoliticizing space in the sense that no body politic can be placed on view, whatever the overt political content of works performed' (p.257). And yet, it arises at the apogee of the enlightenment project in theatre, with the individual performer/character – the human subject – cut out of social context, his or her motives and actions proximate and in plain view, though in a circumscribed locale.

Perhaps its very blackness has encouraged address in monochrome. Cardiff Laboratory Theatre's *Whose Idea Was the Wind?* (1978) – 'a performance limited to the area of a table top' – was 'a quiet telling of stories to an audience of fifteen people' (Pearson 1979a: 4) in a short cycle of poems and writings involving birds, drawn from Native American and Inuit sources. On a black tablecloth were pieces of bark, cones, and twigs illuminated by four candles, the audience sitting closely around. Into this environment, a single human face intruded. Here too anatomical relics of the natural world: the bones of crow, owl, gull and wader, feathers and wings. Bird skulls were manipulated – usually between forefinger and thumb – and rudimentary creatures evoked by the placing of feathers between other fingers. Modulations of the voice and movement of the bones wrought subtle changes in character: the crow began with white feathers, the story of his charring concluding with the substitution of black.

Brith Gof's *Du a Gwyn* (*Black and White*) (1986) was performed during a period of refit: in the video, the walls are pocked with white plaster filler. Presented on a free-standing scaffolding dais backed by a projection screen, it focused upon Humphrey Jennings's film *The Silent Village* (1943) in which he recreated the Nazi destruction of the village of Lidice in Czechoslovakia – following the assassination of Reinhard Heydrich in May 1942 – in the mining community of Cwmgiedd. Jennings used limited though effective dramaturgical means: a single car with a loudspeaker denotes German occupation; the narrative develops as households listen to radio announcements in domestic interiors. The Czech villagers speak Welsh, the men singing defiantly as they assemble before the firing squad. In the opening section of *Du a Gwyn*, possible versions of the un-witnessed assassination were enacted; later, against the film's projection, performers in white boiler suits attempted to intervene and influence the course of events.

In Brith Gof's *In Black and White* (1992), one able-bodied and one disabled man performed a series of duets inspired by the stop-motion photographs of Eadweard Muybridge. Set against a gridded wall reminiscent of the backdrops Muybridge employed to discern trajectories of animal and human movement, the scenario moved from exploratory encounters – mirroring, copying, pulling, pushing, carrying – to a final pas-de-deux in which Dave Levett performed upside down, propelled in his speeding chair.

For Wiles, the black box is 'a historically specific architectural statement' that contemporary practice 'must struggle to accommodate' (Wiles 2003, 255). Rather than utopia, perhaps it has now become the ultimate 'non-place': 'creating neither singular identity nor relations; only solitude, and similitude' (Augé 1995: 103). 'The "non-place" [...] cannot *hold* real lives and stories. It lacks the "thickness" or "density" of situation, in a fabric of connectivity, as a relay in multiple virtualities' (Read 2006b: 61).

Four Pearson/Brookes productions – *Carrying Lyn* (2001), *Polis* (2001), *Raindogs* (2002) and *Who are you looking at?* (2004) – sought to reconfigure Chapter Theatre: the seating bleachers were retracted and audiences were free to arrange themselves, and often to move as participants to a greater or lesser extent.

In *Carrying Lyn*, the videos and Polaroid photographs of performers on the street returned by cycle couriers, and transcriptions of texts spoken in periods of tape rewind, were progressively available for scrutiny on a gridded table down the centre of the space, as a documentary map of the event gradually unfolded.

In *Polis*, four tables – each dedicated to an individual performer – were available for the deposition of photographic and video material returned by audiences from encounters in the city. In concert with texts, maps and diagrams, they revealed the biographical profile of each figure and their role in the overall story: 'Gradually, from the assemblage of poorly shot videos, characters began to emerge, and a narrative started to form, a story of past lovers searching for each other across the city' (Roms 2004: 177).

In *Raindogs* and *Who are you looking at?* all technical playback apparatus was present – in view and in operation on the theatre floor – as was its operator. Bernard Tschumi's cinematic 'frames' were referenced in the precisely painted white screens on the walls upon which pre-recorded sequences of discrete actions and events of precise durations appeared: linked through appearance and locale, the spectator nevertheless had both to scrutinize them and to engage them imaginatively in order to discern connections and to create associations between places, figures and occurrences. However: 'A sense of dissociation and dislocation is performed in the very medium itself: this is a territory of exile, where the performance is divided between screen and stage and the spectator finds "no home" to rest her or his gaze' (Roms 2008: 120).

For Roms, these are panoptic visions of 'a city awash with rain and litter, lost loves and disappeared locations' (ibid.). Pictures of the city entering a space once defined by exclusivity, now become porous. But partial, fragmentary, oligopticon rather than panopticon: views from Henri Lefebvre's 'window' – 'to *hold* this fleeting object' (1996: 219), rather than Jeremy Bentham's – 'great and constant fund of entertainment to the sedentary and vacant in towns …' (Bentham 1995: 45).

Mike Pearson, *Fuji Musume*, Tokyo, July 1980

8. The Gym

The orange letterhead of Cardiff Laboratory for Theatrical Research bears medieval woodcuts of alchemists at their stills; the 'First Statement', dated October 1973 (Gough 2006a: 264), declares the company's two-fold purpose:

> Firstly, it will concentrate on research, even for the sake of research, without the restrictions of performance dates and rehearsal schedules. A permanent performance group will apply the fruits of research to experimental theatre pieces …
>
> Secondly, it will have a major teaching role to make completed research more widely available. Workshops will be arranged whenever required, preferably in a permanent home, if the laboratory succeeds in finding one.

Building-based institutions – Grotowski's Teatr Laboratorium in Wroclaw, Poland and Eugenio Barba's Odin Teatret in Holstebro, Denmark – are the models.

> Obviously, such a venture will eventually require a permanent home, a small plain space to fulfill the following functions:
> 1) Training, rehearsal and research work in a stable atmosphere.
> 2) Performance by members of the laboratory to small numbers of initially sympathetic public. These will be experimental in setting, subject matter and delivery.
> 3) Public demonstrations of technique. Regular workshops open to the public.
> 4) Seminars concerning the development of experimental theatre.
> 5) Guest performances and workshops by other groups and individuals working in the field of physical theatre.
> 6) A meeting place and forum for those concerned about the future of theatre. The pre-requisite to all this is of course that we have a building and a permanent foundation, which can be allied with other laboratories around the world, in a network of interchange involving the exchange of ideas, personnel and findings upon theatre.

The school's gymnasium was never part of the Chapter settlement; in 1978, Cardiff Laboratory Theatre secured it independently from the city council. It would, in time, host Grotowski and Barba and Peter Brook, though the ropes, wall-bars and beams in the rented space survived untouched until the late 1980s.

The acquisition of a closed space had immediate impacts upon practice: conceptual and rehearsal periods became protracted, and scenic devices elaborated.

Cardiff Laboratory Theatre's first major touring production *Moths in Amber* (1978) was created in the Gym. To address the anticipated problem of playing in a variety of venues – from black box to proscenium stage – the performance was housed in a self-contained module: a cocoon-like tent of muslin and bamboo, enclosing both action and audience. Spectators sat on wedge-shaped seating units at the four corners of a square; over their heads were arched poles – fixed to the rear of the units like extendable fishing rods – that joined at the centre and from which the canopy was suspended. Performers perched on podiums between them – resembling performing animals – each with a tree branch upon which hung personal effects. The module carried its own lighting, with external lamps giving a diffuse light through the canopy and more intimate lanterns highlighting performers inside. It looked like an outsized Victorian food cloche: a sealed theatrical context with its own conventions, where anything might happen.

Rehearsals for *Moths in Amber* lasted three months. Initially, performers worked alone: inventing acts, collecting objects, and designing extravagant costumes in which colour was now favoured within the white envelope. The accent was on the creation of unusual fragments, entertaining in their strangeness – painting the tongue with food dye, animating a fox fur with two walking sticks, 'a transformation through human agency' (Gough 2006a: 273) – rather than on the acquisition of circus skills: a set of humorous and disturbing 'turns' lacking any coherent narrative. We called it an 'opera' as there was almost continuous live sound: from homemade instruments (copper pipework saxophones and wooden rattles); from improvised and abstract vocal expression accompanying sections of movement; and from songs derived from field recordings of ethnic musics that without pastiche we attempted to mimic: Pygmy hunting calls, work-songs from Russia, and Romany ballads from the Balkans.

With audience and performers always in the same configuration, it was possible to develop precise choreographies, to plan moments of interaction with spectators, and to programme the exact transition of scenes. This was a sociopetal space in which both groups were thrown together and always mutually on view.

The presence of performers throughout had several repercussions. First, the performer was continuously engaged: on his podium, he might observe and comment theatrically upon the central action; or he might be immersed in personal activities with no connection to the main event. This necessitated close attention to the dynamic modulation of 'on' and 'off'. Secondly, anyone might be watching at any time: the spectator was at liberty to attend either to the soloist, or to the other performers on their podiums, or to the responses of fellow spectators. The overlapping of sections prompted sudden shifts in attention – one act commencing at a podium before that previous had finished.

As the audience entered through a flap, action in this hermetic world had already commenced. Throughout, the spectator's presence was acknowledged in acts involving proximity to, and touch by, performers: surreptitiously invited to look at dirty postcards (the catacombs of Palermo), or to suck sweet black liquid through a transparent straw from a blown egg.

The faux exotica was influenced by Barba's growing interest in eastern theatre techniques that resulted in his actors travelling to India, Indonesia and Japan to study: their training in *kathakali*, Balinese dance and *kabuki* informed *The Million* (1978–84), loosely based on the exploits of Marco Polo, and instigated the foundation of the International School for Theatre Anthropology (ISTA).

In 1980, I too spent three months in Tokyo studying *noh* theatre with Kanze Hideo. I learned a section of *Kanawa* (*The Iron Crown*) – following Kanze behind and to his right as he repeatedly demonstrated without explanation; trying to assume through imitation the prescribed hand gestures and steps. The contact between *tabi*-shod foot and the highly polished hinoki-wood floor of the *noh* stage is almost frictionless, resulting in the characteristic gliding movement. And as all *noh* stages have similar dimensions, so even the location of the performer has significance. All difficult to invoke on the Gym's worn surface.

Unbeknown to colleagues, I also studied the *odori* dance *Fuji Musume* (*Wisteria Maiden*) performed by *onnagata* (men in female roles) in *kabuki*. I learned the complete dance in a one-room school in north Tokyo; I returned with full costume, make-up, props and wig, all of which had been specially made to match my stature. I first demonstrated it in the Gym during Odin's residency in August 1980. I remember the look of astonishment on Barba's face as I stepped out. It didn't go well, the choreography deserting me in the unexpectedly enlarged space: I extended my steps too far, revealing my legs. Afterwards, Barba was gracious – he suggested I was a *samurai* in disguise.

In the 1990s, Brith Gof merged training exercises accrued since 1970 – in the Gym and elsewhere – into a method entitled 'In All Languages': a series of physical languages of gestures and interactions that can be articulated (by applying more or less time, energy etc.) and mediated (through changing spatial and environmental conditions etc.) in which Dave Levett's physical disability became a form of a priori articulation. Less overtly, they survive as enduring personal predilections, preferences and attitudes. Archaeological intimations of practice.

With stripped floor and black walls, the Gym is now Chapter's Studio Theatre.

Architectural detail, 'The Corporation', March 2013

9. Cowbridge Road

The clue to the district's earlier function is in the names: Market Road, 'The Butcher's Arms'. From 1859, the plot upon which Chapter now stands was Cardiff's livestock market. Howard Spring, who lived in a lost street behind Market House, Chapter's annex, describes the scene as local children – drawn by the 'dreadful sights and sounds and smells' of the slaughterhouse – beg a pig's bladder from a neighbor, 'an apparition from Hell' (Spring 1956: 23).

The population of Canton grew from 250 in 1841 to 33,000 by 1892 (see Jones 2003): 'The threat of crime and a crisis in public health in Roath and Canton gave the corporation the push it needed and the new suburbs joined the borough in 1875' (Evans 1984: 366–67). The proximity to such noisome procedures and the need to maintain the city's social well being was policed by lasting byelaws:

> For instance, have you ever: ridden a bicycle in a pleasure ground or had a religious discussion in a pleasure ground or kept a boil uncovered whilst piercing someone's ear or climbed a wall in a cemetery or employed a child in a slaughterhouse or failed to place undried guts in a galvanised iron receptacle or smoked in a tattoo parlour or fallen asleep in the library …
>
> or loitered in a convenience or used soap in any swimming baths or spilled kitchen waste in the street …
>
> or kept swine near a dwelling house or pissed in the street, spit in a waiting room, annoyed a church goer, dropped a stink bomb in a cinema, driven an eleven month-old bull in a subway, placed a poster on a tree, dropped lime on the highway, played an offensive game near traffic, skateboarded on the carriageway or drunk intoxicating liquor in Roath Park?
>
> If so, then you've broken the law in our city. You have offended against the common good. (*Polis* 2002)

As Canton expanded, a suite of Gothic buildings was erected on the southern edge of the stockyards: the turreted Police Station (1883), demolished in 1962; 'The Corporation' (1889), with carved medieval heads and four curved, arched shop fronts; Canton Branch Library (1906) – 'Given to the citizens by Andrew Carnegie LL.D 1906'. The library which cost £5,000 was designed by E. M. Bruce Vaughan 'whose ecclesiastical preoccupations are apparent' (Newman 2004: 280). At Capel Salem (1909–11) – the Welsh Calvinistic Methodist Chapel – Madame Clara Novello Davies played the organ.

Cardiff's inner suburbs resemble Kevin Lynch's 'districts': their very names 'enhance imaginability' and 'crystallize identity' (Lynch 1960: 108) – Canton, Cathays, Riverside, Butetown. Splott. Built quickly – eighty-two streets were laid out in Canton between 1881 and 1891 – they are indeed 'structured with nodes, defined by edges, penetrated by paths, and sprinkled with landmarks' (p.48). Street networks prescribe route-ways (though there are always short-cuts); their edges are defined by river and railway and major road. Each district has a slightly different ambience: in repetitions of form, fabric and house type, in continuities of components.

Amongst Canton's signature features is St John's Church (1855), with its towering steeple. Somewhere between landmarks and 'primary reference points' (ibid.) are long-standing commercial concerns on Cowbridge Road, two of which survived until recently – Pope's photographic shop, opened in 1925 in the former Barclays bank; and Harding's hardware store, supplying everything to maintain the domestic – from light bulbs to cooking utensils, from paint to bath plugs – and providing the buckets, nails and fabric dye for theatre productions. There were always charity shops, source of costumes and shoes – 'dead men's shoes' – that bring other times and experiences – their own shadowy stories – into performance.

> I was drawn to objects that seemed to emerge into the daylight from dusty attics, mouldy sheds, damp garages and, most of all, the junk shops along Cowbridge Road. I liked the patina, the sense of use and purpose, the scars and markings of an object well used, of functionality and distress; objects abandoned, discarded, rejected and forlorn. (Gough 2006b: 13)

In Brith Gof's *Ymfudwyr* (*Emigrants*) (1983–85), a group of Welsh emigrants meet at a point of immigration. They wear the heavy black of nineteenth-century Europe and carry all possessions – personal repertoires of objects – in suitcase, bundle, parcel. For the woman – flat irons, crockery, accordion; for the preacher – Bible, barbed wire, wooden stakes, axe; for the labourer – sledgehammer, chain, potatoes; for the exile – harmonica, gramophone, black earth. Their words are taken from original letters, religious tracts, guidebooks, official reports. A single row of seated audience delineates a rectangular performance space, for actions both simultaneous and sequential – solos, duets, group dances and processions – disclosing hopes and fears, dreams and fantasies about the future and nostalgia for the past, for abandoned family and community: tensions descried in the range of objects.

> There is the Kodak camera that enables the family to 'immortalise' themselves on the picture, or a gramophone which in a dramatic moment of the play draws the family into a frenetic dance. And the sensual devouring of a forgotten peach … And the selling to one another the postcards with the landscapes of their native land which turns into a kind of passionate stock-market auction … And dividing the banknote into four useless pieces to have enough to go around … The father of the family has a suitcase in which there is soil from his native land. The suitcase opens and the soil falls out. One of the sons kneels over. With solemnity he takes it in his hands. He nears his face to it. He spreads the soil over his face. He takes his hands away from his dirty face. Now he is a miner. (*Scena*, Warsaw, Autumn 1985)

In 1986, *Ymfudwyr* was presented in small Welsh towns in Patagonia. We took costumes, bags and some items; others we sourced locally. Not difficult to find a sledgehammer or an enamel bowl in a land where stores are stacked with the paraphernalia of pioneer life. But at the Latin-American Theatre Festival in Cordoba, there was allegedly neither hammer nor bowl to be had in the whole city. Unable to countenance the use of found objects on stage within established conventions of production, the municipal theatre workshop made a bowl from papier mâché and a hammer from folded tin-plate: replicas, substitutes. For us, no orientating sound of water poured on metal, the ring of bowl on floor, the splash patterns after washing feet; and no weight in the hands, no engagement of muscles in upper back and neck. Disorientation, crisis …

Then our interpreter, who had lived close-by as a child, remembered a Jewish family who, twenty years previously, had possessed such a bowl. He found their house. They were astonished. Boy grown to man, lives to relate and his only interest an enamel bowl. They hadn't seen it for years; thought it might be in the attic. A furious search ensued, in vain. And then he opened the skylight. There on the roof, filled with decaying leaves, was the bowl. The resulting scene might be a painting by Chagall, as a young man crawls across a Jewish roof in a South American dusk.

On Friday 16 April 1993, the aged blue suit, bowler hat and black boots I wore in performances of *Ymfudwyr* in Patagonia, in which my role was invested, were stolen from a car in Canton.

'The Ivor Davies', March 2013

10. 'Llwyn yr Eos'

Cardiff's blue plaques mark the sites and passing of noted places as much as occupancy by celebrated inhabitants.

The plaque for the Palladian 'new' Town Hall (1853–1905) – opened by John Batchelor in 1854 and including assizes, county courts, post office, police station and fire brigade – is on Hodge House, headquarters of the late Cardiff businessman Sir Julian Hodge on St Mary Street. The Town Hall appears in a ceramic mural in 'The Golden Cross'; in May 1856 Jenny Lind, the 'Swedish Nightingale', sang there. Upon demolition, the marble sculpture 'Distressed Mother' by J. Evan Thomas, sculptor of the 2nd Marquess, was moved to City Hall; the cast iron public drinking fountain – a gift of mayor William Alexander in 1860 – first went to the bridge over the Glamorgan Canal in Mill Lane in 1908. Though no longer functioning, it is now built into the wall of Greyfriars Bridge over the dock feeder on the edge of Cathays Park: the seated figures in gold are of Christ and a woman of Samaria; the text is from John IV, 13–14 – 'Whosoever drinketh of this water … ' (Morgan 2006: 104).

The plaque for the County Goal on the entrance to Cardiff's indoor market remembers a 'scene of brutal punishment and religious and political martyrdoms'. Donated by the National Union of Mineworkers in 1980, it commemorates the execution of Dic Penderyn (Richard Lewis) for the alleged wounding of a soldier during the 1831 rebellion by mineworkers in Merthyr Tydfil when the red flag was flown for the first time: 'The funeral cortege was over a mile long'.

Cardiff's plaques are generally oval; only one is circular and devoted to an individual. At 95 Cowbridge Road East – 'Llwyn yr Eos' ('Nightingale Grove') – opposite the former Royal Infirmary, is the dedication to composer, film star and matinee idol Ivor Novello, who was born here on 15 January 1893. It reads: 'This boy became a Ruritanian king who gave his people dreams and songs to sing.' There are outlines of harps in the metal railings and depictions on glass door panels.

The son of music teacher Madame Clara Novello Davies – christened by her father after a visiting Italian soprano – he adopted her name by deed poll. He was the writer of songs such as First World War favourite 'Keep the home fires burning'; 'We'll gather lilacs in the Spring'; and 'Crest of the wave', famous for its frenetic rendition, with accompanying gestures, at the annual Boy Scouts' jamboree. His musical theatre works include *Glamorous Night* (1936) and *The Dancing Years* (1939).

Novello featured in D. W. Griffiths's film *The White Rose* (1923) as a divinity student who after becoming a clergyman gives up his calling to return to the girl whom he has made pregnant and who has been disowned by her family. He was cast as the suspect in 'the first true Hitchcock film' (Sinyard, 2012: 2), the suspense thriller *The Lodger: A Story of the London Fog* (1926), in which he plays the prototype of many of the filmmaker's leading men: 'Dark handsome creatures who sometimes have turbulent psychological depths and hints of a murderous melancholy beneath the surface charm' (p.7), though Hitchcock admits that it was impossible, after period expectations, to present Novello against type as the perpetrator (p.6). In this early silent film, several of Hitchcock's subsequent dramaturgical motifs are present: the pursuit of the wrong man; a double hunt, pursing someone who is pursuing the perpetrator; the ineffectuality of the police; cool blondes, 'who seem to magnetise male violence' (p.14); the contamination of guilt; the theme of the double. There are novel filmic devices such as the inclusion of documentary footage of printing presses; enigmatic text in flashing lights – 'To-Night "Golden Curls"'; and views of anxious pacing, shot upwards through a glass floor.

The plot concerns a number of female murders by 'The Avenger' – 'Tall he was, and his face all wrapped up' – and Novello's arrival as the lodger in Homburg hat, scarf and cape, with Gladstone bag, arouses suspicions. His performance is Expressionist in tone, with echoes of Max Shreck in *Nosferatu* (1922), in the elaboration of a physical vocabulary to accompany or to replace speech: a precise economy of gesture, exaggerated steps, speed of expression, use of pauses and freezes, tension in patterns of breathing and histrionic responses in a city of fog and shadow, all of which are abandoned as he makes his escape. Falsely accused, he is pursued by crowds – 'Quick before they tear him to pieces' – and in an extraordinary finale, he is left hanging in handcuffs from a railing between two mobs – 'Thank God I was in time'. He suffers a breakdown: 'But his youth and vigour will pull him through'.

These are conventions of physical expression that provide an analogue for the essentially silent performances of Theatre in Transit and RAT Theatre: helping locate their practices – and their potential analysis – as other than the presumed incomplete presentation of inept drama.

Novello died in 1951 only a few hours after completing a performance of *King's Rhapsody* (1949). The dedication on the effete statue – Novello sitting with toes pointed – beside Cardiff's Millennium Centre reads: 'In this city was born a king who gave his people dreams and songs to sing'; the plaque at his home in Windsor curtly notes 'Composer, dramatist, actor and man of the theatre'.

Cardiff's plaques are readily effaced: that to author Howard Spring on the wall of Barclays Bank in Canton is bare. That to William Burges on 20 Park Place is marked only by a dirty, residual shadow. But there is a further unexpected mode of remembrance. There are in Canton two recently established public houses. 'The Goscombe' is named for sculptor W. Goscombe John who was born on Union Street and whose father Thomas was a woodcarver in the Bute workshops that furbished Cardiff Castle and provided furniture and panelling for family houses in Scotland. Directly opposite is a J. D. Wetherspoon house called, somewhat cryptically, 'The Ivor Davies': the black-and-white sign shows a glowering Novello, cigarette in hand.

On City Road in Roath is Wetherspoon's 'The Ernest Willows', named for the pioneer airman born at 11 Newport Road in 1886, whose workshop was at East Moors in Splott. Willows was the first man to cross Cardiff by air; on 4 June 1910, he flew from Splott, landing his airship 'Willows II' – an innovative craft with twin swivelling propellers to facilitate steering – in front of City Hall, thus winning the £50 prize contributed by city fathers including Viscount Tredegar and Lord Ninian Crichton-Stuart. The event is captured in incongruous photographs of the airship in the civic centre, and on a film lasting twenty-one seconds. In August 1910, he flew from Cardiff to Crystal Place, London in a flight lasting ten hours; in November, from London to Paris in 'Willows III', renamed 'City of Cardiff'. He died in a ballooning accident in 1926.

Willows was the subject of Marc Rees's *Willows III - Waiting for take off* (2000) presented in the Temple of Peace in Cathays Park. To represent the voyage to France, Rees first videoed a long tracking shot over a detailed model of the landscape between London and Paris – with prescient battlefield scenes – using a camera facing vertically downwards. In performance, a down-facing projector threw a small image onto the floor as it moved: in a view as if from the airship.

1 Queen Street East
2 Queen Street West
3 Hayes Island
4 Morgan Arcade
5 Caroline Street
6 Central Station
7 St Mary Street
8 Westgate Street
9 Cardiff Castle
10 Parks

CENTRAL

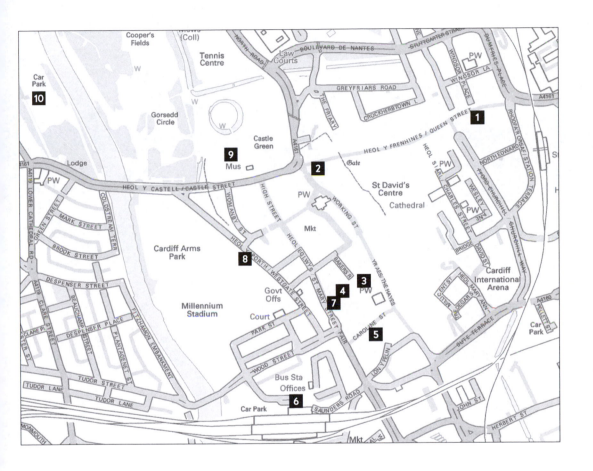

Cardiff Laboratory Theatre, *Hunt the Wren*, December 1978

1. Queen Street East

Four figures on Queen Street: the first, in winged bowler hat and tail-suit, carries a white umbrella topped by a holly-bush and plays the trumpet raucously – he has the strut of a New Orleans marching band leader; a woman with a stuffed seagull on her hat and suit covered in down plays tenor horn; a drummer is clothed in strips of coloured paper and rags; a man in a bird-like mask of bones and feathers carries a tall staff decorated with ribbons, bells and greenery. It is Christmas 1978 and Cardiff Laboratory Theatre mounts a mock Wren Hunt.

> We'll hunt the wren says Robin the Bobbin,
> We'll hunt the wren says Richie the Robin,
> We'll hunt the wren says Jack of the Land,
> We'll hunt the wren says everyone.

The noisy procession is punctuated by several stops where its purpose and theme are elaborated and repeatedly reiterated in a sequence of songs, instrumental music and actions, and echoed in costumes and objects: an episodic structure, with varying modes and intensities of dramatic activity, that includes a call to follow, the hunt, the capture, the distribution of feathers, and the lament.

It recalls a Welsh and Irish luck-bringing calendar custom in which groups of men went out on St Stephen's Day (26 December) to hunt the small bird. Although the practice varied regionally, the wren was usually captured, killed and carried round the neighbourhood in a specially decorated box or wren-house by a singing procession. A feather – to be worn as a protective charm – was offered to households in exchange for food or coins. The corpse was finally buried to the singing of dirges and with circular dances.

At the first station, *Hunt the Wren* begins quietly: horn and trumpet play a gentle duet to draw the attention of passers-by. Gradually the steady beat of the drum takes over and the Calling-On song commences – a loud proclamation of objectives, with an invitation to follow. A snaking procession proceeds, accompanied by trumpet and drum.

At the second station, the main wren song – compiled from several sources – is sung in three-part harmony; it is followed by a rhythmic, staccato choreography as they seek out the bird. Then off again in a syncopated dance.

At the third, the song is presented in full, relating the narrative of a perfect hunt. There is a roll on the drums and a wren – fashioned from clay and pheasant feathers – flies up, suspended from the end of the staff. There is a frantic, humorous attempt to capture the swooping bird that is eventually charmed by whistles and lures. After an instant's remorse at its demise, feathers are handed out to spectators; the cadaver is placed in a wren house, made from a hollowed bread loaf.

The funeral cortege assembles and the figures walk slowly and sorrowfully to the beat of the drum. At the last station, the solo tenor horn sounds, and a song warns all those intent on hunting the wren.

This work of faux-folklore – intrinsic social purpose turned ludic – was one of several street-works enacted on Cardiff's increasingly pedestrianized streets that used British customary pursuits not only as a source of subject matter but also in suggesting modes of performative utterance, spatial organization and dramaturgical structure to inform contemporary practices.

The paradigmatic practice in street-work was that of Eugenio Barba's Odin Teatret: in August 1980, they performed their 'itinerant performance' *Anabasis* – 'a group of strangers making their way amongst strangers' – on Queen Street.

> At times the giant figures on stilts collapse to the ground, while other figures suddenly appear on balconies or roofs, high on church spires, let themselves down into the square or street on a rope, start marching in the opposite direction, disperse, disorientate the people following them. (Odin Teatret, 2013)

But *Hunt the Wren* was intriguing rather than spectacular and its inspirations more immediate: Welsh Folk Museum curator Trefor Owen's *Welsh Folk Customs* (1987) in which he not only describes performative traditions such as the Mari Lwyd – house-visiting by a white shrouded creature based on a horse's skull – but also the threat posed by intolerant nineteenth-century non-conformist evangelism. The museum possesses one of the few beribboned wooden wren houses to survive. The performance was a small act of homage rather than cynical appropriation.

Other influences included the harmony singing of The Watersons on the LP *Frost and Fire: A Calendar of Ceremonial Folk Songs* (1965), and the music of Mike Westbrook's Brass Band on *For The Record* (1976).

Significant too was Richard Southern's *Seven Ages of Theatre* (1962) in which he characterizes theatre as dependent on 'a concentrated effort on one particular occasion' (Southern 1962: 23) – involving the employment of the personal resources of the player – voice, gesture, appearance, instruments/properties – and the secondary resources of place, stage and scenery. Southern analyses dramaturgical structures: identifying a pattern of introduction – combat – death – cure – resurrection – collection, in the plays of English mummers that would be employed in the company's *The Bear Hunt* (1979).

In the opening moments of theatre, Southern suggests, there is *visitation* at a particular season by men in disguise. He recommends the circle as a basic spatial arrangement: 'allowing the best sightlines and closest proximity for the largest number of people' (Pearson 1980: 52). The genesis, delineation and formalization of such space pragmatically organized in provisional locales affect the type, nature and quality of the activity and its reception: performers may need to walk and turn whilst speaking; or stand at the centre to declaim. However, 'any one spectator's vision will include other spectators, architecture and street furniture all of which are likely to distract the attention if the action is not strong enough' (ibid.).

> Street theatre must be loud, immediate and direct, vigorous and ebullient in action, brilliant of costume, a collision of overstated elements, if it is to capture and hold the passer-by and change his status into that of spectator (ibid.).

A contemporary adage asserted that no street performance should last longer than seven minutes – either the time that someone en route might be willing to linger at an incident encountered by chance, or the time it would take the police, once alerted, to arrive. Momentarily recast as spectator, the passer-by might experience the proximity of performers as – watched by others – she receives a feather.

With shifting audience and background, the aim was to engender an evanescent vivacity – performance creating an impression, stating its intention, staking its claim to space, becoming its own point of reference – that deflected notice away from the displays of shops and hoardings, through a captivating though uncomplicated narrative; a demonstration of musical expertise; and a comic tone that could nevertheless switch to pathos. And into which random things might intrude: people, vehicles, and other activities.

Hunt the Wren occurred in the midst of Christmas shopping, close to the Salvation Army band: an unanticipated oddity, but festive and appropriately seasonal, prompting a glance if not a pause.

The ambition was to intrude into and interrupt quotidian flows, enacting Lefebvre's notion of the festive as distanciation from daily preoccupations, as transcendence; a playful inversion of social and cultural conventions.

In the photographs: frontages all now changed; and the Cardiff crowd in period attire.

Pearson/Brookes, *Raindogs*, November 2002

2. Queen Street West

He remains stock-still. The police CCTV operator finds him immediately: the camera seems drawn to him. He is doing that most provocative of things in this flow of consumption, of gazing and grazing – nothing. He is not playing the game; he must be 'loitering with intent'. For him I write:

> His city is all nightmare. He has a feeling for the uncanny auras of the past. And here history seems close to the surface, threatening to return and engulf him with its chaos and plague. His city is shallow but its geology is exotic: communities built on ballast – rock returned in empty coal transports – from the world. What contagion might lurk just below the surface, or behind that facade? You just can't tell by looking.
>
> He knows that others have lived and died here before him: he sees their handiwork, their laughable claims to immortality. In order not to disturb them he walks cautiously, edgily, unnerved: history ever dogging his steps, threatening to leap out, burst out – like molten lava – and turn lives to ashes in its path. As he walks his city into existence, deep maps guide him: records of the events of its past that orientate him. He holds his breath in British Home Stores for instance, never buys drink there because it's built on a cholera cemetery; sings along to Bob Dylan playing the Capitol – in Benetton; Tom Paxton in the Cory Hall – in H&M. (*Raindogs* 2002)

In *Raindogs*, each actor is required to stand erect, without moving or speaking. But he never knows from which of multiple available viewpoints he is being observed and recorded, and exactly when: he must survive in the public domain, stationary for a bracketed period of up to ten minutes, before receiving a telephone message to relax or move on. Without either precise direction or resort to rhetorical devices, he is obliged to use his actorly skill simply to be present: mute, refraining from express display. Preserving his anonymity, he makes no attempt to address any one camera or particular audience.

At a time of increased quotidian circumspection, he is stilled, his energy restrained. Reserved, in repose, yet alert and vigilant: his clothes 'almost anonymous as a uniform', closer to 'a costume which inhibited vigorous action, and which action ruffled, uncreased and spoilt' (Berger 2009: 38). After John Harvey's *Men in Black*, his black apparel is perhaps 'associated at once with intensity and with effacement: with importance, and with the putting on of impersonality'. It is the older black too of mourning, of spiritual grieving: 'for grief is another way of discovering, as it were behind the daylight, a universe of absence and insatiable want' (Harvey 2009: 257).

He wears dark glasses in some attempt at disguise: either to guard against identification and closer scrutiny, or to restrict the ingress of the full impact of this situation of exposure. In large part, he remains un-remarked. Perhaps his attire, the day wear of *homo urbanis*, is suggestive of camouflage; or perhaps deflects the observing eye – as in Japanese *kabuki* theatre where the stage is sometimes populated by numerous shadowy assistants, or *bunraki*, the black-garbed puppeteers who hover around their charge – it induces a sense of invisibility. More likely, it is because he is not making a scene, an exhibition of himself.

He is both embedded within and aesthetically distinct from the urban flux, quietly resisting the circulations around him: he feigns indifference, a provocation to surveillance itself.

On video, attention is deflected towards the crowd and its make-up, to the kinetics and choreographies of public mobility, to the details of architectural style, composition and fabric, apprehended by a spectatorial eye turned *forensic*: to 'a potentially overwhelming "harvest of clues"' (Doyle 2005: 15). Is this loitering an aftermath of acts unwitnessed, or a presentiment of those to come? Who is the criminal-in-waiting? He does of course resemble one of the suited protagonists in Quentin Tarantino's film *Reservoir Dogs* (1992). Mr Pink – 'Why can't we pick out our own colour?' Joe: 'I tried that once, it don't work. You get four guys fighting over who's gonna be Mr Black.'

And is this interrogative mode, the consequence of our already having witnessed too much surveillance – 'the endless recycling of violent images *collected through* CCTV into people's living rooms' (Roms 2008: 120) – a more apposite way to regard such fragmented performance, in which narrative coherence is forfeited?

The texts of *Raindogs* are elegiac: they describe and commemorate an urban geography and town plan largely vanished. They recall venues such as the Capitol cinema where emergent rock bands performed in the early 1960s – Bob Dylan is on his way there as he poses in dark glasses at the Aust Ferry over the Severn in Barry Feinstein's photograph of May 1966; and the Temperance Hall, sponsored by shipping magnate John Cory. Both disappeared when a whole city block was demolished in 1983 and rebuilt as the Capitol Exchange shopping mall, 'a gimmicky display of 1980s polychromy' (Newman 2004: 217). Of 'The Lexington' where Keith Wood presented *The Gospel According to Lenny* [Bruce] (1976), there is no trace. Only the portrait plaques of Dutchmen from the Dutch Café survive, incorporated into the brickwork.

The figures in *Raindogs* stand on the footprint of former streets that persists ghostly in the orientation of new malls and pedestrian walkways. Texts summon old atmospheres: the sickly sweet smells of Brain's Cardiff Brewery. They allude too to significant events: from the farewell banquet to celebrate Scott's departure for Antarctica to Lynette White's murder.

In the pavement are outlines marked in black of shops and houses removed in the nineteenth century. The name was changed from Crockherbton Street in 1887 in celebration of Victoria's Golden Jubilee; until pedestrianized in the mid 1970s, it was the main trunk road to the west – '20 ton steel lorries carrying steel coils, suburban bus stop, pedestrian crush' (Morgan 1994: 50).

At street level, the scene changes repeatedly: the shop in which Theatre in Transit performed *The Odyssey* as part of a programme to stimulate interest in Chapter in 1970 is now an optician. But above, the Victorian and Edwardian city is still evident. Most extraordinary are Nos. 24–26 designed by Charles F. Bernard in 1878 with shafts, ogee windows and pinnacles in Venetian Gothic, inspired by John Ruskin's *The Stones of Venice* (1851–53), close to where the Glamorgan Canal passed beneath.

The street furniture is regularly altered: arrangements of benches, bollards and signs that orientate and direct patterns of movement and pause. Most recent are maps showing distances as minutes of walking in concentric circles – to landmarks and further retail destinations.

Of statues, Robert Thomas's bronze socialist/realist figures – 'Miner' and 'Mother and Son' – feel heroic but burnished of the marks of personality and aging.

In *Carrying Lyn* (2001), Aneurin Bevan – 'Founder of the National Health Service' – is one of our ports-of-call. We pause beneath him and pose for a black-and-white Polaroid photograph as he tilts pugnaciously:

> Despite this, he points seriously at the earth of Wales where
>> His feet are rooted –
> to the land he came from – but on a frantic Friday
> no-one in the city's listening. (Reynolds 2005: 176)

But as we position ourselves outside a Queen Street sex emporium, we are challenged: an assistant has spotted us on the shop's CCTV system.

Pearson/Brookes, *Raindogs*, November 2002

3. Hayes Island

He sits at a table in the open-air snack bar on Hayes Island, an older man, in suit and tie. For him, I write:

> His city is film-set: he's always on camera, in a movie of his own imagining. He recreates scenes especially for the surveillance watchers – bored policemen, tired security guards: *Roma, Open City*; *Rififi*; *Wings of Desire*; *Bullitt*. Striking poses, gesturing wildly. His magnum opus is to be *Tiger Bay*, a full-length version, on location. But he just can't find it. As he stands in the flower-bed that was once The Custom House pub, he thinks he hears the clatter of girls from The Salutation, The Lifeboat, The Greyhound; Victor Parker's guitar sliding from the Quebec; John Silva's bass thumping from the New Moon. But it's just traffic. Maybe he should do Godard's *Weekend* or try Jacques Tati instead. Maybe he should just go to Newport. That's what J. Lee Thompson did anyway: Horst Buchholz riding the 'transporter' bridge. And he wonders when, and if, it ever was 'Tiger Bay': caged, urgent, burning bright. (*Raindogs*, 2002)

He glances nervously, unsure of from whence he is being watched. After viewing the video recording, I add:

> He hired that *Big Issue* seller to sit with him, likes the mongrel on a string, thinks it adds a touch of gritty social realism to his latest project, the film of his life story. He's decided that if he sits on Hayes Island long enough, everyone he has ever known – even the dead – will pass by, will greet him.

The imperative for inactivity is inconceivable within his tradition of theatre-making: he has asked the seller to engage him in 'patter', or 'business' in the *patois* of theatre.

The wooden snack bar was built in 1911 as the Tramway Parcel Express Office; it was converted in the 1950s as trolley buses took over. Hayes Island is one of Cardiff's *nodes* or 'conceptual anchor-points' (Lynch 1960: 102); a *plaque tournante* – a turntable that occasions a 'mixing of populations which is the favourable environment of cultural exchanges' (Sadler 2001: 88). A locus that conspires 'layering and overlap with respect to its position within infrastructures; a layering that will allow it to support multiply folded, complicated, implicated, interaction' (Read, 2006a: 61). It is an old, familiar place to which inhabitants are drawn: 'This is the life. Pavement society. Rickety iron tables under the trees, and the pigeons, and the down-and-outs. A real whiff of Paris' (Bush 2005: 40); 'The City's answer to the Costa del Sol but with added rain' (Finch 2004: 69).

Buildings of different periods press closely:

– St John the Baptist Church where the fifteenth-century pillars are as old as Cardiff gets outside the castle; an alleyway to the market splitting the old graveyard, brass numbers in the pavement marking the sites of former family plots;

– Edwin Seward's Bath stone Free Library, Museum, and Schools for Science and Art (1882; extended 1884) – 'a design of real originality and weighty presence' (Newman 2004: 211) – that opened with a public holiday (Jones 2007). Decorated externally with figures and panels of printers William Caxton and Wynkin de Worde, cherub-like workers (ploughman, smith, merchant, musician) and illustrations of Agriculture, Manufacture, Commerce, Culture, Music and Architecture; and internally by the faience tiles of Maw and Co., with designs by Walter Crane depicting 'The Seasons' and the 'Times of Day';

– City of Cardiff Electricity Showrooms and Offices (1937), refashioned by Percy Thomas in the former fish, poultry and vegetable market of 1901, and until its recent demise, home to furnishers Habitat;

– St David's Hall (1978–82) – 'one fine bit of late Brutalism' (Hatherley 2010: 272), where Brith Gof premiered *PAX* (1990);

– Tabernacle Welsh Baptist Church (1865), a key location in the religious revival of 1904–6: 'About 11 o'clock there are a large influx from the streets, and the chapel became very crowded. The meeting lasted until nearly one o'clock on Sunday morning, during which there were 33 conversions' (*Baptist Times* 20 January 2012);

– the functioning department store of James Howell (1895–96); and the converted premises of David Morgan (1899);

– St David's 2 mall (2009) that replaced the brick Oxford Arcade where, on 21 March 1970, Cardiff students staged an event to commemorate the tenth anniversary of the Sharpeville Massacre in South Africa. With plastic machine guns and without warning, we shot down members of a mock demonstration.

Here too is ship-builder and Liberal John Batchelor (1886), who as mayor in 1853 challenged Bute hegemony and brought sanitation to the city, helping to combat frequent cholera outbreaks. His statue was an affront: after paint was thrown in 1887, both he and the 2nd Marquess had to be protected from 'sectional vandalism' (Evans, 2003, 116).

But Hayes Island repels as much as it appeals. Below the snack bar are the public toilets, opened by the city corporation in 1898: impossible to escape the miasmas that emanate, though they were formerly ameliorated by the sweet smell of Brain's brewery. This is as close to subterranean as Cardiff gets: a contaminated underground that 'encapsulates the jumble of dirt and disease which threatens us in the city' (Bhattacharyya 2000: 195). What lurks in its dark recesses, in 'the pit that introduces further narrative about the city … other ambiguities and ambivalences, bound up in life and earth, purity and foulness' (Pile 2001: 267)? 'And overhead, a gridded skylight ceiling of thick ale-greenish glass crossed by foot-soles and dim shadows, all the city's numberless destinations' (Bush 2005: 42).

Scenes in Ed Thomas's play *Song from a Forgotten City* (1995) are set here: 'A bog. Hayes Island cubicle three, frosted glass looking up the street' (Thomas 2002: 13). Thomas augments a 'Cardiff noir': 'Against a seedy setting of suppressed violence, *Song* celebrates excess, gender confusion and erotic desire, all conventionally associated with a transgressive urbanism' (Roms 2008: 118).

Two characters – Night-Porter and Bellboy – are here on the day of an international rugby game: 'I estimate at least ten thousand walked above me with the heavy dread of defeat' (Thomas: 14); 'On match day this is a surging sea of red and beer' (Finch 2004, 69).

> The Night-Porter – that unlikely figure from *film noir* – recalls the traumatic experience of hearing about the defeat from an 'underground' place: a place that simultaneously evokes the Gothic underworld *and* the world of the Welsh miner. But this underground place is concretely and comically imagined as a toilet cubicle in the Hayes where the Night-Porter is smoking a spliff, drinking lager, eating liquorice allsorts, and looking up through the frosted glass at the street above him. (Williams 2002: 424)

'The Veritable' urinals are by Thomas Crapper and Co: 'But, of course, we should know from the urine soaking the subways and alleyways across our cities that the body never waits' (Bhattacharyya: 196).

At Hayes Island, Cardiff is at its densest: here one might observe the manifold comings and goings and encounters that Georges Perec lists in *An Attempt at Exhausting a Place in Paris* (2010). For another Raindog, I write:

> He wants to rush up to passers-by and demand: 'Who do you love?' 'When were you last jealous, or frightened, or cruel?' 'How do you embrace?' 'What is the one thing you wished you'd said in the most important event of your life?' 'How would you want to be remembered?' 'Have you ever said "I love you" and lied?' 'Was the telegrammic address of Clark's Pies really "Clarpie, Cardiff"?'

Morgan Arcade, March 2013

4. Morgan Arcade

My German academic colleague was delighted to discover nineteenth-century architectures that Walter Benjamin would have appreciated. In the Royal Arcade, outside Wally's delicatessen store – a cornucopia of produce from Eastern Europe and beyond, founded by Austrian Jew Ignatz Salamon and developed by his son Walter, which once stood on Bridge Street – he began to take photographs of the roof. Almost immediately, we were approached by a woman who told him to desist. The reason: we were on private property; what appears to be a public thoroughfare is a commercial emporium patrolled by plain-clothes security officers. A threshold had been crossed: here certain practices are proscribed, doubtless 'to discourage non-consumers from appropriating the site' (Miles in Savage 2009b: 6).

The burgage plots of medieval Cardiff were long and narrow, their width attested by the frontages of the later premises that occupy their sites on St Mary Street. By the mid-nineteenth century many were in-filled with densely populated tenements and slums, allotments and paths.

> There are several courts, alleys and lanes behind the principal streets occupied by families bordering on pauperism, and a similar class of people is found even in some of the new streets, such as Charlotte Street, Caroline Street, and Irish Town and near the Canal.
>
> ... there will always be a shifty and pauper population in its suburbs in consequence of the description of labourers required for loading and discharging the vessels, for attending on the wharfs, and for other casual occupation (contemporary report quoted in Lee 1998: 42–43).

In a *Western Mail* article of February 1864 entitled 'The Architectural Growth of Cities, and the Future of Cardiff' (see Savage: 2009a: 12), architect Edwin Seward professes an ambition to replicate the architecture of Paris: 'by developing the city's back lands and narrow streets into fashionable shopping areas and boulevards'.

Arcade building would colonize the plots laterally: with the installation of twin rows of shops to increase commercial frontage along a covered pavement, and a glass roof to provide shelter and light. In arcades: 'The two great advances in technology – gas and cast iron – go together' (Benjamin 1999: 151).

The Royal Arcade was already operating in 1858. Built in 'Nash villa' style (Newman 2004: 214), it replaced 'a jumble of ugly courts, poor cottages, tiny shops and public houses' (Savage: 105) and brothels. Then came Castle Arcade (1882; 1889), High Street Arcade (1885), Wyndham Arcade (1887), Morgan Arcade (1896–99), and Duke Street Arcade (1902).

Cardiff's arcades were built piecemeal and in a variety of styles: the entrance to High Street Arcade resembles a souk; the Castle Arcade – a Grade 2 listed building

– has three storeys, large end mirrors; and a tier of businesses on a balcony. Here National Theatre Wales has its offices.

The arcades present 'a place of refuge for the unprepared, to whom they offer a secure, if restricted, promenade – one from which the merchants also benefit' (Benjamin: 31). They are as much anthropocentric in character as architectonic in structure, offering feelings both of containment and security, of familiarity, in a world of consumption. They stimulate movement and circulation: shoppers do what they have long done here, regarding 'a thousand little stages ... which performed the magic of transforming pedestrians, step by step, into customers. The agents of this manipulation were architecture: space, form, light and material' (Wall in Savage 2009a: 48). This is Benjamin's 'world in miniature', with no outside, resembling a dream (Benjamin: 406), 'wholly adapted to arousing desires' (p.42); building and action interpenetrating to become 'a theatre of new, unforeseen constellations' (Amin and Thrift 2002: 9).

Morgan Arcade is in a 'fussy Jacobean classical style' (Newman: 214) but it has 'some wonderfully imaginative moments – the point where the ferro-vitreous roof of Edwin Seward's 1879 [sic] Morgan Arcade curves round the street line is fantastical' (Hatherley 2010: 277). Walter Benjamin posits 'arcades as origins of department stores' (Benjamin: 37) – the *boutique* becoming the *magasin* – but here the two are contemporaneous: the arcade is built into David Morgan's department store, devouring Barry Lane in the process.

Morgan Arcade retains its original windows in exotic hardwoods; the names of Victorian manufacturers appear on fixtures and fittings. Though the shop windows are brightly illuminated, the lighting on the pathway is subdued and gas-like. And it is possible to feel vague atmospheres of the past here: the persistence of an acoustic quality in the sudden shuttering of traffic. The arcades often seem hushed, though doubtless the sound of leather on flagstones had a different tenor. Olfactory sensations endure too: the cooked meats in Wally's and the humidors in the tobacconist's evoke times past. What has changed is the rhythm of shopping: the arcades are now locked at 6pm.

But all is not quite as it appears. The Royal and the Morgan contain hidden voids explored by artist Jennie Savage in her extended *Arcades Project: A 3D Documentary*.

> There are 3 cities other than, or beyond the visible city. 1. In the Royal Arcade there is a door marked 'David Morgan Works'. Through this door is Pigeon Alley which connects with St Mary Street. 2. Above the arcades semi derelict rooms and corridors reveal the traces of the David Morgan Department Store. 3. Below the arcades. A subterranean city of interlinked basements and corridors. In a basement in Morgan Arcade you can listen to hairdressers in their staff room which is at the back of a shop on Saint Marys Street. (Savage 2009a: 82)

Passageways, workshops, store rooms, meeting places – a warren of corridors run. South of the Morgan Arcade lie abandoned furniture repair shops, lost storerooms, boarded cellars, service passages that mirror the arcades themselves. Above are cobwebbed rooms, halls full of wrecked fitments, places where women once sat with sewing machines and stacks of cloth and men with pens checked lists and bills of lading, a world of dust and despair. (Peter Finch in Savage 2009b: 5)

A world where leftovers accumulate and adhere: cached, forgotten, and surplus to current requirements.

Cardiff extols its arcades, and the new malls position themselves within their history: they are no less destructive of existing patterns of occupancy. In St David's 1, something of the footprint of former streets persists in the plan. In the towering St David's 2, the foundations are deep, the Victorian city effectively obliterated. And yet as one approaches the east entrance, along the attenuated Bridge Street, idling on a customary route, an image of greasy cafés and second-hand bookshops – and then a second of the multi-storey car parks that replaced it and where an audience met a performer in *Polis* (2001) – is suddenly projected in the mind's eye.

In the instructions for their participatory performance *Where would you take a stranger?* (in Savage 2009b: 5), Daniel Ladnar and Esther Pilkington recommend:

4.3 Places to take strangers in Cardiff: the arcades, the market, the castle and the steelworks at night with their orange glow …

6. A place to avoid 6.1 St Mary Street, at 4 in the morning on a Saturday Night. Caroline Street – Chippy Lane – on match days. But then, you might have had some of your best conversations there. 6.2 If you are going for chips on Chippy Lane, try Dorothy's or Tony's.

Caroline Street, March 2013

5. Caroline Street

As groups of audience leave Chapter in five taxis to locate and video performers in the city, I regale those remaining – who will venture out when the others return – with reminiscences of Cardiff.

> I found it almost immediately – 'Cardiff: City of Jazz'. That autumn – 1968 –it was Tubby Hayes at 'Les Croupiers', barely able to blow a note, barely able to stand, blocked up, three months away from his OD, though we thought he was just a bit pissed; blues guitarist Victor Parker at 'The Quebec'; and at the New Moon Club – the John Surman Quartet; the Don Rendell and Ian Carr Quintet; the Graham Collier Sextet as well as local boys Professor Terry Hawkes on drums, solicitor Dave Greensmith on bass and local Docks legend John Silva on just about everything, from flute to vibraphone. Mind, by this time the only license the New Moon could get was as a supper club – they used to shove a hot-dog in your hand on the door, if you ever got that far. It was on the top floor of a warehouse at the end of an alley, where 'business' was always brisk. But don't go looking. It's gone. To the best of my reckoning, it stood exactly beneath the South-East corner of the Marriott Hotel. (*Polis* 2002)

The intersection of The Hayes, Bridge Street, Mill Lane and Caroline Street was an early locale of notoriety: 'Drinking, prostitution, crimping and violent crime found their home there' (Evans 2003: 112).

> This used to be full of various seedy little back streets, with their run-down cafes, dubious book-stores and down-and-out boozers, Frederick Street, Bridge Street and the rest. All gone. (Williams 1995: 32)

Until its initial redevelopment in the 1970s, it offered vicarious pleasures: it is repeatedly invoked by Cardiff writers as a touchstone of old Cardiff – the black and white city, flaking, peeling, past its best. Rhodri Morgan recalls 'the aromatic and highly flavoured atmosphere of 1960s Bridge Street after dark' (Morgan 1994: 42). John Williams describes a scene then close to disappearance: 'The old Bridge Street was a hundred-yard stretch of dodgy second-hand "bookshops", smokey cafés, scrumpy pubs and "medical supply" shops that lost half their trade when they legalised abortion' (Williams 2003b: 122). The New Moon club – 'where the phrase "cheap, sweaty fun" could well have been coined' (Briggs 2002: 154) – was up a spiral, cast iron staircase above a textile warehouse (p.17): 'it was historical, in a god-awful kind of way' (Williams 1995: 178).

The junction is now a piazza in front of the new library. Coffee drinkers in John Lewis's store look out onto the twenty-five metre high sculpture – a circular hoop and inclined metal arrow – by Jean-Bernard Métais entitled 'Alliance' (2009). The hoop is sunk into the pavement. A mechanism programmes its liquid contents to rise and fall with the tide; it is reputedly partially submerged into the canal below, whose course is attested by the railings with blue wave-like motifs erected on Mill Street – 'Cardiff's Amsterdam' (Finch 2004: 135).

> At night, projectors from inside the arrow beam down text in Welsh and English by Cardiff-based writer Peter Finch evoking the layers of Cardiff's urban history and present. The bodies of passers-by will act as screens thus symbolically enveloping visitors to the city centre in Cardiff's progress through time. (*Wales Online*, 16 November 2009)

St David's 2 commissioned this new 'landmark': the project director extols 'an iconic symbol that will represent the city on a national and even international level.' 'Good public art is like a door to the senses that makes the entire space, the place and the people in it resonate together' (ibid.) the sculptor declares.

Aldo Rossi describes how dispositions of historical elements continue to orientate municipal circulation:

> Cities tend to remain on their axes of development, maintaining the position of their original layout and growing according to the direction and meaning of their older artifacts, which often appear remote from present-day ones. Sometimes these artifacts persist virtually unchanged, endowed with a continuous vitality; other times they exhaust themselves, and then only the permanence of their form, their physical sign, their *locus* remains. The most meaningful permanences are those provided by the street and the plan. (Rossi 1982: 59)

But the purpose of 'Alliance' is to fill a design gap rather than providing direction. Perhaps Rossi's persistent 'artifacts' – that attract and deter and determine circulations – are cultural as much as architectural. Traditional behaviours and practices, with a historical dimension, that generate the tenor of urban spaces: drunkenness, fighting, 'looking for business' …

> The drunken brawl, alas, is still heard on our streets – the curse of liquor still fills our workhouse, infirmary and asylums … "the bitter cry of outcast Cardiff" is a cry for which drink is chiefly responsible. (Cardiff Temperance and Prohibition Association Annual Report 1886, in Evans 2003: 113)

Bridge Street has been deleted, The Hayes pedestrianized and Mill Lane gentrified, but much that was evident in 1886 can still be witnessed in Caroline Street, Lardner and Pilkington's 'Chippy Lane' (Savage 2009b: 5): 'A sixty-yard stretch of chippies and shops selling army surplus or dirty mags, populated this time of night by very drunk people trying to get a little ballast into their stomachs and even drunker people busy unloading their stomachs into the gutter' (Williams 2003a: 1).

The redeveloped north side was once Brain's brewery. The south is much as it has long been: Dorothy's (est. 1953); Tony's; the Red Onion, supplying 'gangs roaming Caroline Street in search of dangerous-looking food – that much hadn't changed at least – and gangs just throwing up in every alley and doorway' (Williams 2000: 204). An enduring scene of fortuitous fumblings, sudden enmities, and quick evacuations, that eschew the regulatory processes that pervade the urban everyday, the 'unperformative norms which reiterate how people should behave in the city' (Edensor 2005: 86). An artifact: of cultural resistances learned as much by custom as by instinct. The pavement forever a greasy slick:

> a flotsam tide of food wrapping
> slops and swirls ankle deep.
> (Ifor Thomas, 'Caroline Street' 2005)

Ed Thomas finds in Caroline Street an urban poetic. Fragments of his text for *Raindogs* (2002) reappear in his drama *Stone City Blue* (2004), in which 'intertwining voices muse on sex, drugs, violence, loneliness, loss and sometimes even beauty, love and tenderness' (*The Stage*, 10 November 2004).

> He's hugged them all
> Christina, Maria, Angelina and Hannah
> Diana, Millicent, Violet and Holly
> Done Lady Margaret, Lady Mary,
> Even Queen Anne and Saint Mary
> He's bathed them all with holy water
> He's made them clean
> It's 4.45am … in the city.
> He's hugging Caroline
> Caroline is the hardest
> Caroline is always difficult
> She's a legend
> People come from far and wide
> To pay homage in blood and bone and spit
>
> With salt and vinegar and broken promises.
> But he loves her more than the others
> He likes it when it's just her and him
> When the night is nearly over
> He hugs her tightly
> His brush against her kerb
> He makes her clean
> The left side then the right
> Up and down and all over
> His cleaning trolley
> One forward, one reverse
> A water-jet. Rotating brushes.
> He's the crawler of kerbs
> The hugger of pavements
> In the city of women's names.

Pearson/Brookes, *Carrying Lyn*, June 2001

6. Central Station

The company name is proclaimed in large letters cut into the imposing Portland stone facade: Cardiff Central railway station (1932–34) was designed by Great Western Railway architects. A place of tiffs, touts and telephones, of staring intently at destination boards before hurrying into action.

Facing out, the view is less auspicious: the bleak piazza and bus terminal of Cardiff Central Square – 'Sgwar Canolog Caerdydd feels like the last gasp of a public realm seen as a design problem' (Miles in Savage 2009b: 6). This was once Newtown or Temperance Town, built in 1846 to accommodate immigrant workers: 'Scrape the Cardiff surface and you'll find shamrocks underneath' (Finch 2002: 165). In 1966, one hundred and sixty-nine houses in six streets were demolished: 'Can a whole district – houses, people, even the name – simply disappear?' (ibid.). Only Wood Street Congregational Church is remembered – on the South Gate House office block.

It is 12 noon on Saturday 2 June 2001, in the foyer of Cardiff Central. In the Polaroid photograph three of us are holding disabled performer Lyn (formerly Dave) Levett whom we have met from the London train. For over two hours, we are videoed and photographed as we carry Lyn on a predetermined route of short journeys of ten minutes duration, and pauses of five, across the city towards Chapter – St Mary Street, Caroline Street, Hayes Island, Queen Street East and West … That evening we repeat the procedure, dispatching footage and still images by cycle courier to the theatre where it is projected in parallel with recordings of the same actions and places at midday. In periods of awaiting the arrival of material and of rewind, my recorded voice speaks texts that attempt some theoretical proposals for a popular audience: 'theory-lite'.

> 1.
>
> John Berger once suggested that the great pilgrimage of the twentieth century is the journey from the village to the city. Most of us now live in cities, some of them vast conurbations of shantytowns: it is the 'urban' that defines our contemporary experience. But if the village is *par excellence* a homogeneous community, a place where everyone knows everyone else, then the city is a congregation of strangers. We can never know more than a fraction of our fellow inhabitants and we can never know the whole geography in any kind of detail. We are destined to be one amongst a great many. And if the village is essentially a monoglot community, defined by similarity, then the city is a place of diversity and multiculturalism. And even the early city was a place of import, not only from its own rural hinterland, but also from far off, attracting the novel and the exotic – you've probably seen the mediaeval banana recently found in London.

This does mean that in order to orientate ourselves, we may be drawn to live in the city with others of our kind – our own race, creed, language, religion, background – in a particular neighbourhood. We may indeed be denied permission to live anywhere else, as in the Jewish ghettos. And here we may attempt to preserve a particular identity through social practice and custom, through our diet, through our calendar celebrations. And all this may give a particular ambience to the neighbourhood: Chinatown, Little Italy ...

2.

Although we may come to know one area of the city in detail – our street corner, local market, recreational facilities – the rest we will only know as isolated locations strung together by journeys. To move around we may even need maps – an A-Z, the Underground plan – and we begin to rely on others – public transport – to get us there. Our urban experience is to know the names of tube-stations that we pass through without knowing their surrounding locations.

Routes, crossroads and centres: whilst they may be found elsewhere, they are all found in the city. The notions of itinerary, intersection, centre and monument begin to describe the urban space.

Thus individual itineraries in the city are constantly drawn towards centres, where they intersect and mingle. [Marc] Augé suggests that there is then the possibility for polyphony, the interlacing of destinies, actions, thoughts and reminiscences.

3.

In cities, history accumulates. Many live on their rubbish, their debris endlessly accreting beneath the feet. Not only does waste gather but also buildings are constantly knocked down and others erected on their site. In some parts of London, the Roman city is twenty feet below the surface.

Most cities are multi-temporal; the remains of the past are all around us. Architecture survives. Here a Georgian town house exists next to a modern designer home. Some buildings are thought worthy of preservation and restoration. And some fragments of buildings become integrated into others as if they are half-digested: stratifications of past occupations, repairs and constructions, the superimposition of different time-scales. Other buildings are repaired, their function changes: a chapel becomes a disco. Their identity is unstable ...

10.

The city is too complex an organism for us ever to fully know it, consisting as it does of endlessly intersecting narratives. A famous Situationist map of Paris demonstrated that most Parisians only ever moved regularly between three points in the city, their entire life circumscribed by a triangle - home, work, shop. We may not feel so constrained but we do tend to stick to particular routes, creating for ourselves a cognitive map of the city, enabling us to get around. I remember the terror at being in Tokyo, a city without street names and plates. The only way I could function was to emerge from a given underground station and then remember my route back there as I explored the surrounding area. The mental maps I devised were then like radiating shoots from a number of points.

But if we are to make work in the city how might we begin to sensitize ourselves to its nature and make effective use of it? For instance, if the dominant theme of the city is trade and commerce, what might the sub-themes be? If we call Cardiff 'The City of Rugby' can we begin to make performance which enhances this theme and which defines our essential role within it?

How might we deal with the fact that the city is often designed for the able-bodied, middle-aged? Can we create projects with the disabled, the young, the old that begin to question this middle ground? Can we, for instance, create environments that are only accessible by wheelchair, lifts that are four feet high and that occasion the so-called able-bodied to squat and bend?

Can we begin to draw maps that take different focal points, creating projects for instance that only operate literally within the sound of Bow bells?

Can we begin to alter the nature of the city itself by planting gardens on derelict sites as has been done in New York, raising questions about environmental degradation?

Or in keeping with traditions of street trading can we try to sell food in a way that is other than simply holding it in the hand?

Can we open a different kind of museum or perhaps a zoo featuring 'urban man' as its prime exhibit? Or perhaps provide an alternative tour of an existing museum drawing attention to overlooked details or creating fictional histories and usages for familiar artifacts and exhibits?

Can we imagine performance for the transport system; or over the tannoy of a tour bus; or in a parked car?

Well can we? Or has the city become such a potentially dangerous environment that any deviance from normal patterns of behaviour might be enough to attract unwarranted attention. Good enough reason perhaps to try.

(Pearson/Brookes: *Carrying Lyn* 2001)

Solomon Andrews's phoenix, Central Market, St Mary Street, March 2013

7. St Mary Street

Outside Sam's Bar – originally The Steam Mill Arms, then The Terminus Hotel, now Peppermint Bar – we pause with Lyn, as policemen pour out of a van behind us. Paul Jeff takes our Polaroid photograph with his Graflex news camera. His personal project is to restore the temporal aspect to photography through a notion he terms atonement (at/one[mo]ment): 'Atonement consists of an instant loaded with significance and capable of swallowing whole narratives in one unifying moment. It is a dense instant not unlike an astronomical black hole' (Jeff 2001: 23). We squat nervously; two hundred football fans await us on Mill Street.

Female performers in *Who are you looking at?* (2004) are also on St Mary Street, named for the first parish church washed away in the sixteenth century.

> They're working hard in their wanderings: five separate trajectories, five
> destinies. Converging.
> Drifting, all-seeing
> Alert to those for whom city is zoo:
> Who pace: foreheads, flanks rubbing the bars;
> Who turn: baring teeth, rattling the cage.
> Flexing, stretching, occasionally yawning.
> Watchers and watched: yellow eye to yellow eye.
> One waiting to throw coins and nuts,
> The other to maul an outstretched hand.
> Spraying the patch with piss up the wall.
> Cocking a leg; burning bright;
> In the heat – in the forest – of the night.
> What binds them is desire – let loose, set free – invisible threads slowly
> winding tighter. (*Who are you looking at?* 2003)

One carries a rucksack: her video camera registers passing men as leering gargoyles, seemingly immune to the cold: 'This is the land of shirts outside your trousers and studs in your nose' (Finch 2002: 13). After seeing the video, I write:

> I'd foreseen Sodom and Gomorrah; blood on the tracks; sex and the city.
> Horror show.
> From the heights of age and moral certainty, I'd have said:
> 'They're skating on thin ice, some of them;
> Watching for black spots, listening for cracks.
> Stepping lightly, then slipping and sliding,
> Coming a cropper, upended, arse-first.'

Another sits framed in the window of a sandwich bar, looking out onto passing traffic; she is videoed from a car parked opposite. For her I write:

I'd imagined a setting from Edward Hopper,
Haunted figures in the diner gazing out on neon streets,
In cinemascope.
I'd wanted them to see those
Who are bowling along, rootless.
Caught in a sudden gust from far south.
Like a hat, an umbrella, the Western Mail,
Rising suddenly, spinning in a vortex, a thermal of hot air.
Floating out of reach.
Then falling …
Caught in a tangle of arms and legs, wrapped round shins;
Ensnared, entrapped, then snatched, kicked free.
Rising again quickly, above it all,
Looking down with lofty detachment.
Seeking the jetstream, fearing a pressure-drop.
But all they ever see is their own reflection in the window.
Nighthawking …

Ten years on, the street is now pedestrianized: to encourage retail circulation, and to assist the policing of the night-time throng – an intense carnivalesque, where stag and hen parties wear matching outfits adorned with name and function.

But above street level, the Victorian townscape endures: 'Architecturally this really is a fabulous place, its impressiveness barely affected – possibly improved, for some – by hordes of screeching petit-bourgeois virgins covered in marker pen groping each other before being sick in the gutter'; 'a great complex urban project … ranging from low countries Gothic to two massive Americanised neoclassical department stores' (Hatherley 2010: 270).

Postcards from the early twentieth century show the emporia, with their large street awnings and passing trams; and night-time scenes too. But these latter are hand-tinted photographs shot in daylight – always a full moon partly hidden by cloud to create a twilit scene; windows as squares of yellow, orange and red spilling onto the street – from the Library and St John's Church, and along St Mary Street. And around frames and architectural features, a thin line of glitter adds an air of enchantment.

Some places on St Mary Street, to set the scene, from bottom to top:

– Jacobs's Biscuit Factory – where the canal once met the city – now an antiques market: some stalls jumbled, others strictly ordered by type. Here an outlet for the Cardiff Reclamation Yard once on Ferry Road, where Egyptian figures from a cinema flanked its entrance. The nineteenth-century city in fragments, from chimneypots to floor tiles, to patch and renovate.

– The facade of Thompson House – home of the *Western Mail* – now masking stand-up drinking places, where an audience seeks a performer in *Polis*. At the door, bald men in black coats with armbands, registered like Hackney carriages:

'They look the part. They've seen the films' (Finch 2004 78).

– 'Le Monde' restaurant: a former coffee warehouse, whose smells mingled with those of Brain's brewery.

– 'The Prince of Wales': opened as the Royal Theatre (1878), and later a sex cinema.

– On the end of Wyndham Arcade: the sales office for apartments in St David's 2 in the shop where the model for Centreplan was exhibited in 1971.

– 'Les Croupiers' casino: now a gentleman's club.

– James Howell's department store, of two periods – the more southerly 'a brilliant exposition of American Beaux-Arts classicism' (Newman 2004: 214) by Sir Percy Thomas (1928–30). This extension absorbed Bethany Baptist Chapel (1864–65): in the menswear department an arch is still apparent, and a dedication in bronze to Rawlings White burnt at the stake for heresy in 1555.

– 'Solomon's Temple': the exotic entrance to the covered market, built by entrepreneur Solomon Andrews, that bears his name and a phoenix rising from the flames. His previous endeavour – with tower and camera obscura built in 1884 – was destroyed by fire in 1885. Andrews's 'vast but ramshackle' business empire was 'integrated neither vertically nor horizontally', growing 'by hunch and whim' (Evans 1984: 356): ever seeking an opportunity, bringing horse trams to Canton. But Andrews's portico only provides access to a structure that was redesigned by city architects in 1890 – with a steel and cast iron frame and, in an early example of surveillance, a central control tower. It was opened on 8 May 1891 by the Lady Mayoress, The Most Honourable the Marchioness of Bute, in a plethora of pomp and tartan. Fruit stalls stand opposite those selling Welsh rugby shirts; Kelly's Records is next to Sunday School Supplies; pet suppliers on the balcony are above the butchers. Most celebrated is Ashton's, selling fish here since 1886. The large clock that reads 'H. Samuels Everite Time' has lost its hands.

A performer in *Raindogs* (2002) stands close by, on the corner of Church Street. For him I write:

> He has decided that he will become a street-greeter, welcoming visitors to the city, a city that only he knows. Here on this spot for instance he will tell them, Captain Scott paused on his way to the civic dinner, feeling an icy blast from far south suddenly scour his heart. He knows a thousand such places, unmarked, invisible to those whose feet grind away the streets each day. And these he will reveal: he will become a 'revelator'. But home? No familiar smells draw him back to Roath or Ely or Grange. He knows only the miasma of odours – burger, urine, blossom – hovering over Hayes Island. So he will endlessly chase his tail there, round and round.

Aberystwyth University students, *Lifting*, 1999

8. Westgate Street

The city is turned red by the favours of the crowd: shirts, scarfs and hats of various vintages. The stalls sell inflatable daffodils, balaclava-like headgear in the shape of that flower – face appearing at the centre of the corolla – and leeks with green topknot and whiskery roots. The face stencillers offer red dragons and fleurs-de-lys. The touts are shouting 'Buy or sell tickets'.

The routines of spectators resemble customary, even ritualized, practices as they pass through traditional haunts of consumption, on an established and immutable circuit, wearing their favourite, luck-bringing attire. In the Brewery Quarter, they drink prodigiously: on the site of Brain's brewery, in national team shirts sponsored by S. A. Brain, embellished with the words Brain's SA, after the company's legendary beer. The renewal of personal leases on life, through vicarious though anticipated extra-daily experiences.

Fifteen minutes before kick-off the city begins to flow inexorably in one direction, towards the river Taff: first a stream then a torrent, impossible to swim against on Westgate Street. The red is dashed with some black and the fluorescent green of police, yellow of vendors, and orange of stewards. The communal expectation is palpable, the immersion and investment in a national event consuming, and potentially threatening if you are not part of it.

Suddenly a troupe of thirty appears, dressed in Welsh kit and masquerading as named players. They play a comic, improvised game as they roll down the street, calling out new instructions, using road markings as try-lines. Here too, incongruously, are mock Friesian cows and their milkmaid: all constituents of good-natured social suspension and misrule that nevertheless might turn satirical and political. A complex metaphor unfolded as the brother-in-law of legendary Welsh full-back Neil Jenkins ('The Ginger Monster') would appear on the pitch before a match in ginger wig and large plastic ears, replicating exactly Jenkins's preparation and run-up – before kicking a toy sheep over the crossbar.

Inside the stadium, long-standing traditions: the military band; the presence of Taffy, regimental goat of the Royal Regiment of Wales. And new innovations: celebratory flame and smoke cannons; large video monitors relaying close-up action. As the teams emerge, the noise of seventy-five thousand voices reaches a crescendo: the crowd is indeed 'the sixteenth man'.

Today, the visitors are the New Zealand All Blacks who begin with the *haka*, a choreographed Maori baiting with slapping, stamping, tongue wagging and gurning. The riposte is the massed rendition of the national anthem 'Hen wlad fy nhadau' ('Land of my fathers') – in harmony.

The whistle blows: the nature of the opposition, and whether the roof is open, will affect strategies and tactics – whether to kick long or play close. Gone the mud-baths of yore.

Rugby Union mixes free running and set pieces such as scrum, lineout and place kick; and semi-structured passages, such as the rolling maul. Both teams attempt to find a rhythm of circulation around the ball, constantly confounded by the opposition.

The tackling is ferocious but the rules are clear: the parameters of what can and cannot be done are refereed closely; all that might be put under pressure mutually understood. Rules give direction and purpose to the release of energy: once they are known, there can be planning and organization to achieve the desired effect. This can lead to specialization and the employment of individual skills and the selection of 'the best person for the job' – hooker, flanker, fly-half. And spectators can appreciate their observance, or violation. The final whistle only sounds after an infringement: in their match against Scotland in 2012, amid increasing crowd elation, Wales cannily managed to keep the ball in play for seven minutes beyond full-time before scoring to win.

Westgate Street was once the bank of the Taff: Quay Street and Golate Street – Cardiff's oldest thoroughfares – ran down to the wharf. The river was realigned by Brunel and the reclamation eventually donated to the city by the Bute Estate for recreational purposes. When Turner's built the Cardiff Central Fire Station (1912) – on the site of the Wooden Circus Theatre – the pile foundations had to be sunk to a depth of twenty feet, as it stood on the old riverbed. Along the present street are 'The Queen's Vaults'; 'The Royal' garage, now a microbrewery, with an Art Deco relief of an aeroplane with whirring propellers, a rushing charabanc and the words 'Carways. Airways'; and the Angel Hotel where the South African Springbok team appeared on the balcony during their controversial tour in 1969, and student demonstrators chanted 'Jump, jump'.

Before devolution, Cardiff Arms Park was 'the principal institution of Welsh nationhood' (Morgan 1994: 17). It was replaced in 2000 by the Millennium Stadium: its cause played against that of the opera house (see Crickhowell 1997); its seats and sections of hallowed turf sold to supporters. A city with a major sports stadium at its heart, and an annual schedule of events during which the civic is engulfed and surrenders – all public transport in the vicinity suspended.

The national obsession provides a recurrent theme for performance:

Brith Gof's *Gwynt, Glaw, Glo a Defaid* (*Wind, Rain, Coal and Sheep*) (1991) included a section performed on a four-metre square of boxed turf in Chapter Theatre, over which it was raining. The choreography of the four male performers was based on rugby set-pieces. They wore black shirts, black gum shields and black electrical tape around the head, in homage to the fearsome Neath team of that time.

In Robert Delauney's painting 'L'Équipe de Cardiff' (1912–13), a blue-shirted forward leaps high in the lineout, beneath an early biplane. *Lifting* (1999), performed by Aberystwyth University students in the Gym, celebrated the once illegal procedure in which catchers are now hoisted to considerable heights by their fellows.

Street Greeks (2002), a Pearson/Brookes collaboration with playwright Ed Thomas, was projected for two locations: street and studio. It was to include twenty new texts, each of one-minute duration, inspired by classic Greek works on tragedy and the city.

In phase one – on each day of performance, at some point during that day – the twenty texts would be performed in the public domain: on the street, in cafés, in taxis, each presentation to be unannounced and negotiated in the context of exposition.

> They will be staged in relation to the architectural fabric of the city, to details of social situation and include passers-by and others, invited and coerced on the spot into taking part in the delivery of the text. Each performer must work within the particular situation or set of circumstances and achieve a clean presentation of the text, however difficult. The presentation of each text will simultaneously be videoed. Twenty minutes of new and original video material must be collected during the day.

A principal ambition was to perform on days of rugby international, both inside and outside the stadium.

> This video footage will then provide the raw material for a formal, indoor theatre work of at least sixty minutes, created and presented on the same day. In performance, the recently recorded video fragments will be juxtaposed to create a coherent story from disparate events that happened at sites across the city. They will also constitute the inspiration and source for the performers, now 'live' in the theatre, who by physically reacting and responding to the recordings of themselves – emulating, copying, challenging – will improvise a new version of the narrative into existence, including the details of the day.

Street Greeks remains unrealized.

Cardiff Castle Banqueting Hall, 2013

9. Cardiff Castle

By the age of twelve, John 3rd Marquess of Bute was an orphan. He grew up withdrawn and bookish, with interests in the Middle Ages, mysticism and spiritualism – he later joined the Society for Psychical Research – and languages – he later learned Welsh and supported the Eisteddfod. Upon coming of age in 1868 and converting to Catholicism, he attended mass daily. He was, incidentally, one of the richest men in Britain, with the time and wealth to pursue his passions.

Cardiff Castle and its grounds were much altered by Capability Brown in the late eighteenth century. But in the 'art-architect' William Burges, the 3rd Marquess found a partner with the skill and vision to express his enthusiasms in further works of renovation. Together, they undertook a sixteen-year building project inspired and informed by themes and images from archaeology, medieval studies, religion, literature, astrology and the occult, and by travels in Europe and the Near East, that were wrought together in an exuberant, aperiodic example of the Gothic revival: 'a feudal extravaganza of painted murals, stained glass, gilding and sculpture all set within the framework of the Norman castle turned mansion' (Williams 2008: 16).

> Here Burges's imagination could run riot. Here the arts were all called into service: painting, sculpture and wood-carving, stained glass, metalwork, inlay. Here marbles, gilding and other surfaces which sparkled or shone found their places. Here, above all, the arts could tell their stories. (Newman 2004: 202)

Their first enterprise was the Clock Tower, designed in 1866 whilst Bute was still a bachelor: polychrome statues of the seven planets stand on plinths bearing their accompanying signs of the zodiac in gold.

Work on the west wing began in earnest in 1872, after Bute's marriage to Gwendolen Fitzalan-Howard: individual rooms were completed over the next ten years, Burges's undertakings completed by William Frame following his death in 1881. The centrepiece is the ornate Banqueting Hall (1875), its fan-vaulted ceiling bearing sixteen carved angels after the manner of East Anglian churches. The elaborate sideboard is intended to double as an altar. The walls bear murals depicting twelfth-century and legendary scenes such as Llywelyn's dog Gelert guarding his infant son against the wolf. The chimneypiece in the form of a miniature castle – six trumpeters on the battlements and a mounted knight on the gate – encapsulates the story of Robert of Normandy.

Throughout the house, no surface is left unadorned: all is modelled, painted, gilded. The profusion of detail, decoration and colour was achieved by local craftsmen, a group of skilled masons, carvers, joiners that included sculptor Goscombe John's father in the Bute workshops in the Docks.

Of other rooms:

– the Arab Room has a stepped 'jelly mold' *muquarnas* ceiling covered in gold leaf that glows in the sun, *mashrabaya* windows and Italian marble floor;

– the Small Dining Room has a chimneypiece with three angels flanked by Abraham and Sarah;

– the Summer Smoking Room has painted tiles showing scenes of classical legends, the elements, stars and constellations and a sun-burst chandelier;

– the Nursery is decorated with tiles by Maw and Co. showing Aesop's fables and heroes and heroines from children's literature;

– the Chaucer Room, an octagonal, top-lit room designed for the Marchioness, is painted with scenes from the *Legend of Good Women*, the *Parlement of Foules* and the *Canterbury Tales*.

One striking feature is the presence of animals: mammals, reptiles, birds, and insects, both real and fabled. Burges's bookcases and tables in the Library have carvings of unusual creatures: platypus, beaver, armadillo and pangolin; on the doorframes, lizards, and monkeys on branches. Each of the naked winged putti on the walls holds the name of one of Bute's favourite authors – Aristotle, Balzac, Byron, Dante, Fielding, Gogol, Molière, Petrarch, Pope, Rabelais, Schiller; the chimneypiece is inset with figures representing ancient languages – Greek, Assyrian, Aramaic – hieroglyphs, runes.

A heterogeneous mixture of symbology and iconography demonstrating one man's range of interests and another's propensity for allegory, allusion, humour and visual puns: the Bachelor Bedroom is decorated on the theme of the pursuit of mineral wealth; Bute's Roman bath adorned with metal sea creatures; the bell push in the Small Dining Room is a howler monkey with a nut in its mouth.

The Animal Wall (1887–88) by Thomas Nicholls was added after Burges's death. It once stood in front of the castle where two lions flanked the gate: the stone creatures – formerly painted, with glass eyes – appear over the crenellation as if escaping from the moat garden, but equally serving as guardians and deterrents, warning 'Keep out'. The wall was moved *en bloc* to the front of Bute Park in 1930, when further creatures were added: lion, lynx, bear, seal, baboon, wolf, hyena, vulture, wombat, jaguar, pelican …

What then is Cardiff Castle? It is a manifestation of wealth, achieved because money was no object and simply because Bute could do it: as ostentation as Charles Foster Kane's Xanadu in *Citizen Kane* (1941). But it is also the three-dimensional projection of a complex psyche, a fantastic external realization of entwined personal preoccupations, not entirely ascetic in nature: electricity was installed in 1883; radiators heated the dwelling space throughout.

But it was intended neither to be lived in long-term nor widely appreciated. The heightening of the curtain wall on the foundations of the Roman fort effectively shut out the city, and the building's exterior betrays little of the extravagant interior: 'This could have been a nineteenth century Disneyland if the Marquess had been letting the public in. But he wasn't' (Finch 2002: 93). And the Butes never spent more than six or eight weeks a year in Cardiff, four in summer and two in winter.

'Burges wrote that the walls of his buildings should "speak and tell a story"' (Williams: 38), and there are narrative sequences here in the wall paintings, friezes, dioramas and statuary. But the castle has a theatrical mien. It gives the impression of a designer's maquette or model box: each room a scenographic set piece or mise-en-scène awaiting the entrance of a medieval figure, or his actorly Victorian counterpart, or the contemporary tourist in a walk-on role.

The concept of mise-en-scène concerns the disposition and arrangement of elements – plastic and human – in order to tell a particular story: eliding scene with script or scenario – that may be more or less dogmatic in its demands – to advance the intentions and desired outcomes of the production; or existing as a counterpoint in manifesting an autonomous existence. It also involves the organization of viewpoint and the perspectives from which the scene is observed and registered.

Michael Shanks takes up the concept: 'The arrangement of things in place to fit the interest of viewing and inspection is a key component of archaeological work, whether it be the trench section cleaned for scrutiny, a reconstruction of a building, or an assemblage of artifacts in a museum' (Shanks 2012: 147).

Bute himself carried out excavations of Blackfriars Priory in the castle grounds, leaving the foundations open for view. His reinstatement of the Roman curtain wall is a major act of reconstruction, never previously attempted. As in all his works of reconstruction and renovation – however convincing – the interface of old and new is marked by a course of red bricks.

As old animosities between 'wharf' and 'castle' cooled, Bute became Lord Mayor in 1890–91, his archaeological ventures helping afford historical roots for Cardiff's growing claims to city status.

"THE NATIONAL PAGEANT OF WALES"
ROTARY PHOTO. E.C.
INTERLUDE 4 SCENE 2 LLYWELYN OLAV AND THE EIGHTEEN OF PONT OREWYN DEC 11TH, 1282
PHOTO COPYRIGHT.
C. CORN, CARDIFF.

Souvenir postcard, National Pageant of Wales, July 1909

10. Parks

Two events at the turn of the twentieth century mark the city's growing confidence and aspirations: the Cardiff Fine Art, Industrial and Maritime Exhibition (1896); and the National Pageant of Wales (1909).

The Exhibition was staged in Cathays Park by permission of the 3rd Marquess, in the period of push towards attaining city status. Its organizing council comprised 'the local men with the money: Solomon Andrews, John Cory, S. A. Brain, and the Lords Tredegar and Windsor' (Pincombe 2007: 76). Edwin Seward planned the site: his own 'Old Cardiff' imagined the city in the medieval period as faux facades.

> We may say that nothing is the creation of mere fancy, but a representation of the town as closely as it can be reproduced from old plans and prints, and what scanty fragments of masonry remain, so faithfully has the designer followed his idea that 'Old Cardiff is reflected in the very pebbles of the road.
> (*Evening Express* 2 May 1896 in Pincombe: 83)

Amongst educative exhibits: a diorama of the Battle of Waterloo; and of the African jungle – 'where one would find a "shooting saloon, lions, tigers, birds and easts of all descriptions, and Zulus and kaffirs on the war path" amongst other delights' (p.86).

Amongst entertaining attractions: Thompson's patent gravity switchback railway, Hotchkiss's patent bicycle railway, Studt's galloping horses. Each night there was a performance such as *Santiago*, a 'grand opera' portraying the sack of that city by Sir Francis Drake in 1585, staged in and around the site's central feature, the artificial lake. Lit by night, if offered boats of many kinds including electric launches. Most ambitious was the one thousand foot-long replica coalmine – including an actual four-foot seam supplied by the United National Colliery Co. – in which visitors carried lamps and wore helmets.

But tragedy struck when Mademoiselle Albertina the parachutist – fourteen year-old Louisa Maud Evans – was blown away in her balloon. Her body was found three days later at the mouth of the River Usk near Newport.

At that time, Cardiff welcomed travelling spectacles: Buffalo Bill Cody brought his Wild West show with sharpshooter Annie Oakley in 1891 and 1903, and again in 1904, the troupe pitching its teepees in Sophia Gardens.

But the National Pageant was of another order: a combination of inflated amateur theatricals, eisteddfod ceremony and tattoo, featuring five thousand performers, horses and a pack of hounds. Staged with the blessing of the 4th Marquess in Sophia Gardens, this was a performance of considerable scale, relating the history of Wales from 50BC to the Act of Union in 1536. A publicity postcard promises: 'Thrilling Episodes. Historic Costumes. Great National Spectacle'. In a period of enthusiasm for pageantry elsewhere in Britain, it included forty thousand costumes; three thousand incandescent lamps; 'five searchlights of 10,000 candle power which will enable the Master to sweep the whole ground from his box' (in Edwards 2009: 98); and a telephone system connecting him with fourteen points on the field.

One characteristic of the production was the casting of living descendants as their forebears – Mr Thurston Basset of Beaupre appeared as the thirteenth-century Basset of Beaupre – and of eminent individuals in central roles: the Lord Mayor of Cardiff as Hywel Dda the law bringer – 'He added to his bearing, without theatricality, the kingly gesture and conviction we instinctively associate with Howel the Good' (*Western Mail*, 27 July 1909, 9). The Chief Constable of Glamorgan was cast, ironically, as the Chief Ruffian, carrying off a girl across his saddle – 'The dramatic and the humorous were skillfully blended with the picturesque' (ibid.). And the mounted Viscount Tredegar as Owain Glyndŵr. There were many supernumeraries: Augusta, the Marchioness of Bute as Dame Wales, a red dragon emblazoned on her dress, entered at the beginning with 'ladies of distinction' representing the counties. And Lord Ninian Crichton-Stuart as Lord-in-Waiting.

The scenario is a combination of tableaux and action sequences often lacking dialogue, with orchestra and chorus functioning to create the mood. The programme provides an essential guide to the order of scenes, the happenings in each sequence, and the historical context. There are five *episodes* each concerning a particular era, each with an *interlude* divided into a number of *scenes*:

> Interlude 4 Scene 3: Davydd ap Gwilym and the fair ones he immortalized.
> The adulatory, not to say amorous, trend of some of his verses are rather too rich to be considered quite delicate from a modern point of view. Nevertheless, those verses immortalised such ladies as Gwenonwy, 'the star-hued nun of the foam-white brow,' and nineteen other charming damsels of the period, who dance on the Pageant Field in pale heliotrope gowns, and execute, with the eminent bard himself, a *pas de vingt-et-un* which is most alluring to gaze upon. (*Pictorial and Descriptive Souvenir*)

> They dance delightfully; then group themselves adoringly round him, and when he has postured poet-wise a little, he flees man-wise from their embarrassing affection. (*The Times*, 27 July 1909, 13)

> Interlude 4 Scene 4: Owen Glyndŵr proclaimed Prince of Wales,
> 20th Sept., 1400.
> It is of great interest that such a loyal and notable Welsh soldier as Viscount Tredegar, who more than fifty years ago rode into 'The Valley of Death' in the immortal charge of the Light Brigade at Balaclava, should today be appearing in the role of the rebel who led his own people so successfully against the English in the fourteenth and fifteenth centuries. (*Pictorial and Descriptive Souvenir*)

As Tredegar rode in, the audience stood and cheered, as much for him personally as for the interlude.

In the souvenir postcard by C. Corn of Cardiff, Merlin 'the Arch-druid' exalts a papier-mâché cromlech, as King Arthur looks on in papier-mâché armour; the audience appears in the far distance.

Most striking was the storming of a mock Cardiff Castle by Ivor Bach in 1178, enacted by five hundred rugby players. A publicity poster commends the 'Footballers' ferocious onslaught':

> Across the field, close on the heels of Ivor Bach's galloping horse, rushed his gallant men, making for the Castle. Their clothes of white and purple fluttered gaily in the breeze. Pike and glaive flashed brightly as they sped. Others brought up the scaling ladders and the paraphernalia of primitive siege. From the east and from the front armed men pressed on the C and scaled its walls. The Norman knights tried in vain to stop the rush. It was wild and irresistible. It was made with all the élan of real battle.
>
> The whole episode from beginning to end was of a most dramatic and thrilling kind, and it is one which no other Pageant is likely to equal. (*Western Mail*, 27 July 1909, 9)

The closing scene:

> This is the most magnificent spectacle of any kind attempted in modern pageantry, and represents a glowing mass of between 4,000 and 5,000 persons – all the performers in all the forgoing [sic] processions and episodes – marshalled together, as in some gigantic ballet scene, on the broad field of the Pageant.
>
> At a given signal, the fairies join hands and form a map of the counties of Wales, with the lady representing each county in the centre of each group of fairies of that county's colour (ibid.).

For site-specific performance, for devised theatre, for physical theatre, for open-air events, for reenactments, for community-engaged work in Cardiff: an originary moment.

REFLECTIONS
AFTER WALKING

CITY

Cities are places of work, consumption, circulation, play, creativity, excitement, boredom. They gather, mix, separate, conceal, display. They support unimaginably diverse social practices. They juxtapose nature, people, things, and the built environment in any number of ways. (Amin and Thrift 2002: 3)

Why city? Because it is contested space. Because it layers commerce, manufacture, leisure, the political sphere – because it demands negotiation, compromise, co-operation, conflict, agreement in order to function, in order to move. (Tim Etchells in Harvie 2009: xii)

For its purposes, *Marking Time* views the city:

- as ground plan; as built environment; as structure;
- as architectures, objects, bodies; movements, forces, intensities; life stories, encounters, prescriptions; as individual anonymity and collective construct;
- as inhabitation: 'Every citizen has had long associations with some parts of his city, and his image is soaked in memories and meanings (Lynch 1960: 1);
- as contrasts and admixtures; as networks and systems, within and beyond its limits. All of which may have 'distinct, generative effects' (Amin and Thrift: 2);
- as sensuous display, ambience and atmosphere: a double condition of 'the random and the systematic, the visible and the obscured, which is the true significance of the city' (Williams 1973: 154);
- as artifact repeatedly transformed by use; as 'an archival form constituted from the fragments and shards of memory traces' (Edensor 2005: 172).

■ As the circumstances and conditions within which performance is – or might conceivably be – enacted, with varying degrees of public visibility and rhetorical projection.

The layout upon which performance might be enacted:

Within urban topography, Kevin Lynch (1960 47) identifies paths, edges, districts, and nodes or junctions that may become conceptual anchor points or symbolic concentrations. Marc Augé (1995) proposes three simple spatial forms to map social space – the line, the intersection of lines, and the point of intersection (p.57). In the city, these correspond respectively to routes and paths that lead from one place to another; to crossroads and open spaces where people pass, meet and gather and that are sometimes large in order to satisfy the needs of economic exchange – as

with markets; and thirdly to monumental centres, places of institutional complexity
– town hall, seat of government, palace, cathedral. Forms, Augé suggests, that
are 'concretized only in and through time' (p.58). He defines places as 'relational,
historical and concerned with identity'. Spaces that cannot be thus figured are
by definition *non-places* (p.94): places of solitary contractuality – prescriptive,
prohibitive or informative rather than social – that can, seemingly, accommodate
all comers.

The social conditions within which performance might be negotiated:

Henri Lefebvre characterizes the city as œuvre ...

> closer to a work of art than to a simple material product. If there is production
> of the city, and social relations in the city, it is a production and reproduction
> of human beings by human beings, rather than a production of objects.
> The city has a history; it is the work of a history, that is, of clearly defined
> people and groups who accomplish this *œuvre, in historical conditions.*
> (1996: 101)

For Lefebvre, every city has an utterance or language, particularities 'expressed
in discourses, gestures, clothing, in the words and use of words by the inhabitants'
(p.115): a distinctive hum. And a form of writing: 'what is inscribed and prescribed
on its walls, in the layout of places and their linkages, in brief, the *use of time* in
the city by its inhabitants' (ibid.). His city is poly-rhythmical or symphonic:
serial, repetitive and cyclical rhythms of occupancy – personal, collective and
administrative – are transected and interrupted by linear events and occurrences.
Its systematizing networks are formed from the mobilities and pauses of people,
commodities and information, travelling and working at different speeds and in
different measures.

■ All this performance might inhabit, complement, or temporarily interrupt.

For Certeau, Giard and Mayol (1998), dwelling is in thrall to archaeologies
of practices and common knowledge (narratives, myths, fantasies), that make
inhabitants believe and do things: 'They are the keys to the city; they give access
to what it is: mythical'; 'With the vocabulary of object and well-known words, they
create another dimension, in turn fantastic and delinquent, fearful and legitimating'
(p.142). 'Living is narrativizing. Stirring up or restoring this narrativizing is thus
also amongst the tasks of any renovation' (ibid.).

■ A renovation that performance might advance: not necessarily by enacting or
   overtly indicating residual cultural phenomena, but by standing adjacent to and
   thus highlighting that which survives or has disappeared.

The material and temporal context within which performance might be staged:

For Aldo Rossi (1982), the city is at once structure and ruin – 'great camps of the living and the dead where many elements remain like signals, symbols, cautions' (p.10), its main permanences being housing and monuments. 'Destruction and demolition, expropriation and rapid changes in use and as a result of speculation and obsolescence, are the most recognizable signs of urban dynamics' (p.22): yet despite rapid transformation some elements may have the power to retard or accelerate the urban process. Cities are modified by functions of time and culture: when these are in action – 'as events and as testimony' – the city is revealed to itself. It becomes 'a giant or collective house of memory' (p.10) – associated with places and objects, both positive and negative but contributing to its constitution.

■ Performance as such an event: potentially revelatory in character.

The city retains the traces of time: neighbourhoods are distinguished by continuities, by concrete signs of ways of life, history and language; the primary elements that distinguish it may be survivals from its past. Its principal *loci* are 'determined by its space and time, by its topographical dimensions and its form, by its being the seat of a succession of ancient and recent events, by its memory' (p.107). The urban artifact begins 'in the event and in the sign that has marked the event' (p.106). The built environment may then be 'a source of evidence that can bear witness to the events that traversed it' (Weizman 2010: 61). But Eyal Weizman sees the difficulty here:

> Since events do not register themselves directly within spatial structures, forensic architecture must conceive of spaces/events as material and temporal hybrids distributed throughout the entire architectural field. Forensic architecture must consider the built environment as being beyond merely the site of, or the backdrop to, violation. (p.62)

Tim Edensor (2005) acknowledges the creative work that might ensue from the ruin, constituted out of a jumble of disconnected things, occurrences and sensations: 'the enigmatic traces that remain, their ghostly presences, invite us to fill in the blanks' (p.58).

■ Performance as a potential mode of enquiry, interpretation and 'filling in the blanks'.

Analogies for relationships between performance and urban environment:

In his critique of characterizations of architecture as the history of style, as the articulation of surfaces or as functionality, Bernard Tschumi suggests that spaces are qualified by actions just as actions are qualified by spaces. To examine this proposition, he has long espoused models that portray the entangled nature of object, human subject, and event, that match 'the abstraction of architectural thought and the representation of events' (1990: 89). The essentially melodramatic aspect of his schema – 'To really appreciate architecture, you may even need to commit a murder' (1994b: XX) – suggests approaches for both the dramaturgical composition and critical understanding of performance.

His acknowledgement of the subversive capabilities of the event was influenced by the evenements in Paris in 1968: 'Erecting a barricade (function) in a Paris street (form) is not quite the equivalent to being a flâneur (function) in that same street (form)' (2003:174); 'Architecture ceases to be a backdrop for actions, becoming the action itself' (1990: 95); 'Events have an independent existence. Rarely are they purely the consequence of their surroundings' (p.99).

His series of 'theoretical projects' – initially termed *screenplays* – simultaneously direct and witness activities and incidents projected onto autonomous spatial architectures: 'intrusions into the architectural stage set'. A creative and instrumental model for understanding, animating and taking responsibility for the relationship between actions and space. In *The Manhattan Transcripts* (1994b) he adopts the discrete frame as a structuring and representational device, juxtaposing maps, plans, axonometric projections, news photos, line drawings, choreographic diagrams, and photographs of people and places in sequences of frozen, temporally suspended moments – to better examine, express and document our discontinuous experience of the city. In these programs he uses a tripartite mode of notation to represent three disjointed levels of reality – space, event and movement – in shifting relationships of reciprocity, when events and spaces are totally interdependent and fully condition each other's existence; indifference, when spaces and events are functionally independent of, or neutralize, one another; and conflict. Through sequences of jump cuts, he supposes that the viewer will maintain memory of the previous frame in the creation of imaginary narratives. He claims to introduce the order of experience and the order of time – moments, intervals, sequences – into exploration of the limits of architectural knowledge. He also envisages transformational techniques – aspects of media such as cinema – that can be applied equally and independently to spaces, events or movements: strategies such as repetition, superimposition, distortion, dissolve, and insertion. Techniques in which the content of contiguous frames can be mixed, superimposed or faded in, elaborating endless relational possibilities. He has a fascination for the dramatic: his explorations frequently involve violence and crime. For him, moments of passion, acts of love, and the instant of death have their own momentum and are rarely the consequence of their surroundings: 'there is no architecture without event, without program, without violence' (1994b: XX).

Tschumi's programs are conceptual and inciting – as 'secret maps and impossible fictions' they envisage and propose action; at the same time – as architectural inquest (1994b: 6) – they document what are also past occurrences. In this they resemble the filmic storyboard and the theatrical scenario – 'All sequences are cumulative. Their "frames" derive significance from juxtaposition. They establish memory – of the preceding frame, the course of events' (1990: 103). The relationship with performance is suggestive. The programs provide models for both conceiving and documenting performance, and informing narrative structures enacted as a series of distinct frames or moments.

■ Performance itself as potentially the most effective manifestation of the multiple articulations of event and space that Tschumi conceives, the transformational techniques he craves.

What performance offers Tschumi is time: it gives dynamic to the frame, and duration to the event. It can suggest simultaneity – difficult to represent on the page – and it draws attention to all that the frame marginalizes: sound, odour, climate; social milieu; historical depth; all that is adjacent; all that is hidden behind the facade; all that makes a place distinctive. Without either pointing to this or that, or attempting to re-enact things that have already happened here, performance reveals places anew, through its singular moment of extra-ordinary visitation, through its contiguous existence, incidentally throwing the spectator's attention from the 'cinematic flow' to what is beside it.

Pearson/Brookes's productions of the early 2000s were resolutely analogue in their application of technology: tapes, discs and photographs were transported around the city. But they do pose questions concerning contemporary dramaturgy and reception.

■ Where was *Polis* generated: in one place or many places? Places from which performers and spectators were variously excluded or absent, where co-presence no longer seems a useful definition of performance.
■ How was *Carrying Lyn* being apprehended: in one place or many places? Places where the potential to monitor response in a loop between performer and spectator no longer seems like a useful definition of performance?

Since their stagings, digital technology has advanced markedly. The 'new mobilities paradigm' in human geography assesses the impact of the societal shift from sedentarism to nomadism and changes in the perception of space pursuant upon the widespread adoption of mobile telephony; of a social life organized through new kinds of transient locations, employing technology 'to organise illicit exchanges, meetings, political demonstrations or "underground" social gatherings' (Sheller and Urry 2006: 213).

Life on the go: in ear, on screen. Place now produced and reproduced through hybrid assemblages of objects, technologies, and socialities combining presences and absences.

■ A two-fold programme then for urban theatre works:

– to apply emergent technologies in hybrid forms that are themselves briefly place-making;

– to evince the transitory and the mundane: to demonstrate for the popular imagination how we ourselves and our immediate environment are part of historical process, how constituents of contemporary material culture exist within overlapping frames and trajectories of time, drawing attention to how we are continuously generating the archaeological record. Whilst little is at risk here, everything of value – communality, generational communication, sense of place – might be at stake.

Such works might resemble small acts of resistance to the excesses of mediated, global culture, drawing attention to the local and particular, identifying and energising regionalized identities, without monopolizing interpretation.

In a renewed sensitivity to ephemerality, to an everyday rendered unfamiliar, an enacted archaeology might provide insights into the personal and the emotive, at scales that as yet escape the scrutiny of CCTV surveillance 'to address tensions, contradictions, exclusions, pains' (Buchli and Lucas 2001: 14); to celebrate the grain of a city, its history and its changing nature ...

... the fact that we do and can still mark – insubordinate to the imperatives of public cleansing, architectural sanitization, social decorum, to 'the continual maintenance and scrupulous restoration of surfaces' (Edensor 2005: 72) – in acts that are colloquial, vernacular, detailed, social; and that, in this, we are not alone.

And perhaps this concern with the dirty and the discarded is a symptom of late modernism, a nostalgia for a public domain in dynamic dialogue with its inhabitants counter to the current genrefication and gentrification of the urban landscape, the deterritorialization of social life, and retreat into the unmarked domain of cyberspace. Dwelling *as is*.

ARCHAEOLOGY

The city's new surface grows over its older scars (Finch 2002: 43).

> & still the city reveals itself. Elephants on queen street, the market's neon clock, twisted chimney pots, the half white brick wall above sam's bar with its ghosts of outline from previous neighbours & architectural pasts, purpose, life, the stained glass, the worlds on offer over upstairs sills & old warped panes. (Robson 2003: 102)

'Architecture obliterates and constitutes the past. It establishes itself in relation to a time and place of origin, and it also endures and is marked by the passage of time and interpretation' (Curtis 2001: 63). Aldo Rossi characterizes the city as a man-made object, the ultimate archaeological artifact (1982: 4), a record of events and a record of time.

> Their spatial structures transport history and manifest memories. Urban spaces are a history book and an impression of contemporary society, they are a palimpsest of history and present day. Those who are able to orientate themselves read them like a book. (Saverio Muratoru in 'Urban Concepts 1908–2008', Museum für Hamburgische Geschichte, November 2009)

City as both material fabric always susceptible to decay – through both long and short-term processes of environmental erosion and human degradation, and as memory – grounded in experience, always susceptible to amnesia.

In cities, the past accumulates: architectures are preserved, restored, ingested into new builds. Or they may persist vicariously, though changed in function, appearance and nomenclature. The corresponding process of recurrent demolition, erasure and development results in European cities that are mound-shaped: Roman London only outcrops in the deepest cellars. At scales from the civic to the domestic, the present is susceptible to curation: conscious decisions about what shall be preserved, and what juxtaposed with what, in which 'the patina of time may be retained, imitated, or removed' (Lynch 1972: 31).

Things endure – 'the survival of "resistances" from a stubborn past' (Certeau et al 1998: 133): material (buildings, parks, statues) and human (practices, traditions, habits, accents) – and their residual rhythms. These 'ghosts of the city' – 'the debris of shipwrecked histories' – can be uncanny as they momentarily open vistas onto another world. Certeau, Giard and Mayol regard them as 'personas' on the urban stage: 'These objects play the roles of actors in the city, not because of what they do or say but because their strangeness is silent, as well as their existence, concealed from actuality'; 'They organize around them the city saga' (p.135). But they go on to critique the process we might term 'heritage' – all that stems 'from a theatrical, pedagogical, and/or scientific operation that pulls objects away from their everyday use (from yesterday or today), objects that it offers up to curiosity, information, or analysis' (p.138).

Over the past twenty years, contemporary and historical archaeology has emerged as a vital field of both subject matter and study: a new domain of which the archaeologist is both researcher and constituent member. It is mirrored in pursuits such as urban exploration – entering abandoned and derelict sites – and 'hauntology' in music – the integration of samples and sonic vestiges in current compositions.

Contemporary archaeology attends to the past that accompanies us and that is more or less apparent: the relics of histories that either hang on, or that are consciously conserved. And to that which happened within memory, recently – the vernacular, the ground level, the short term that results from our own actions. It involves a 'relation of proximity maintained regarding places, objects, ways of life or practices that are still ours and still nourish our collective identity' (Olivier 2001: 175); it is 'an archaeology of us' (Buchli and Lucas 2001: 89), even though 'It makes the familiar strange' (Buchli 2007: 115). The present here as multi-temporal, with elements of material culture existing within overlapping frames and trajectories of time. As a field of enquiry, it involves a renewed sensitivity to the fabric of the present and attention to those details – distinct and differentiated – that signal habitation and presence but that we may consciously disattend or casually ignore or collectively forget.

For Rodney Harrison, the domain of contemporary archaeology is 'a physical stratum that contains not only the present, but all its physical and imagined pasts combined' (Harrison 2011: 154). This 'tactile plane' or assemblage in which different occupations are mixed has 'past and present as a single surface in which all of the components of the assemblages at the surface are equally implicated in the production of the past and present' (p.156). The image of palimpsest is apposite in Cardiff, a city that lacks deep stratigraphy. If archaeology conventionally equates with excavation and metaphors of depth, there is a shift to 'archaeology-as-surface-survey' – 'as an allegory for a creative engagement with the present and the spaces in which the past intervenes within it' (p.144).

■ The documents and places of performance as co-present – with us, now.

In the city, the archaeological record is generated continuously. At the most intimate of scales, we inscribe the urban surface with varying degrees of permanence. The physical surroundings of both private and public domain are marked – both consciously and inadvertently, repeatedly and accidentally – by our presence and by our passing. In the touch of flesh on metal and stone, we leave signature traces: the prints of our bodies. In certain places, our marks accumulate – the signs of our regular and habitual contact. In others, our bodies abrade and erode. In the very passage of pedestrians, in places of multitudinous swarming, the pavement is ground down. Elsewhere, there are the marks of singular actions – traumatic events, transitory occurrences; of movements, moments, events, encounters.

These are the authentic inscriptions of the performance of everyday life: the result of tradition, ritual, happenings; of long-term evolution and unconnected short-term ruptures and singularities; of nearness; of dwelling.

They may result from unreflexive, routinized sequences of movement, the repetitive inscription of personal and collective paths: quotidian choreographies, dressage (Lefebvre 2004: 38–45). Or 'place ballets' – 'an interaction of time-space routines and body routines rooted in space, which becomes an important place of interpersonal and communal exchanges, actions, and meanings' (Seamon 2006; see also Edensor 2010: 8) – in which 'when, how often, how long, in what order and at what speed' (Edensor: 2), are governed by habits, routines and conventions. Or they are the marks of momentary accidents and punctual inscriptions.

These are the spoors of the performance of *homo urbanis*: 'short-term ephemeral consequences of daily life at the scale of the individual, household and immediate community' (Buchli 2007: 117). But they are unevenly distributed: the cityscape is 'thick' and 'thin'. It includes places of congregation and flocking and of desertion and liminality; dense pathways and uninhabited borderlands – 'a thousand vanishing points, each unique, each alive, each pregnant with riches and wonders and time' (Manaugh 2009: 63); 'There are other places in Manhattan that are thick with recurrences, points that seem magnetized by a genius loci. In our time prostitutes walk where prostitutes walked a hundred years ago' (Sante 1998: xiv). From Walter Benjamin's solo *flâneur* to Elias Canetti's surging crowds …

Such marking results from 'various (and uneven) networks of time stretching in different and divergent directions across an uneven social field' (May and Thrift 2001: 5), as individuals 'repeatedly couple and uncouple their paths with other people's paths, institutions, technologies and physical surroundings' (Mels 2004 in Edensor 2010: 1–2).

Henri Lefebvre's *Rhythmanalysis* (2004) is instructive in understanding the interaction of place, time and expenditure of energy, in 'investigating the patterning of a range of multiscalar temporalities – calendrical, diurnal and lunar, lifecycle, somatic and mechanical – whose rhythms provide an important constituent of the experience and organisation of social time' (Edensor: 1): '*cyclical*, with big and simple intervals, within more intense, *alternating* rhythms with short intervals' (Lefebvre 1996: 221).

> It recognises consistencies, repetitions and reproductions, moments of quietude, notwithstanding the furious work that goes into the sustenance of stable arrangements, and is open to moments of chaos, dissonance and breakdown; moments of arrhythmia. (Edensor: 18)

So whilst rhymthanalysis is primarily concerned with repetitions and conformities, it acknowledges reprises and the unforeseen, surges and periods of quietude within an ever-changing mix of interactions, materialities and motilities of both human and non-human; in the city as – after Crang – 'polyrhythmic ensemble' (see Edensor: 3), that in its rhythms generates marking.

The synchronization of practices in collective choreographies or in familiar manoeuvres may result from and be constitutive of shared cultural assumptions. Reiteration may be constitutive of community; the contemporary may contain residual rhythms of the past. But rhythms need not be ossified – there is room for improvisation and adaptation: 'The disruption of accepted rhythms – a motionless body in a crowd, a blockage in the road, a power cut – makes apparent that those rhythms that usually hold sway have been thwarted' (Edensor: 17).

The key task of contemporary archaeology is to perceive 'the ways in which points of detail can emerge from the broader and generally anonymous processes of cultural change' (Schofield 2009: 1). It is to draw out of the background that which is concealed, hidden or immersed within contemporary superfluity and excess, in an uncovering of 'all the non-discursive, inarticulate, delinquent and disregarded elements of the history of a given site' (Holtorf and Piccini 2009: 17).

There is a re-politicization here of a discipline – that has its origins in processes of nation-state building – as a form of active apprehension, a particular sensibility, at a time of 'a state of overwhelming superfluity that renders many aspects of human experiences silent and invisible' (Buchli 2007: 115). As it poses the question 'Who made these marks?' it addresses social and ethical issues, engaging with questions of identity, community, class and gender – a significant early project was Buchli and Lucas's investigation of the personal effects left behind in a recently abandoned council house in London (2001). In an examination of the relationship between material culture and human activities, it inevitably concerns endeavours and experiences that are non-discursive, resulting from practices of labour, trade and social life. It might reveal inarticulate, unregarded or disregarded practices – anonymous, silent, silenced, suppressed, forgotten, ignored – such as patterns of social smoking or profligate street urination or covert sexual activity. It might challenge familiar categorizations – such as assigned usage and the spatially constructed order – through the identification of delinquent events and practices – shortcuts, transgressions and acts of trespass that privilege the route over the inventory: the lateral skids of skate-boarders, places where the bye-laws of the city are clearly broken by chewing gum chewers and public drinkers and drug users. It might presence absence, indicating the traces of those departed or who live a life of a different timetable, such as night workers and club-goers. It might indicate small acts of stylistic defiance in the personalization of domicile and business. It might demonstrate the partiality of our understanding of the occupancy of the city, revealing that which escapes usual discourses of urban planning. It might be redemptive and therapeutic, but equally alienating, troubling and disruptive in addressing the overlooked, taken for granted, conflicted, subaltern: 'To do the archaeology of the contemporary past is to engage directly with its raw and extremely painful nerves – such as homelessness, social exclusion, war crimes, or reconciliation' (Buchli: 116) With the accent on detail – on that barely noticed – the archaeologist might enquire of inhabitants and workers about the marks their activities and occupations produce and about how such traces reveal difference and distinctiveness; about the genesis and history of existing marks within the locale and how they serve as a mnemonic for the events that caused them, leading to a fuller appreciation – through the stories and experiences of others – of the micro-chronologies and polyphonic geographies that make up the urban present. The city as a temporal as well as a spatial phenomenon. In all the above, the ethical dimension is crucial as it attends to those who may have fallen out of discourse.

■ In these traces, can we discern the movements, moments and encounters involved in their making? In the restoration of an absent present, do we engage in a 'melancholic resistance to the inevitability of the march of time and progress' (Holtorf and Piccini 2009: 17)?

■ In dialogue with contemporary archaeology, the description and analysis of performance can find new approaches: aesthetic performance and its sites as relics within the urban landscape; the performance of everyday life discernible in its traces.

■ But what kind of trace does performance – as an ephemeral, transitory phenomenon – leave?

■ Can return to places occasion archaeological recollection: site stimulating memory – 'It happened right here' – or memory of performance picturing sites as they once were – 'This wall wasn't there': 'a process of discrete iterative acts of recollection, present moments prompting connections with something that remains' (Shanks and Svabo 2013).

■ Remembering that 'all the components of the assemblages at the surface are equally implicated in the production of the past and present' (Harrison 2011: 156): performance as a function of, and co-constituent with, architecture, neighbourhood and social ambience.

Practice-based investigations such as fieldwork – being afield with archaeologists – may, reciprocally, enrich ways to experience, imagine, question, animate and represent places, and offer insights to inform, extend and enhance appreciation and interpretation. This may involve itinerary (walking and talking together), visitation, encounter (expressing sensibilities), apprehension (following connections), evocation (revelation; drawing places out of the everyday through physical presence and focused aesthetic attention, and rendering them momentarily significant through 'pointing to' and 'pointing out') and account (aesthetic exposition). Raising ghosts: absences, hauntings, faint traces glimpsed in the sea of background noise.

■ What happens here; has happened here; might happen here?

Then, as a representational and interpretive practice, performance might:

☐ precipitate rapid shifts in attention to, and account of, the nature of places, in detail and in general;

☐ elide regional and local knowledge – drawing together and combining narratives from popular sources (anecdotal, reflective, celebratory) with academic perceptions and bureaucratic data sets to better reveal the imbricated nature of cityscape, the entanglement of place, human subject and event, the contested relationships between design, experience and identity – in forms where meanings may be sequentially and simultaneously presented, represented, questioned, inverted and invented;

☐ embrace aspects of other disciplinary perceptions, stances and knowledges – phenomenological and canonical – within accessible frameworks of exposition, helping describe the complexities of places;

☐ explicate and problematize the multiplicity of meanings that resonate within and from locales;

☐ elaborate conflicting definitions of, and attitudes to, cityscape and illuminate the historically and culturally diverse ways in which it is made, inhabited and interpreted;

☐ enact the intimate connection between personal biographies, social identities and the biography of place.

In an essentially expressive rather than explanatory mode, the varying rhetorical devices of performance can facilitate shifts in viewpoint, attitude and emphasis; empirical in nature – grounded in things – it can articulate connections across time and in space. And it can occasion creative frictions between what is *of* the place and what is brought *to* the place.

■ Performance as a key component in the methodological apparatus – the tool-kit – of contemporary archaeology.

In *The Archaeological Imagination* (2012) – as in *Theatre/Archaeology* (2001) – Michael Shanks espouses the forensic as a mode of enquiry, the scene of crime as a frame of scrutiny: 'A forensic connection between place and event involves a task of distinguishing and sorting evidence from irrelevancy; what is significant from what is garbage; signal from noise; figure from ground' (pp.146–47). In addition, he casts the mise-en-scène as a narrative locale concerned with 'the disposition, arrangement and relationships between people, artifacts, places and happenings' (p.106).

For Shanks, the entropic process is crucial; he regards archaeology as dealing with alterity and abjection, a rummaging in 'the decaying garbage heap that is history' (p.92) that may even cause disturbance and nausea and that may inform the style of writing.

> Rather, layer is piled on layer so that the weight will create metamorphosis or *decomposition*, as the pieces grind at each other, as catalysts (word, themes, images, metaphors, whatever) take effect and amalgams or connections emerge, where probably there should be none. (Shanks 2004: 152)

Such perceptions incidentally reflect a further shift in archaeology: towards a concern with the formation processes of the archaeological record as much as the record itself, towards taphonomy.

■ How does performance decay and disappear? How and why do certain elements of its record survive? What might be deduced from their singular examination and collective incorporation?

After Emile Locard's adage – 'When one object comes into contact with another something is exchanged between and taken away by both objects' (see Pepper 2005: 5) – we suppose that performance leaves its marks on bodies, places, things, witnesses and records, and they on each other. From a play of event, site, document and recollection, useful accounts might proceed.

Forensic investigation involves the observation and interpretation of details – in a particular sensitivity to location that accompanies actuality, and in the association of place and event. Not here as scrutiny of the aftermath of performance immediately upon the departure of the performers, though this might, in the stratigraphy of what is left overlaying what, indicate a sequencing of causative events. Rather, as the perception of performance as a demarcated historical moment that endures in both material and immaterial traces as an imaginary construct.

Traces produced by performance include conscious acts of recording for the purpose of establishing evidence, such as photography; and chance survivals with varying degrees of durability and veracity – 'Time in its passing casts off particles of itself in the form of images, documents, relics, junk' (Sante 1992: ix); 'There is an idea advanced that remote documents may hold the key to comprehending human actions, events, and so on' (Bond 2009: 2).

■ What survives and why?

■ What went to the archive, what to the rubbish dump, what to a personal hoard?

■ What escapes through oversight or wilful exclusion?

■ Who is written out of the account?

■ What is best left outside contemporary contemplation in the public domain?

■ What is the tension between memory and document?

In *Theatre/Archaeology*, our one admonition – after my late colleague Clifford McLucas – was to recognize and disaggregate that produced before, during and after performance: resisting the tendency to conflate documents that may have had different (political) purposes and be intended for distinct audiences at the time, into a contemporaneous substantiation of the real-time event.

Forensic enquiry is a particular way of looking – 'There can be no categorical hygiene in the forensic imagination' (Pearson and Shanks 2001: 61). Simply, '*at scene of crime anything could be relevant*. And anywhere could be a scene of crime' (Shanks 2012: 103). This involves intuition: seeking '*clues* to the pattern of interaction, clues that allow us to gain a practical hold on the situation' (Pile and Thrift 2000: 308). Forensic investigators 'turn space into evidence' (Doyle 2005: 15); 'But it is by no means obvious, often, what is evidence. *Anything*, potentially, could be evidence' (ibid.). Even the faintest of impressions can be revealing, though recognizing this may then depend upon regarding in oblique ways. The overall aim at a location is to establish the chain of events: investigatory questions concern entrances and exits, possible motives, what was done, modus operandi, who witnessed what happenings.

> They are a species of space where we ask – what happened here? As much as a focus on a past happening, this attitude towards place is about potentiality. We ask – what could have happened here? We imagine and look forward – what could happen here? Far from being empty spaces, these are place/ events, with a history and a future, articulations of site, agents/actors, props, (possible) events. (Shanks: 104)

The first task may be to decide upon the extent of the scene (of performance). Where does it begin and end, in the momentary manifestation of long-term ambitions, processes of research and devising, genealogies of practice. Then how might it be delineated and secured.

At the scene, as anything could be of interest – depending on the focus of that interest – there is a democratization of subject matter (Bond: 12). As anything – however negligible – may feasibly be mobilized, the scene becomes 'a symbolic battleground' (Doyle: 20); 'a rarified space in which the banal is almost completely eradicated (or annihilated)' (Bond: 4). 'Ordinary locations are brought into significance by events' (Pearson and Shanks: 61), 'where the familiar codifications of the quotidian is diminished and ordinary expectations are challenged' (Bond: 65). A place where people and things are out of their ordinary place, out of kilter: 'Is the position of the body "sensible"?' (Ribowsky 2007: 83).

Picture the stereotypical scene-of-crime: the constant vigilance and unceasing effort under an anxiety to document as much as possible, because we don't actually know what is, has been, or might be going on, and may never know. What here is significant? There is always doubt whether there is enough evidence to warrant the reconstructed sequence of events and attribution of motivation, or enough even to gain any kind of insight. And scrutiny might always produce false leads or over-concentration on insubstantial elements. If as Walter Benjamin asks 'But is not every spot of our cities the scene of a crime? Every passerby a perpetrator?' (1985: 256), then forensics might even scope everyday life itself, with the scene as field of view.

In *Lacan at the Scene* (2009), Henry Bond describes types of crime scene through Jacques Lacan's categorization of human mental functioning – neurotic; perverse; psychotic (p.31). The perverse crime scene resembles a film set, addressed to a future audience: 'a distinctively artificial place that is designed and art-directed, literally constructed' (p.41). At the psychotic crime scene, there are 'relentless – almost systematic disruptions and mutilations to the familiar everyday objects depicted' (p.95); there is 'no need to limit the flow of detritus, dirt, waste liquids, and so forth, that become juxtaposed with surprising objects in unexpected contexts, resulting in a continuity (no gaps) or a superimposition of the everyday' (p.101). Here disorder results from improvisation, and a punctuated string of actions that may be dissociated. At the neurotic crime scene, there is a 'pathological privileging of certain objects': 'a communication, but one that the subject *does not wish to make directly*' (p.141).

■ All three categorizations of crime scene apply in attending to performance: both as real-time event, and to its subsequent reimagining from documentary remains.

The crime scene is 'photographed for the purpose of establishing evidence' (Benjamin 2002: 108) – 'a fragment scissored from time' (Doyle 2005:13). 'Photographs serve three purposes: they contribute an understanding of how a crime transpired and define the geography of the crime scene for future reference; they also furnish proof on behalf of the prosecution that a crime actually took place' (p.15). They record places, victims and criminals but their frame is selective – they ignore what is happening beyond its edges. The purpose of their focused scrutiny is 'to help witnesses recall events and to assist in clarifying the statements of witnesses' (Pepper 2005: 26): 'images that were used as part of the forensic evidence to map the mise-en-scène of the crime' (Mort 2008: 320). 'Every detail of these pictures, relevant or not, has a weight, as if it had been chosen, and the compositions can seem impossibly definitive' (Sante 1992: 61). Photographs 'linger analytically over scenes of mayhem with a rational gaze and steady hand' (Doyle: 16). To establish entrances and exits, chains of events, the narrative of the event ...

For performances of the 1970s, the photographic record predominates. In still images, the perpetrators are present though their motives often remain obscure. But in the freeze frame, we might appreciate the kinetic trajectory, literally frozen (Bond 2009: 2), the energetic engagement now expired. The challenge, after Benjamin, is to go beyond 'free floating contemplation' and scrutinize them to exhaustion. And this is often difficult as such images are inevitably melancholic: 'Haunted voids reverberating with sadness' (p.13).

In contemplating performance photographs:

- What escapes our immediate attention if we focus solely on the human subjects that naturally attract us?
- What is discerned by shifting the focus to scenographic elements – to objects, their forms and functions? And what of the other 'things' – the non-human actants, their effects and side-effects – that impact upon theatrical composition and upon its reception: scale, surface, temperature, acoustics?
- Within a place of performance what was operative in the constitution of affect and meaning? What else impacted, contributed or pertained? What were the contributory factors?

And if we cannot discern the physical marks of past aesthetic performance, we might at least muse on how it inhabited a place, oriented itself, found affordance, and how performance itself might have drawn attention to the local and particular. To evince an imaginary mise-en-scène – the distribution, arrangement and relationships between people, artifacts, places and happenings. Complexities of intent, application and interpretation, of environment, people and things, in what Ian Hodder has termed *entanglement* (2012).

And these imaginings – part-fact, part-fiction, archaeology as creative disposition – are the substance of *Marking Time*.

> The detective is a creature of the city. More than that, it is the detective who makes the modern city thinkable. It is not just a question of detective stories as topography, re-creating cities in writing or, more likely, writing imagined cities into being. (Donald 2000a: 56)

CODA

> You can have an affair here and no one will spot you. You can commit a murder and not be caught. (Finch 2004: 12)

This appeal to crime and forensics is not intended to be prurient; it seems apposite, as in the late 1980s Cardiff was a violent place.

The murder of Lynette White in James Street in February 1988 was followed on 21 December 1990 by that of shipping clerk Geraldine Palk, who worked close by. Shortly after, I interviewed a scene-of-crime officer, who stressed the importance of the book of documentary photographs that enable subsequent detectives to revisit the various 'scenes' – the site of death, the mortuary ... Crucial, as the investigation was to last twelve years.

Early on, DNA samples were taken from 5,000 men in one of the largest screening programmes undertaken by a British police force up to that time; I was one of those men, selected because of the proximity of our offices. Unbeknown, we inhabited the same cityscape, in the urban congregation of strangers.

The murderer Mark Hampson was finally identified in 2002, again pursuant upon advances in mitochondrial DNA analysis and after random swabbing at Dartmoor Prison where he was serving a four-year sentence for assault. He was arrested upon release at the prison gates; he died in Wakefield Prison in 2007.

POSTSCRIPT

For the 2012–13 season, Cardiff City swapped its blue shirts for red, and included a dragon in its emblem, at the insistence of its new Malaysian owners who regard it as a more auspicious colour, and with an eye to new markets: 'In Asia, red is the colour of joy, red is the colour of festivities and of celebration. In Chinese culture, blue is the colour of mourning' (Vincent Tan, *The Guardian*, 6 April 2013, p.7). On 16 April 2013, the team was promoted to the Premier League. Rumours still abound that the owners intend to rename the 'Bluebirds', 'Cardiff Dragons'.

REFERENCE

LIST OF PERFORMANCES

Theatre in Transit, *The Odyssey*, February 1970

Principal performances discussed: listed by company, roughly chronologically, with date of premiere.

Theatre in Transit: *The Odyssey* (1970); *Welcome to the degree factory* (1971).

Transitions: *Captain Confusius* (1971); *Jack Russell's' Circus* (1972); *Dracula's Castle* (1972).

Keele Performance Group: *Hunchback* (1971).

Keith Wood: *Coyote Saloon* (1971).

RAT Theatre: *Hunchback* (1972); *Blindfold* (1973).

Llanover Hall Theatre Workshop: *The Ancient Mariner* (1973).

proto-Cardiff Laboratory for Theatrical Research: *Image* (1973).

Cardiff Laboratory for Theatrical Research: *Abelard and Heloise* (1974); *The Lesson of Anatomy* (1974); *Mariner* (1974).

Keith Wood Group: *The Philosopher's Stone* (1974); *The Nighthawk* (1974).

Cardiff Laboratory Theatre: *Bricolage* (1975); *Roundabout and Circular* (1977);

Death of a Naturalist (1977); *Moths In Amber: Glimpses of a Nomad Opera* (1978); *Whose Idea Was the Wind?* (1978); *Hunt the Wren* (1978); *The Bear Hunt* (1979).

The Pip Simmons Theatre Group: *Woyzeck* (1977).

IOU: *Between the Floods – the Churning of the Milky Ocean* (1978); *The House* (1982).

Pauper's Carnival: *Dark Corners: a fantasy for grown-ups* (1979).

Brith Gof: *Ymfudwyr* (*Emigrants*) (1983); *Boris* (1985); *Du a Gwyn* (*Black and White*) (1986); *Gododdin* (1988); *PAX* (1990); *Gwynt, Glaw, Glo a Defaid* (*Wind, Rain, Coal and Sheep*) (1991); *Patagonia* (1992); *In Black and White* (1992); *A death in the family* (1992); *Arturius Rex Project 1: DOA* (1993); *Arturius Rex Project 2: Camlann* (1993); *Arturius Rex Project 4: Cusanu Esgyn* (1994); *Arturius Rex Project 5: Arturius Rex* (1994); *Prydain: The Impossibility of Britishness* (1996).

Moving Being: *Tiger! Tiger! Burning Bright* (1985).

Pearson/Brookes: *Dead Men's Shoes* (1997); *Body of Evidence* (1997); *Carrying Lyn* (2001); *Polis* (2001); *Raindogs* (2002); [*Street Greeks* (2002)]; *Who are you looking at?* (2004)

Ed Thomas/Y Cwmni: *Song from a Forgotten City* (1995); *Stone City Blue* (2004).

Marc Rees: *Willows III - Waiting for take off* (2000).

Mike Pearson: *Be Music, Night* (with Peter Brötzmann Chicago Tentet) (2004).

André Stitt: *The Institution* (2005).

Eddie Ladd: *Cof y Corff/Muscle Memory* (2007).

National Theatre Wales: *Coriolan/us* (2012); *De Gabay* (2013).

National Theatre Wales *Coriolan/us*, August 2012 (Marc Douet)
Directed by Mike Pearson and Mike Brookes

BIBLIOGRAPHY

Abse, D., *Ash on a Young Man's Sleeve* (Cardigan: Parthian, 2006 [1954]).

Amin, A. and Thrift, N., *Cities: Reimagining the Urban* (Cambridge: Polity Press, 2002).

Anderson, J., 'Talking whilst walking: a geographical archaeology of knowledge', *Area*, 36, 3 (2004), 254–61.

Andreotti, L. and Costa, X., (eds), *Theory of the Dérive and Other Situationist Writings on the City* (Barcelona: Museu d'Art Contemporani de Barcelona, 1996).

Anon., *Superb Buildings: E. Turner & Sons, Ltd., Builders and Contractors, Cardiff* (London: J. Burrow & Co. Ltd., 1929).

Anon., *Radical Arts: Art & Politics* (Birmingham, 1971).

Ansorge, P., *Disrupting the Spectacle: Five Years of Experimental and Fringe Theatre in Britain* (London: Pitman, 1975).

Asquith, R., 'The Arena of Exploration: Children's Theatre' in S. Craig (ed.), *Dreams and Deconstructions: Alternative Theatre in Britain* (Ambergate: Ambergate Press, 1980), 86–94.

Augé, M., *Non-places: Introduction to an Anthropology and Supermodernity*, (London: Verso, 1995).

Babot, P., 'Remembrance, Rupture and Catharsis' in A. Stitt (ed.), *Substance: Residues, Drawings and Partial Objects 1976–2008* (Exeter: Spacex, 2010), 288–93.

Bachelard, G., *The Poetics of Space* (Boston: Beacon Press, 1969 [1958]).

Bailey, D., *Improvisation: Its Nature and Practice in Music* (Moorland Publishing: Ashbourne, 1980).

Barker, C., 'Pip Simmons in Residence', *Theatre Quarterly*, IX, 35 (1979), 17–29.

Benjamin, W., *One Way Street and Other Writings* (London: Verso, 1985).

Benjamin, W., *The Arcades Project* (Cambridge, MA: Belknap Press/Harvard University Press, 1999).

Benjamin, W., 'The Work of Art in the Age of Its Technological Reproducibility: Second Version' in H. Eiland *et al.* (eds), *Selected Writings Volume 3 1935–1938* (Cambridge, MA: Belknap Press/Harvard University Press, 2002).

Bentham, J., *The Panoptic Writings* (London: Verso, 1995).

Berger, J., *About Looking* (London: Bloomsbury, 2009 [1980]).

Berger, J., 'Boris' in B. Bruford (ed.), *Granta 9* (Harmondsworth: Penguin, 1983), 21–51.

Betsky, A., *The Complete Zaha Hadid* (London: Thames & Hudson, 2009).

Bhattacharyya, G., 'Public toilets' in S. Pile and N. Thrift, (eds), *City A–Z* (London: Routledge, 2000), 194–96.

Bond, H., *Lacan at the Scene* (Cambridge, MA: The MIT Press, 2009).

Bonnett, A., 'Dust (1)' in S. Pile and N. Thrift, (eds), *City A–Z* (London: Routledge, 2000a), 62–63.

Bonnett, A., 'Graveyards' in S. Pile and N. Thrift, N. (eds), *City A–Z* (London: Routledge, 2000b), 91–93.

Bowsher, J., 'Encounters between Actors, Audience and Archaeologists at the Rose Theatre , 1587–1989' in L. McAtackney, M. Palus and A. Piccini (eds), *Contemporary and Historical Archaeology in Theory; Papers from the 2003 and 2004 CHAT conferences,* Studies in Contemporary and Historical Archaeology 4. BAR Int. Ser. 1677 (Oxford: Archaeopress, 2007), 63–66.

Boyle, M., <http://www.boylefamily.co.uk> [accessed 11 January 2013].

Briggs, J., *Before the Deluge* (Bridgend: Seren, 2002).

Buchanan, C., *Cardiff: Development and Transportation Study* (London: Colin Buchanan & Partners, 1966) (six volumes).

Buchli, V. 'Afterword: Towards an Archaeology of the Contemporary Past' in L. McAtackney, M. Palus and A. Piccini (eds), *Contemporary and Historical Archaeology in Theory; Papers from the 2003 and 2004 CHAT conferences,* Studies in Contemporary and Historical Archaeology 4. BAR Int. Ser. 1677 (Oxford: Archaeopress, 2007), 115–18.

Buchli, V. and Lucas, G., *Archaeologies of the Contemporary Past* (London: Routledge, 2001).

Burt, S. and Barker, C., 'IOU and the New Vocabulary of Performance Art', *Theatre Quarterly,* X, 37 (1980), 70–94.

Bush, D., 'Hayes Island' in P. Finch and G. Davies (eds), *The Big Book of Cardiff* (Bridgend: Poetry Wales Press, 2005), 40.

Butler, C. and Davies, M., (eds), *Things Fall Apart* (Cardiff: National Museum Wales, 2006).

Canetti, E., *Crowds and Power* (Harmondsworth: Penguin, 1992 [1962]).

Cardiff City Hall, *City Hall Cardiff: Visitor Information Guide* (Cardiff: The City and County of Cardiff, 2006).

Casey, E., *The Fate of Place* (Berkeley: University of California Press, 1998).

Casey, E., 'Between Geography and Philosophy: What Does It Mean To Be in the Place-World?', *Annals of the Association of American Geographers,* 91, 4, (2001), 683–93.

Certeau, M. de., *The Practice of Everyday Life* (Berkeley: University of California Press, 1984).

Certeau, M. de, Giard, L. and Mayol, P., *The Practice of Everyday Life Volume 2: Living and Cooking* (Minneapolis: University of Minnesota Press, 1998).

Childs, J., *Images of Wales: Roath, Splott and Adamsdown* (Stroud: Tempus, 1995).

Childs, J., *Roath, Splott and Adamsdown: One Thousand Years of History* (Stroud: The History Press, 2012).

Cohn, R., 'The Triple Action Theatre', *Educational Theatre Journal*, 27, 1 (1975), 56–62.

Craig, S., (ed.), *Dreams and Deconstructions. Alternative Theatre in Britain* (Ambergate: Ambergate Press, 1980).

Crickhowell, N., *Opera House Lottery: Zaha Hadid and the Cardiff Bay Project* (Cardiff: University of Wales Press, 1997).

Curtis, B., 'That Place Where: Some Thoughts on Memory and the City' in I. Borden *et al.* (eds), *The Unknown City* (Cambridge, MA: The MIT Press, 2001), 54–67.

Dakowicz, M., *Cardiff After Dark* (London: Thames and Hudson, 2012).

Daunton, M. J., *Coal Metropolis: Cardiff 1879–1914* (Leicester: Leicester University Press, 1977).

Daunton, M. J., 'Coal to Capital: Cardiff since 1939' in P. Morgan (ed.), *Glamorgan County History* (Swansea: The Glamorgan County History Trust, 1988), 203–24.

Davies, I., 'Caroline Street' in P. Finch and G. Davies (eds), *The Big Book of Cardiff* (Bridgend: Poetry Wales Press, 2005), 192.

Davies, J., *Cardiff and the Marquesses of Bute* (Cardiff: University of Wales Press, 1981).

DeLillo, D., *Mao II* (London: Vintage, 1992).

Dixon, S., *Digital Performance* (Cambridge, MA: The MIT Press, 2007).

Donald, J., *Imagining the Modern City* (London: The Athlone Press, 1999).

Donald, J., 'Detectives' in S. Pile and N. Thrift, (eds), *City A–Z* (London: Routledge, 2000a), 56–58.

Donald, J., 'Memory' in S. Pile and N. Thrift (eds), *City A–Z* (London, Routledge, 2000b), 149–50.

Doyle, P., *City of Shadows: Sydney Police Photographs 1912–1948* (Sydney: Historic Houses Trust of New South Wales, 2005).

Edensor, T., *Industrial Ruins: Spaces, Aesthetics and Materiality* (Oxford: Berg, 2005).

Edensor, T., (ed.), *Geographies of Rhythm: Nature, Place, Mobilities and Bodies* (Farnham: Ashgate, 2010).

Edwards, H. T., *The National Pageant of Wales* (Llandysul: Gomer, 2009).

Eliade, M., *Shamanism* (Princeton: Princeton University Press, 1964).

Evans, E., *South with Scott* (London: Collins, 1921).

Evans, N., 'The South Wales Race Riots of 1919', *Llafur*, 3, 1 (1980), 5–29.

Evans, N., 'The Welsh Victorian City: The Middle Class and Civic and National Consciousness in Cardiff, 1850–1914', *Welsh History Review*, 12 (1984), 350–87.

Evans, N., 'Region, Nation, Globe: Roles, Representations and Urban Space in Cardiff, 1839–1928' in A. Fahrmeir and E. Rermbold, (eds), *Representations of British Cities: Transformation of Urban Space, 1700–2000* (Berlin: Pluto, 2003), 108–29.

Farley, P. and Roberts, M. S., *Edgelands: Journeys into England's True Wilderness* (Jonathan Cape: London, 2011).

Finch, P., *Real Cardiff* (Bridgend: Seren, 2002).

Finch, P., *Real Cardiff Two: The Greater City* (Bridgend: Seren, 2004).

Finch, P., *Real Cardiff Three: The Changing City* (Bridgend: Seren, 2009).

Finch, P. and Davies, G., (eds), *The Big Book of Cardiff* (Bridgend: Poetry Wales Press, 2005).

Fitz-Gerald, G. F. and Coxhill, L., *The Poppyseed Affair* (Rare, Raw Revox A77 Recording and Film: Reel Recordings, 2011), CD/DVD.

Geertz, C., 'Art as a Cultural System', *Modern Language Notes*, 91, 6 (1976) 1473–1499.

Geertz, C., *Local Knowledge* (New York: Basic Books, 2000).

Gough, R., *Dream Train: A Photographic Record of the Guizer Project* (Cardiff: Cardiff Laboratory Theatre, 1977).

Gough, R., *Cardiff Laboratory Theatre: Prospectus '78-'79* (Cardiff: Cardiff Laboratory Theatre, 1978).

Gough, R., 'Perfect Time: Imperfect Tense' in J. Christie, R. Gough, and D. Watt (eds), *A Performance Cosmology: Testimony from the Future, Evidence of the Past* (London: Routledge, 2006a), 266–82.

Gough, R., *Perfect Time: Imperfect Tense* (Black Mountain Press: Aberystwyth, 2006b).

Graham, S., 'Surveillance' in S. Pile and N. Thrift, (eds), *City A–Z* (London: Routledge, 2000), 246–49.

Grotowski, J., *Towards a Poor Theatre* (London: Methuen, 1969).

Hadid, Z., 'Internal terrains' in A. Read (ed.), *Architecturally Speaking: Practices of Art, Architecture and the Everyday* (London: Routledge, 2000), 211–31.

Hall, S., 'The Social Eye of *Picture Post*', *Working Papers in Cultural Studies*, 2 (1972), 71–120.

Harrison, R., 'Surface Assemblages: Towards an Archaeology in and of the Present', *Archaeological Dialogues*, 18, 2 (2011), 141–96.

Harvey, D., *Paris, Capital of Modernity* (Abingdon: Routledge, 2006).

Harvey, J., *Men in Black* (London: Reaktion Books, 2009 [1980]).

Harvie, J., *Theatre & the City* (Basingstoke: Palgrave Macmillan, 2009).

Hatherley, O., *A Guide to the New Ruins of Great Britain* (London: Verso, 2010).

Hawkes, T., *Metaphor* (London: Methuen, 1972).

Hawkes, T., *Shakespeare's Talking Animals* (London: Edward Arnold, 1973).

Hodder, I., *Entangled* (Oxford: Wiley-Blackwell, 2012).

Holloway, L. and Hubbard, P., *People and Place: the Extraordinary Geographies of Everyday Life* (Harlow: Pearson, 2001).

Holtorf, C. and Piccini, A., 'Introduction' in C. Holtorf, and A. Piccini (eds), *Contemporary Archaeologies: Excavating Now* (Frankfurt am Main: Peter Lang, 2009).

Hooper, A. and Punter, J., (eds), *Capital Cardiff 1975–2020* (Cardiff: University of Wales Press, 2006).

Hulton, P., *The RAT Theatre Archives* (Exeter: Exeter Archives, 2007a), EDA/RT/1–5, DVD.

Hulton, P., *The RAT Theatre Symposium* (Exeter: Exeter Archives, 2007b), EDA/RT/1–5, DVD.

Hunt, A., *Hopes for Great Happenings: Alternatives in Education and Theatre* (London: Eyre Methuen, 1976).

Itzin, C., *Stages of the Revolution: Political Theatre in Britain since 1968* (London: Methuen, 1980).

Jahangeer, D. A., 'architecturewithoutwalls' in Noever, P. (ed.), *Urban Future Manifestos* (Ostfildern: Hatje Cantz, 2010), 1–3.

Jeff, P., 'Carrying Lyn' *Performance Research*, 6, 3 (2001), 23.

Jones, B., *Images of Wales: Canton* (Stroud: Tempus, 2003).

Jones, B., '"Rooms at the Top" Cardiff's Municipal Museum, 1862–1912', *Llafur*, 9, 4, (2007), 26–46.

Jordan, G., *'Down The Bay': Humanist Photography and Images of 1950s Cardiff* (Cardiff: Butetown History and Arts Centre, 2001).

Kasner, C., 'Eddie Ladd: Cof y corff/muscle memory', *Ballet magazine* <http://www.ballet.co.uk/magazines/yr_07/mar07/ck_rev_eddie_ladd_0207.htm> [accessed 13 February 2013].

Kastner, J. and Wallace, B., *Land and Environmental Art* (London: Phaidon, 1998).

Kaye, N., *SiteWorks: 288 events/sites, San Francisco 1969–84* <http:siteworks.exeter.ac.uk> [accessed 16 August 2013]

Kerr, J., 'The Uncompleted Monument: London, War, and the Architecture of Remembrance' in I. Borden et al. (eds), *The Unknown City* (Cambridge, MA: The MIT Press, 2001).

Kershaw, B., *The Politics of Performance: Radical Theatre as Cultural Intervention* (London: Routledge, 1992).

Kittlausz, V., 'No Place like Home' in P. Healy and G. Bruyns (eds), *De-/signing the Urban: Technogenesis and the Urban Image* (Rotterdam: 010 Publishers, 2006), 183–200.

Knapp, B., *Antonin Artaud: Man of Vision* (Athens: Ohio University Press, 1980).

Koolhaas, R. and Mau, B., *S M L XL* (New York: Monacelli Press, 2002).

Kwinter, S., *Requiem: For the City at the End of the Millennium* (Barcelona: Actar, 2010).

Latour, B., *We Have Never Been Modern* (New York: Harvester Wheatsheaf, 1993).

Latour, B., *Reassembling the Social: An Introduction to Actor-Network-Theory* (Oxford: Oxford University Press, 2005).

Lawton, E., 'Underneath the skin of the material world', *The Architects' Journal*, 206, 12 (1997), 38–39.

Lawton, E., *Work in Progress: Selected Exhibitions* (2006), self-published DVD.

Lee, B., *Central Cardiff* (Stroud: Tempus, 1998).

Lee, B., *Butetown and Cardiff Docks* (Stroud: Tempus, 1999).

Lefebvre, H., *Writings on Cities* (Oxford: Blackwell, 1996).

Lefebvre, H., *Rhythmanalysis: Space, Time and Everyday Life* (London: Continuum, 2004).

Lefebvre, H., *Critique of Everyday Life* (London: Verso, 2008 [1961]).

Lewis, E., 'Freedom' in P. Finch and G. Davies (eds), *The Big Book of Cardiff* (Bridgend: Poetry Wales Press, 2005), 128.

Lichtenstein, R. and Sinclair, I., *Rodinsky's Room* (London: Granta, 1999).

Long, M., 'About the People Show', *The Drama Review*, 15, 4 (1971), 47–57.

Lorimer, H., 'Herding memories of humans and animals', *Environment and Planning D: Society and Space*, 24, (2006), 497–518.

Lynch, K., *The Image of the City* (Cambridge, MA: The MIT Press, 1960).

Lynch, K., *What Time Is This Place?* (Cambridge, MA: The MIT Press, 1972).

Macfarlane, R., *The Old Ways: A Journey on Foot* (London: Hamish Hamilton, 2012).

Mainwaring, A., *Llanover Hall* (Cardiff: HTV, 1974), television broadcast.

Manaugh, G., *The BLDG BLOG Book* (San Fransisco: Chronicle Books, 2009).

Margolles, T., <http://artesmundi.org/en/artists/teresa-margolles> [accessed 11 January 2013].

Massey, D., 'The political place of locality studies', *Environment and Planning*, 23, 2 (1991), 267–81.

May, J. and Thrift, N., *Timespace: Geographies of Temporality* (Routledge: London, 2001).

McLaughlin, E., 'Crime' in S. Pile and N. Thrift, (eds), *City A–Z* (London: Routledge, 2000a), 49–50.

McLaughlin, E., 'Police stations' in S. Pile and N. Thrift, (eds), *City aA–Z* (London: Routledge, 2000b), 186–89.

Miller, D., *The Comfort of Things* (Cambridge: Polity Press, 2008).

Moore, G., *City Trilogy* (Cardiff: Moving Being at St. Stephen's, 1982), production programme.

Moore, G., *Moving Being: Two Decades of a Theatre of Ideas* (Cardiff: Moving Being Ltd., 1989).

Moore, G., 'The Space Between – Work in Mixed Media: Moving Being 1968–1993' in A-M. Taylor (ed.), *Staging Wales: Welsh Theatre 1979–1997* (Cardiff: University of Wales Press, 1997), 153–59.

Morgan, D., *Memories of Cardiff's Past* (Derby: Breedon Books, 2006).

Morgan, R., *Cardiff: Half-and-half a Capital* (Llandysul: Gomer, 1994).

Mort, F., 'Morality, Majesty and Murder in 1950s London: Metropolitan Culture and English Modernity' in G. Prakash and K. Kruse (eds), *The Spaces of the Modern City* (Princeton: Princeton University Press, 2008), 313–45.

Mumford, L., *The Culture of Cities* (New York: Harcourt, 1938).

Nancy, J.-L., *The Ground of the Image* (New York: Fordham University Press, 2005).

Newman, J., *The Buildings of Wales: Glamorgan* (New Haven: Yale University Press, 2004 [1995]).

Odin Teatret, <http://www.odinteatret.dk/> [accessed 11 January 2013].

Olivier, L., 'The archaeology of the contemporary past' in V. Buchli and G. Lucas (eds), *Archaeologies of the Contemporary Past* (Routledge: London, 2001), 175–88.

Opie, I., *The People in the Playground* (Oxford: Oxford University Press, 1993).

Opie, I. and Opie, P., *Children's Games in Street and Playground* (Oxford: Oxford University Press, 1969).

Owen, T. M., *Welsh Folk Customs* (Llandysul: Gomer, 1987 [1959]).

Palfrey, C., *Cardiff Soul* (Talybont: Y Lolfa, 2006).

Pearson, M., 'Community arts projects: Their methods and techniques with special reference to children' (unpublished Master's thesis, University of Wales, 1973).

Pearson, M., 'Notes on Physical Preparation' (unpublished document, Cardiff: Cardiff Laboratory Theatre, n.d.).

Pearson, M., 'Owls Started This' (Cardiff: Cardiff Laboratory Theatre, 1979a).

Pearson, M., 'The Summer Project 1979' (unpublished document, Cardiff: Cardiff, 1979b).

Pearson, M., *Glimpses of the Map: Cardiff Laboratory Theatre 1974–1980* (Cardiff: Cardiff Laboratory Theatre, 1980).

Pearson, M., 'The Dream in the Desert', *Performance Research*, 1, 1 (1996), 5–14.

Pearson, M., *'In Comes I': Performance, Archaeology and the City* (Exeter: University of Exeter Press, 2006).

Pearson, M., 'It came apart in my hands: Reflections on *Polis* by Pearson/Brookes', *About Performance*, 7 (2007), 13–23.

Pearson, M., *Site-Specific Performance* (Basingstoke: Palgrave Macmillan, 2010).

Pearson, M., *Mickery Theater: An Imperfect Archaeology* (Amsterdam: Amsterdam University Press, 2011).

Pearson, M., 'Raindogs: Performing the City', *Cultural Geographies*, 19, 1 (2012), 55–69.

Pearson, M. and Levett, M., 'Devices and Desires', *Contemporary Theatre Review*, 11, 3+4 (2001), 81–92.

Pearson, M. and Shanks, M., *Theatre/Archaeology* (London: Routledge, 2001).

Penrose, S., *Images of Change: An Archaeology of England's Contemporary Landscape* (Swindon: English Heritage, 2007).

Pepper, I., *Crime Scene Investigation: Methods and Procedures* (Maidenhead: Open University Press, 2005).

Perec, G., *Species of Spaces and Other Pieces* (Harmondsworth: Penguin, 1997).

Perec, G., *An Attempt at Exhausting a Place in Paris* (New York: Wakefield Press, 2010).

Piccini, A., 'Guttersnipe: A Micro Road Movie' in C. Holtorf, and A. Piccini (eds), *Contemporary Archaeologies: Excavating Now* (Frankfurt am Main: Peter Lang, 2009), 183–99.

Pile, S., 'The Un(known) City or an Urban Geography of What Lies Buried Below the Surface' in I. Borden, et al. (eds), *The Unknown City* (Cambridge, MA: The MIT Press, 2001), 262–79.

Pile, S. and Thrift, N., (eds), *City A–Z* (London: Routledge, 2000).

Pincombe, I. M., '"Success in Art and Industries?" The Cardiff Exhibition, 1896', *Llafur*, 9, 4, (2007), 72–88.

Pountney, J., Robertson, K. and Gibbard, A., *Cardiff before Cardiff* (Talybont: Y Lolfa, 2012).

Punter, D., *Metaphor* (London: Routledge, 2007).

Punter, J., 'Cardiff Bay: An exemplar of design-led regeneration?' in A. Hooper and J. Punter (eds), *Capital Cardiff 1975–2020* (Cardiff: University of Wales Press, 2006).

Pywell, G., *Staging Real Things* (London: Associated University Presses, 1994).

Read, S., 'The Form of the City' in P. Healy and G. Bruyns (eds), *De-/signing the Urban Technogenesis and the Urban Image* (Rotterdam: 010 Publishers, 2006a), 74–90.

Read, S., 'The Urban Image: Becoming Visible' in D. Hauptmann (ed.), *The Body in Architecture* (Rotterdam: 010 Publishers, 2006b), 48–65.

Redknapp, M., *Discovered in Time: Treasures from Early Wales* (Cardiff: National Museum Wales, 2011).

Rees, S., 'Threshold – on the work of Eve Dent', *Platfform*, I (2003), 24–29.

Rendell, J., *Site-Writing: The Architecture of Art Criticism* (London: I. B. Tauris, 2010).

Reynolds, E., 'Nye' in P. Finch and G. Davies (eds), *The Big Book of Cardiff* (Bridgend: Poetry Wales Press, 2005), 176.

Ribowsky, S., *Dead Center* (New York: Harper, 2007).

Robinson, J., *Mapping the moment: Performance culture in Nottingham 1857–1867* <http://www.nottingham.ac.uk/mapmoment> [accessed 16 August 2013]

Robinson, T., *Connemara: Listening to the Wind* (London: Penguin, 2008).

Robson, L., 'A Stain on the Map' in F. Rhydderch (ed.), *Cardiff Central* (Llandysul: Gomer, 2003), 95–104.

Roms, H., 'Performing *Polis*: Theatre, nationness and civic identity in post-devolution Wales', *Studies in Theatre and Performance*, 24, 3 (2004), 177–92.

Roms, H., 'From map to Trace: Situating performance art in Wales' in A. Stitt (ed.), *Trace: installaction artspace 00–05* (Bridgend: Seren, 2006).

Roms, H., 'Staging an urban nation: Place and identity in contemporary Welsh theatre' in N. Holdsworth and M. Luckhurst (eds), *A Concise Companion to Contemporary British and Irish Drama* (Oxford: Blackwell, 2008).

Roms, H., 'What substance is substance? André Stitt's material performances' in A. Stitt, *Substance: Residues, Drawings & Partial Objects 1976–2008* (Exeter: Spacex, 2010).

Roms, H., 'What's Welsh for Performance?' <http://www.performance-wales.org> [accessed 13 January 2013].

Rossi, A., *The Architecture of the City* (Cambridge, MA: Opposition Books/The MIT Press, 1982).

Rowlands, E., Hansard vol 773 cc572–82 (1968) <http://hansard.millbanksystems.com/ commons/1968/nov/13/roads-cardiff> [accessed 11 January 2013].

Rubin, J., *Do It: Scenarios of the Revolution* (New York: Simon and Schuster, 1970).

Sadler, S., *The Situationist City* (Cambridge, MA: The MIT Press, 2001).

Sante, L., *Evidence* (New York: Farrar, Straus and Giroux, 1992).

Sante, L., *Low Life* (London: Granta, 1998).

Savage, J., *Depending on Time* (Cardiff: Safle, 2009a).

Savage, J., *Nutopia: Exploring The Metropolitan Imagination* (Cardiff: Safle, 2009b).

Schechner, R., *Performance Studies: An Introduction* (Routledge: London, 2002).

Schlögel, K., *Moscow* (London: Reaktion Books, 2005).

Schofield, J., '1115 hrs, 24 June 2008: Drama and the moment' in J. Schofield (ed.), *Defining Moments: Dramatic Archaeologies of the Twentieth-Century*, Studies in Contemporary and Historical Archaeology 5. BAR Int. Ser. 2005 (Oxford: Archaeopress, 2009) 1–8.

Seamon, D., 'A Geography in Lifeword in Retrospect: A Response to Shaun Moores', *Particip@tions*, 3, 2, 2006 <http://www.participations.org/volume%203/issue%20 2%20-%20special/ 3_02_seamon.htm> [accessed 18 April 2013].

Sekar, S., *Fitted In: the Cardiff 3 and the Lynette White Inquiry* (London: The Fitted In Project, 1997).

Shank, T., 'The Pip Simmons Group', *The Drama Review*, T-68 (1975), 41–46.

Shanks, M., 'Three rooms: Archaeology and performance', *Journal of Social Archaeology*, 4, 2 (2004), 147–80.

Shanks, M., *The Archaeological Imagination* (Walnut Creek: Left Coast Press, 2012).

Shanks, M. and Svabo, C., 'Mobile media photography: new modes of engagement' <http://archaeography.stanford.edu/MichaelShanks/454> [accessed 12 February 2013].

Sheller, M. and Urry, J., 'The new mobilities paradigm', *Environment and Planning A*, 38, 2 (2006), 207–26.

Simmons, P., 'Superman' in H. Barker *et al.* *New Short Plays 3* (London: Eyre Methuen, 1972), 89–111.

Sinyard, N., 'The Lodger: A Tale of the London Fog' in A. Hitchcock, *The Lodger* [1926] (BFI/network, 2012), DVD insert.

Southern, R., *The Seven Ages of the Theatre* (London: Faber and Faber, 1962).

Spring, H., *Heaven Lies about Us* (London: Collins, 1956).

Stewart, K., *A Space on the Side of the Road: Cultural Politics in an 'Other' America* (Princeton: Princeton University Press, 1996).

Stitt, A., *The Institution* (Cardiff: Chapter, 2005).

Stitt, A., (ed.), *Trace: installaction artspace 00–05* (Bridgend: Seren, 2006).

Stitt. A., (ed.), *Substance: Residues, Drawings and Partial Objects 1976–2008* (Exeter: Spacex, 2010.

Stitt, A., (ed.), *Trace: Displaced* (Cardigan: Parthian, 2011).

Stokes, B., *Tale of the Tiger* (Cardiff: HTV, 1985), television broadcast.

Taylor, A-M., 'Out of the Box Rooms', *Planet*, 105 (1994), 70–76.

Theatresurvey, 'Guide to Underground Theatre', *Theatre Quarterly*, 1, 1 (1971), 61–5.

Thomas, D., *Under Milk Wood* (London: J. M. Dent & Sons Ltd., 1954).

Thomas, E., *Selected Work '95–'98* (Cardigan, Wales: Parthian Books, 2002).

Thomas, E., *Stone City Blue* (London: Methuen, 2004).

Thomas, H., 'Spatial structuring in the Capital: Struggles to Shape Cardiff's Built Environment' in R. Fevre and A. Thompson (eds), *Nation, Identity and Social Theory* (Cardiff: University of Wales Press, 1999), 168–88.

Thomas, I., 'Caroline Street' in P. Finch and G. Davies (eds), *The Big Book of Cardiff* (Bridgend: Poetry Wales Press, 2005), 192.

Thompson, J. L., (dir.) *Tiger Bay* (ITV, 2004 [1959]), DVD recording.

Trace Gallery <http://www.tracegallery.org> [accessed 12 February 2013].

Tracey, S., *Under Milk Wood* (London: EMI, 1965), audio recording.

Troutman, A., 'Inside Fear: Secret Places and Hidden Spaces in Dwellings' in N. Ellin (ed.), *Architecture of Fear* (New York: Princeton Architectural Press, 1997), 143–57.

Tschumi, B., *Questions of Space* (London: Architectural Association, 1990).

Tschumi, B., *Architecture and Disjunction* (Cambridge, MA: The MIT Press, 1994a).

Tschumi, B., *The Manhattan Transcripts* (New York: Academy Editions, 1994b).

Tschumi, B., 'Six Concepts' in A. Read *Architecturally Speaking: Practices of Art, Architecture and the Everyday* (London: Routledge, 2000), 155–76.

Tschumi, B., *Architectural Concepts: Red is not a Colour* (Rizzoli: New York, 2012).

Tschumi, B. et al., (eds), *Bernard Tschumi, Zénith de Rouen* (New York: Princeton Architectural Press, 2003).

Walton, D., *Revolution 69* <http://web.onetel.net.uk/~davewalton/archive/local/1969.html> [accessed 13 January 2013].

Weizman, E., 'Forensic Architecture' in Noever, P (ed.), *Urban Future Manifestos* (Ostfildern: Hatje Cantz, 2010), 61–62.

Whybrow, N., *Street Scenes: Brecht, Benjamin & Berlin* (Bristol: Intellect, 2005).

Whybrow, N., *Art and the City* (London & New York: I. B. Taurus, 2011).

Wiles, D., *A Short History of Western Performance Space* (Cambridge: Cambridge University Press, 2003).

Williams, B., <http://www.bedwyrwilliams.com> [accessed 13 January 2013].

Williams, G. A., *When Was Wales?* (Harmondsworth: Penguin, 1985).

Williams, H., *The Speakers* (London: Robin Clark, 1982 [1964]).

Williams, I., *Captain Scott's Invaluable Assistant: Edgar Evans* (Stroud: The History Press, 2012).

Williams, J., 'Fantastic Fictions: Wales and Welsh Men in the plays of Ed Thomas' in E. Thomas *[Selected] Work '95–'98* (Cardigan, Wales: Parthian Books, 2002), 408–55.

Williams, J., *Bloody Valentine* (London: Harper Collins, 1995).

Williams, J., *Five Pubs, Two Bars and a Nightclub* (London: Bloomsbury, 1999).

Williams, J., *Cardiff Dead* (London: Bloomsbury, 2000).

Williams, J., *The Prince of Wales* (London: Bloomsbury, 2003a).

Williams, J., 'Young Marble Giants in the Casablanca' in F. Rhydderch (ed.), *Cardiff Central* (Llandysul: Gomer, 2003b), 85–93.

Williams, J., 'The Legend of Tiger Bay' in P. Finch and G. Davies (eds), *The Big Book of Cardiff* (Bridgend: Poetry Wales Press, 2005), 217–34.

Williams, M., *The Essential Cardiff Castle* (London: Scala, 2008).

Williams, R., *The Country and the City* (Oxford: Oxford University Press, 1973).

INDEX